THE END OF ENDS

Giovanni Battista Piranesi, *Carceri d'invenzione di G. Battista Piranesi archit. vene.* Plate VII (F 30), etching, 1835, owned by the National Museum in Kraków.

TADEUSZ BRADECKI

The End of Ends

and a few beginnings
in the Land of Fiction

Translated by
Tadeusz Bradecki and Kate Sinclair

This edition first published in 2024
by CB editions
146 Percy Road, London W12 9QL
www.cbeditions.com

Cover: Simon Bradbury as Clov in *Endgame* by Samuel Beckett at the Irish
and Classical Theatre in Pittsburgh, directed by Tadeusz Bradecki in 2006.
Photograph from the author's archive. Design: Mikołaj Kosiński.

Printed in England by Short Run Press, Exeter

ISBN 978-1-909585-59-1

Contents

Preface vii

Introduction ix

The End of Ends 1

Index 249

Acknowledgements 255

Preface

KATE SINCLAIR

Tadeusz Bradecki (1955–2022) was a director, actor and writer. He studied at the State Drama school in Kraków, graduating first in acting and then in directing. He was also part of the programmes of ongoing development with Grotowski and Peter Brook at the famous Theatre of Nations workshops in Wrocław in 1975.

He went on to direct over a hundred plays, operas and musicals internationally in a career spanning forty-five years. He was the Artistic Director of the National Theatre in Kraków, Stary Teatr (1990–96) during one of its most creative periods, Director at the National Theatre in Warsaw (2003–7) and Artistic Director of the Teatr Śląski in Katowice (2007–13). Seminal productions included *Poor Folk* by Dostoevsky, *Spring of Nations*, *Woyzeck*, *The Manuscript found in Saragossa*, *Fantazy*, *As You Like It* and *The Metaphysical Pattern of Evidence*, several of which he wrote or adapted. At Teatr Śląski his productions of *Polterabend* in Silesian dialect as well as *The Taming of the Shrew* and *Art* received critical acclaim.

He spoke five languages fluently and regularly directed abroad. His thirteen productions at the Shaw Festival Theatre in Canada included *Guys and Dolls*, *The Crucible*, *Candide* and *Princess Ivona of Burgundy*. He worked in the US on Beckett's *Endgame*, in the UK, and in Italy on the premiere of *Maximilian Kolbe* by Ionesco, as well as directing shows in France, Russia, Romania and Korea. He was given many awards for directing and acting (over twenty-three). These included awards for directing at festivals both in Poland (Wrocław, Opole, Szczecin,

Torun) and internationally (Sarajevo, Mess Festival). He won the Swinarksi Award for directors, the Silver Gloria Artis Medal for services to culture and the Polish/ITI/UNESCO award for championing Polish culture abroad. In 1993 he was made a Chevalier des Ordre des Lettres et Arts in France.

As an actor he was nominated for the best actor's prize at Cannes in 1980 for the film *Konstans* (*The Constant Factor*), which was written for him. His awards for acting in theatre, TV and film included the Leon Schiller Award and the Golden TV award. He performed in over forty films directed by Krzysztof Kieślowski, Krzysztof Zanussi, Andrzej Wajda and Stephen Spielberg. He wrote several award-winning plays: *The Pattern of Metaphysical Evidence*, *Saragossa*, *In the Sandpit* and *Nocturne*. He also wrote columns for twenty years for the Polish literary publication *Dialog*.

He was Associate Professor at the State Drama school in Kraków and continued to work as a freelancer. His recent productions of *Hamlet* and *The Servant of Two Masters* at the Dramatczny Theatre in Warsaw received great critical attention.

§

Tadeusz wrote this work, *The End of Ends*, in the last year of his life. It was published in Poland in September 2021 by Żywosłowie Press. He then prepared the English translation of the text with me, his wife, in London.

Tadeusz was an exceptional artist and, moreover, human being, which is altogether rarer. He was once described on a work visa as 'An Alien with Extraordinary Capabilities', something he found very funny.

I am grateful for the support of CB editions for their careful help in getting it published in a language he loved. Any errors in the English version are mine; Tadeusz tended not to make mistakes.

Introduction

TADEUSZ BRADECKI

Between 2001 and 2020 I was a columnist for the renowned Polish monthly *Dialog*. During that time, I wrote more than 170 texts, mostly dedicated to both history and the present state of the theatre, with many references to various cultural issues.

Reviewing those texts after the end of that cycle (usually after several years) I noticed that surprisingly many of them deal with the returning theme of narrative techniques in the theatre and in literature. Nature and the genesis of the story, of the theatre story, as well as more traditional stories – their various forms and ways of influencing, their differences, colours and often unexpected connections – interested me continuously during those years.

After some hesitation, I decided to use some of those materials, placing them in a decidedly different order, giving them a new context and adding to them some related topics only touched on before. These include the end of modernity, the so-called end of grand narratives, the story-within-a-story or the theatre-within-the-theatre. As a result, a concise book was created, which I have titled *The End of Ends*, and which is dedicated to a reflection upon the human passion for storytelling and performing.

If a fellow traveller journeying through the Land of Fiction would like to ponder for a while, with me, the many paths that pass through it, I would consider my intentions to have been fulfilled.

[2021]

The End of Ends

1   Suddenly, in the lockdown, the indispensability of writing. Writing understood as the overwhelming necessity of making some kind of verbal expression. Its most natural, spontaneous form is a conversation with oneself, that is, something like a diary, often practically a diarrhoea of words. To expel this 'something' from oneself, to write it down, to leave it behind. This action, we tell ourselves, is a work in progress or an experiment and maybe 'something' will come out of it. Yet in the meantime – let's be honest – it is simply excrement.

Speaking rationally, it is better to write, even in this excremental way, than not to write. Expulsion, or the action of pouring words onto paper, brings back, to some extent, balance. At the end, something has been done. It is better to 'do' than not to 'do', we say to ourselves; it is better to 'be' than to torment oneself with a potentiality which never finds vent.

To give vent. This sounds like bloodletting during some illnesses centuries ago. A form of sanitation, done through an extraction. What's more, all these metaphors seem to be underlined by a sexual urge, by longing for a dose of dopamine, for the lazy relief of 'afterwards'.

This something which we expel consists mainly of accumulated frustration. Everything remains blocked, closed, forbidden in this lockdown. Therefore, one wants to break through these barriers, to crush them, to force them open. It is like a sequence of scenic gestures in *To the Actor: On the Technique of Acting* by Michael Chekhov: one has managed to commit so many gestures of closure, of defensive huddling up, that now one would desire to open oneself, to grow in space, to expand, both with the body and the voice.

Every state of closure, no matter the circumstances, is a state of imprisonment. Usually, it is an imprisonment in space, but often also in time. The stereotypical image tells us that the prisoners count the number of days remaining until they are free by drawing marks upon their cell walls. That would be, however, the optimistic version: one remains closed for so many days, months, years, expecting to be released at the end. In such a version there is a great feast, an Exodus, a liberation at the end of the allotted time. Yes, but a certain Hamm in Beckett's *Endgame*, for example, perceives his sentence as a lifelong one. The eventual counting of the days will not bring closer his end, nor will it postpone it. For Hamm, as for Albert Camus, the only serious philosophical dilemma is suicide.

Wait, wait, please, just a moment. A suicide, nothing less? Because of the bloody microbe, because of the lockdown? It would be better to produce excrement.

2 Cursing and swearing is often the most spontaneous and natural form of conversation with oneself. Could it be a chain of Witkiewicz-like, flipping, abusive and deeply insulting linguistic blots, for example? It is not easy to construct such a chain, believe me. One has to sweat a lot before all these 'cock-counting, bum-fluffing, fluff-banting', all these overblown flibbertigibbets agree one with another to form a perfect musical sequence. It is not easy, and therefore the natural state, or seemingly spontaneous character of the primordial rant (unspoiled by the suffering of culture) can be easily undermined. One has to know how to spit accurately – a critic might say – and a truly wild gush, impressive and pre-Neanderthal in its authenticity, requires a refined composition of colours – he might add.

The perversion of pure negativity may be yet another possible way of expressing frustration. Imagine nothing born of nothing. The sound of the rain behind a window is like a metronome, awful and relentless, but inside nothingness reigns. Nothing yesterday, nothing today, nothing tomorrow. The resulting negativity is like taking centre stage in an 'Anyone can sing' talent contest. Even if there are better candidates in the wings, we sit in the spotlight glued to our chairs, and no one can touch us. Are we out of tune? Even if we are, so what? Let the others rebel backstage, they cannot do anything. Yes, such a strategy of negativity is nerve-wracking, this is true, but it is also shockingly effective.

It becomes evident very soon that we do not so much want to talk to ourselves, but rather that we desperately need someone to talk to: an interlocutor. Or perhaps we need an audience for whatever we have to say. What we are seeking, in fact, is the possibility of any dialogue. There is a Polish proverb: a man talks to a picture, but the picture never talks back to him. No matter how long that proverbial fool talks to the picture, his motive must be his strong faith in the possible miracle of an answer. His absurd monologue only makes sense in the context of such a faith.

So why not imagine God as an interlocutor? The first one to do this was St Augustine, just before the end of the fourth century. Public confessions of sins were known before him among the Israelites and were also present from time to time among some citizens of Rome. But the *Confessions* of St Augustine, a thick tome of literature carefully written in the form of a prayer, was a sensation. Nothing like it had ever been written before, or was again for a very long time afterwards. And no modern narcissistic excesses, using the monologue form of 'I', starting with Jean-Jacques Rousseau's *Confessions* (1770) and ending with Gombrowicz's *Kronos* (2013), could have appeared without Augustine's work.

To find an audience for our moral anxiety becomes therefore indispensable. One does not even need to invent a particularly elevated audience: Krapp in Beckett's *Krapp's Last Tape* records himself for himself and listens to himself. He is both the sender and the receiver. Although his juggling of times and places is pretty refined, his existential situation remains simple. He is writing a letter, or, more precisely, he is recording a message addressed to himself in the future. His recording on the magnetic tape is just like he is writing a letter and putting it into a bottle to be thrown upon the ocean's waves. The only difference is that Krapp's tapes land peacefully in his library, while letters sent in bottles may traverse thousands of miles for dozens of years, or dozens of miles for hundreds of years, before they reach any destination.

3 I am writing a letter and immediately I am finding myself in a literary situation. Even if I am the future receiver, like Krapp, I need somehow to imagine myself in the future. I need to imagine a version of myself who, in the future, will agree to receive my letter. Will I be really old when I read it? 'Hello, you old codger!' — I could start this way in such a case — 'you may not remember me, but here I am reminding you of myself!' Yet the letter might also reach me much earlier, maybe even quite soon, so how should I start it then? 'I know that you imagine that you know the content of this letter from memory, but I shall surprise you — because no doubt you have erased this from memory: you forgetful old sieve!'

And what would happen if I were to imagine a receiver of my letter who is not me?

4 'I am entrusting my note, Madame, to your discretion and I am signing it as your lifelong admirer' – with these words I have imagined Madame de Merteuil. This is not easy, to create all her life and her background, her form, her movements, the sound of her voice, her laughter, the inclination of her head, her glance. She becomes someone very close to me. I know her habits, her faults, her numerous weaknesses, little sins, hesitations and shameful secrets; I am becoming her author and Madame de Merteuil appears in my dreams as a fully autonomous, living being. She suggests to me her actions, teaches me her expressions; it will not be difficult for me to write yet another letter, seemingly created by her hand, her courteous answer to the letter of the Vicomte de Valmont. And by writing to Valmont as Madame de Merteuil, I also had to create the person of Valmont himself. Holy smoke, the whole world of *Les Liaisons Dangereux* starts to exist on my laptop. Ladies and Gentlemen, it may already be literature …

5 By conjuring Valmont writing to Madame, I have enabled the existence of a literary game. I have created his and Madame de Merteuil's refined and cruel Paris; I have created their world. Yet another reality was created earlier by the letters of a certain Portuguese nun, and later still a completely different one in Russia through the letters of Makary Dievushkin and Varvara. In his *Poor People* (1848), Dostoevsky develops the convention of the novel-in-letters to perfection. As in *Les Liaisons Dangereux* by Laclos (1782), what the sender of the letter wants to convey to the receiver often becomes a manipulation of facts. It is often close to emotional blackmail. What starts to matter is the so-called subtext, that is, not what the sender wants to convey, but what he or she would like to hide. What starts to matter is what the correspondents omit from the page.

The exchange of letters between the recipients becomes a complicated dialectical record of both their quavering consciousnesses and their repressed subconsciousness. Both their truths and their lies evolve in time. Here we have human relationships in their *in statu nascendi* form. What remains unsaid often says more about their situation than solemn declarations and oaths. What remains misrepresented, or even blatantly falsified, may in fact be more truthful than the alleged 'truth'.

6 There is a literary game, and there is a game-within-a-game. In the kingdom of literary games, the game of alleged authorship is one of the oldest. It starts with a most simple, even brutal trick: for example, Apocrypha. Pseudo-Philo, Pseudo-Plato, Pseudo-Dionysius the Areopagite and many others. Here, the author who created the work is cunningly hiding and wanting their work to be taken as that of some more famous author. Does this come from modesty? I don't think so. I suspect it started from the ancient law of supply and demand: what has sold successfully once should sell even better the next time. Let's create something in the style of the earlier hit and people will buy it, no doubt. Also, one cannot exclude a more noble motivation; let's say that I adore some unfinished thoughts and the message of the original author so much that I feel the need to add to them. I want to explain the difficult parts, to make the complicated concepts more accessible. It may be that this more pious intention was dominant in the early ages, the ages of manuscripts. It may be that only in *The Gutenberg Galaxy* the easily reproduced book becomes an object worth falsifying.

Thanks to this process, it became possible that Don Quixote could listen with amazement in the 'Second Part of His Adventures' to the bachelor Samson Carrasco telling him about readers snatching the 'First Part' of the book out of the hands of booksellers. What is more, the authorship of the 'First Part of

His Adventures' was claimed to be not by Cervantes but by a certain Hamet Banengeli of Arabic descent! A further game-within-a-game is the form of the sequel. *The Merry Wives of Windsor* is a sequel to *Henry IV*, consciously produced by Shakespeare to exploit the success of the actor playing Falstaff. The owners of the rights to the late Ian Fleming's James Bond series commissioned numerous authors to write apocrypha which sell brilliantly. The American thriller author Robert B. Parker successfully wrote sequels to Raymond Chandler's thrillers featuring Philip Marlowe. Nowadays, after Parker's death, other authors create new titles with the lyrical and deadly Spenser living on in the role of the main gumshoe.

Both apocrypha and sequel seem, therefore, to be the first contenders of this game-within-a-game. But there are more sophisticated players in this contest: *The Manuscript Found in Saragossa* by Jan Potocki (1805–1815), for example, or *The Narrative of Arthur Gordon Pym of Nantucket* (1838) by Edgar Allan Poe. Similarly, Stanisław Lem's *Memoirs Found in the Bathtub* (1961) and *The Private Memoirs and Confessions of a Justified Sinner* (1824) by James Hogg also provoke in the same way. What is different in this quite plentiful subgenre is that a subtle agreement is being made by the author with the reader: let's agree, says the real author of the novel, that it was not I who wrote this work – although my name is printed on the first page – but some other, the supposed author of these pages, accordingly Alphonse Van Worden, Gordon Pym or Lem's anonymous narrator.

Even bigger subtleties are possible here. In Poe's case, it is not Poe who presents the printed version of the text but the alleged 'finder' of Pym's papers. Lem's *Memoirs Found in the Bathtub* is preceded by the introduction of the Editor from some future millennium on Earth, while in the case of Potocki, a short prelude by the publisher of Van Worden's diary remains anonymous. This subtle agreement is nothing more than Samuel Coleridge's 'willing suspension of disbelief', formulated in 1817. His famous definition is understood as the intentional avoidance of critical thinking or logic in examining something surreal, such as a work of speculative fiction, in order to believe in it for the sake of enjoyment. Without this willing suspension of disbelief it is practically impossible to participate in any theatrical event. Therefore, all these examples of the use of the literary ploy of multi-levelled authorship, lead us – in the spacious building of storytelling – straight to the room named 'Literature' or to yet another room named 'Theatre'.

7 In the beginning was the beginning, which was called the *incipit*. These were the first few words of the ancient or medieval manuscript, often colourful, permitting the identification of the text. So, for example, if the text began with the words *Agnus Dei*, it meant that the text was a notation of that prayer. This practice remains alive to this day in the Papal decrees. Also, we are used to recognising a melody from its first few notes, which are also its *incipit*. There used also to be an *explicit*, which contained the information about the author, or about the copier, or about the patron and other circumstances, which was usually placed on the last page and called a colophon.

The colophon tended to be automatically moved to the same place in printed books. The new invention of print and the printing industry were gradually changing habits through many experiments and mistakes. And so the colophon was finally moved from the last to the second or third page. The shape of the first and last pages, the practice of adding empty pages and the graphic ornamentation of the front page were continuously evolving. For example, a play published in a quarto in London in 1594 did not have on its front page the brief words, *Henry VI, Second Part*, but a much longer description, exquisitely formed into a handsome pyramid:

The First part of the Contention betwixt the two famous Houses of Yorke and Lancaster, with the death of the good Duke Humphrey: And the banishment and death of the Duke of Suffolke, and the Tragicall end of the proud Cardinal of Winchester, with the notable Rebellion of Jack Cade: and the Duke of Yorke's first claim unto the crowne.

The extensive title of the book explained its content and invited the potential client to purchase it. It did not sound very different to a street crier's raucous refrain on some platform in front of the theatre. Let's imagine him, with a drum, under a vividly painted canvas (one can see such advertisements on the engravings from St Bartholomew's fair), when – in between pounding the drum – he keeps exclaiming, like a costermonger:

The Tragedy of King Richard the Third, containing His treacherous Plots against his brother Clarence, the pitiful murder of His innocent nephews, His tyrannical usurpation, with the course of His detested life, and most deserved death.

This is exactly how the title page of the Quarto edition, printed soon after the play's opening, reads. The practice of this new technology, print, with its titles, introductions, lists of contents, etcetera, started to imitate, in the most surprising manner, the oldest stunts of the theatre, with its prologues, interludes or the traditional, final *Bergamasca* dance. The process was fuelled by both sides. The theatre eagerly imitated the solemnity of books, while at the same time literature or, more precisely, the novel was discovering, incredibly quickly, the usefulness and efficiency of presenting events in the form of a sequence of scenes divided by the flow of time. Milan Kundera has described this process in detail in his *Testaments Betrayed* and *The Curtain*, starting from Cervantes and reaching to Dostoevsky and Flaubert. The nineteenth century indeed refined the technique of writing 'a scene after a scene' almost to perfection: Kundera rightly notes that the moment of appearance of Prince Myshkin, let's say, in the sitting room of Nastasia Filipovna, can be identified with horological accurateness, at quarter past two, let's say, no more, no less. This is why the process of adapting the prose of Dostoevsky for the theatre is basically so easy – one needs only to cut the unnecessary descriptions, to shorten the dialogue a little, and the work is done.

Cervantes, who was himself both a prose writer and a playwright, enjoyed playing with this parallelism of literary and theatrical forms a lot. So here we have a main title, *Don Quixote from La Mancha*, and immediately afterwards the first act, that is 'Volume One' with its 'Chapter I', which – attention, please! – '*treats of the character and pursuits of the famous gentleman Don Quixote of La Mancha*' …

The author, exactly like a man at the theatre's entrance, feels obliged to offer a synopsis of his story in one sentence before he moves to the proper narration:

> In a village of La Mancha, the name of which I have no desire to call to mind, there lived not long since one of those gentlemen that keep a lance in the lance-rack, an old buckler, a lean hack, and a greyhound for coursing …

Every new chapter in the adventures of the Knight of the Rueful Countenance includes the description of the next event at the head of the page. And so, for example, '*Chapter VIII, Of the good fortune which the valiant Don Quixote had in the terrible and undreamt-of adventure of the windmills, with other occurrences worthy to be fitly recorded*' starts from a dramatic confrontation:

> At this point they came in sight of thirty or forty windmills that there are on that plain, and as soon as Don Quixote saw them he said to his squire, 'Fortune is arranging matters for us better than we

could have shaped our desires ourselves, for look there, friend Sancho Panza, where thirty or more monstrous giants present themselves, all of whom I mean to engage in battle and slay, and with whose spoils we shall begin to make our fortunes; for this is righteous warfare, and it is God's good service to sweep so evil a breed from off the face of the earth'.

I am comparing here the author, whose importance is continuously fortified by the technology of print, to the theatrical herald; even more so, to the Master of Ceremonies, who distributes his encouragements and praise to the audience. The power which this Magus holds over the listener – comparable to the power of Prospero over the audience in *The Tempest* – has grown over the centuries. The modern authors understand this new power of theirs very well, and they love to woo and beguile their readers with spectacular stunts and flights of rhetoric.

Let's see – for example 'Chapter VIII' of 'Volume Two' ends with the words:

In the end, Don Quixote made up his mind to enter the city at nightfall, and they waited until the time came among some oak trees that were near El Toboso; and when the moment they had agreed upon arrived, they made their entrance into the city, where something happened to them that may fairly be called something.

Having our curiosity sharpened, we turn the page. The next one, along with our expectations, presents 'Chapter IX', where in the place of the usual short synopsis included in the first line we read: 'Wherein is related what will be seen there.'

Shameless Cervantes! He got bored, this selfish, egoistic demigod, with composing the next courteous portion of introduction and so here he dares to put me, his reader, off, with an impatient gesture of his pen! And then only to pick up the topic again in a moment, as if nothing has happened:

'Twas at the very midnight hour – more or less – when Don Quixote and Sancho quitted the wood and entered El Toboso. The town was in deep silence, for all the inhabitants were asleep, and stretched on the broad of their backs, as the saying is.

(Trans. John Ormsby)

The stressing and emphasising of the position of the author-conjurer in literature was growing throughout the sixteenth, seventeenth and eighteenth centuries. In 1759, the first of nine parts of *The Life and Opinions of Tristram Shandy, Gentleman* by Laurence Sterne appears and it is, arguably, the equilibristic record of the author's tightrope walk on the narrative line. Nine volumes presented in the first person (purportedly supplied to the printer by Tristram Shandy), nine volumes of an extra-terrestrially crazy tale which departs, returns, jumps forward, gossips, quotes, distorts, remembers, mentions, retorts and spins. And all that time it does not move beyond the moment of birth of the title character! A masterpiece of verbosity, it is an open and provocative challenge to the reader. A refined mix of *pastiche*, remix, marvellous improvisation, insouciance and a proof of the divinity of creative writing. A perfidious masterpiece: one could not go any further along this path. For the next step on this catwalk of charming, blasphemous arrogance, one will have to wait until the middle of the twentieth century: 'Monday: me. Tuesday: me. Wednesday, Thursday, Friday: me' (Gombrowicz, *Diaries*).

8   There is a literary game, there is a game within that game and there is theatre-within-a-theatre. It has always been known within the theatre that its activity happens in a theatre. What is also always understood is that the first task of the theatre is to competently bring the spectator to the wilful suspension of disbelief. Therefore, only after the long introduction from the

Watchman and the Chorus can the proper action of *The Orest-eia* start. In an analogical way, some suggestions of the Chorus first have to transport us to Verona, before Samson and Gregor, servants of Capulet, can slowly enter the stage. However, stories written in prose – in the form of a letter, tract, novel or dialogue – seemed to recognise more slowly, and much later, the incredible potentialities hidden in the story-within-the-story.

This concept itself was never a revolutionary novelty. For example, Plato knew very well the benefits of quoting the statements of others in his stories. At the beginning of his dialogue *Symposium*, Apollodorus describes to his friend the long discussion which took place at the feast of Agathon, which was held when Apollodorus and his friend Glaucon were still children. Glaucon seems to be someone who heard the story of Apollodorus some time ago, even before the friend asked for it. And now Apollodorus tells the story all over again to his friend, assuring him that he has heard about it from Aristodemus, 'that from Kydatenaion, that not very high one, always with bare feet'. Then Apollodorus repeats in incredible detail to Kydet his friend (in fact, to us readers) almost every word of all the participants who were there. He describes very accurately who and how many times they spoke, what was said and what for, as if he himself were there.

This multi-layered shroud of stories, allegedly heard from some or other persons, serves, I suspect, mainly as a cover, as an invention, blurring the real authorship of the *Symposium* because of the context of the political and social manners of Plato's time. 'If anybody asks' – the author seems to say – 'I have only written what somebody, somewhere, may have heard from somebody else. In fact, nobody knows from whom, and it happened so many years ago anyway, so who really knows what happened?'

The *Symposium* uses the frame of the story-within-a-story as a trick which is supposed to shield the author from eventual repression. We are still a long way from the narrative licence to use the multi-level, box-within-a-box structure which we see in many works of modern times.

Anyway, a certain Lucian from Samosata, writing after the year AD 120, knew the conscious juggling of alleged authorship very well and he cultivated the subtle dialectics of literary truth and fiction with great skill and refinement. In the introduction to his *True History*, he writes about being shocked by some fantastic lies in the descriptions of distant, exotic lands found in the works of earlier authors, including Ctesias, Iambulus and even Homer. 'What surprised me most', he writes about his predecessors, 'was their confidence that nobody will notice that they are lying'. Lucian assures readers that his work is:

> about things, which I have never seen, nor ever experienced, nor ever heard about them from anybody else; what's more, about the things, which in fact do not exist and which never could have existed. Therefore my readers cannot believe in any of my words.

Paradoxically, immediately afterwards, he presents the description of his alleged journey beyond the Columns of Heracles, the sequence in which he visited the islands and finally the various kingdoms and monsters which live in them. Then he travels with companions to the Moon and reports about the war there between the locals and their rivals from the Morning Star. At last, he lands again in the Earth's ocean, only to be swallowed by an enormous whale. Paraphrasing Gombrowicz:

> Who believed him, who read him alone,
> Is a stupid idiot, and is a trombone!

This general process of 'borrowing' from other writers' material was creeping through the centuries slowly, but was creeping nevertheless. If one can borrow (and divulge) one letter, why not borrow three of them? Diogenes Laërtius copied and divulged three letters of Epicurus, and only three of his original letters have reached us from the abyss of time. If one intriguing story about some fascinating adventures can be circulated, why not seven, or even ten of them? The anthologies of stories start to appear, for example, the exempla for imitation, composed for young clerics and collected after some time into a tome, *Disciplina clericalis* (thirteenth century). In the thirteenth century, a further set of moralising tales appeared, entitled *Il libro dei sette savi*, in which a young man faced with a verdict of death had to listen to lectures about righteous and immoral ways of behaving. Contemporaneously, a continuous stream of Greek, Hebraic and Latin translations from the East started to flow. These stories were not always pious, were often salacious (*Panchantra*, *Tales of the Thousand and One Nights* and the cycle *Brihat Katha*). After 1280, the Italian collection *Novellino* was published, a collection known also as *Il libro di novella et di bel parlar gentile* or *Cento novelle antiche*. And so, when Boccaccio starts writing his *Decameron* in 1347, the game of a story-within-a-story is already a widely known and is a popular convention. Not long afterwards, dozens, if not hundreds of imitators – Chaucer and Shakespeare included – will borrow from Boccaccio.

Therefore, Cervantes is already strongly embedded in this competition when, at the very beginning of the seventeenth century, he proposes at a certain moment of his novel:

Don Quixote gave the promise for himself and the others, and with this assurance he began as follows: 'My name is Cardenio, my birthplace one of the best cities of this Andalusia, my family noble, my parents rich, my misfortune so great that my parents must have wept and my family grieved over it without being able by their wealth to lighten it; for the gifts of fortune can do little to relieve reverses sent by Heaven. In that same country there was a heaven in which love had placed all the glory I could desire; such was the beauty of Luscinda …'

This is how the story of Cardenio starts, the classical additional story, inserted into the primary narrative of the novel. And yet some time later, in the fifth chapter of the fourth volume, the same knight Cardenio, the Ragged One, becomes – within the main story about Don Quixote – a witness of an unexpected discovery:

The landlord was carrying away the valise and the books, but the Curate said to him, 'Wait; I want to see what those papers are that are written in such a good hand.' The landlord taking them out handed them to him to read, and he perceived they were a work of about eight sheets of manuscript, with, in large letters at the beginning, the title of 'Novel of the Ill-advised Curiosity.' The Curate read three or four lines to himself, and said, 'I must say the title of this novel does not seem to me a bad one, and I feel an inclination to read it all.' To which the landlord replied, 'Then your reverence will do well to read it, for I can tell you that some guests who have read it here have been much pleased with it, and have begged it of me very earnestly; but I would not give it, meaning to return it to the person who forgot the valise, books, and papers here, for maybe he will return here some time or other; and though I know I shall miss the books, faith I mean to return them; for though I am an innkeeper, still I am a Christian.'

'You are very right, friend,' said the Curate; 'but for all that, if the novel pleases me you must let me copy it.'

'With all my heart,' replied the host.

While they were talking Cardenio had taken up the novel and begun to read it and forming the same opinion of it as the Curate, he begged him to read it so that they might all hear it.

'I would read it,' said the Curate, 'if the time would not be better spent in sleeping.'

'It will be rest enough for me,' said Dorothea, 'to while away the time by listening to some tale, for my spirits are not yet tranquil enough to let me sleep when it would be seasonable.'

'Well then, in that case,' said the Curate, 'I will read it, if it were only out of curiosity; perhaps it may contain something pleasant.'

Master Nicholas added his entreaties to the same effect, and Sancho too; seeing which, and considering that he would give pleasure to all, and receive it himself, the Curate said, 'Well then, attend to me everyone, for the novel begins thus.'

That 'beginning of the novel', announced by the author, who is Cervantes himself, is the fourth chapter of the fourth volume of the story about Don Quixote. It is a chapter which starts immediately and which the Curate reads to the others:

Chapter thirty three: The novel of the ill related curiosity.
In Florence, a rich and famous city of Italy in the province called Tuscany, there lived two gentlemen of wealth and quality, Anselmo and Lothario, such great friends that by way of distinction they were called by all that knew them 'The Two Friends.' They were unmarried, young, of the same age and of the same tastes, which was enough to account for the reciprocal friendship between them. Anselmo, it is true, was somewhat more inclined to seek pleasure in love than Lothario, for whom the pleasures of the chase had more attraction …

A question arises: does the Curate indeed read to the others the words '*Chapter thirty three, The novel of the ill related curiosity*'? Maybe he reads them only the title: '*The novel of the ill related curiosity*'. Or maybe he skips all these words and starts directly from: 'In Florence, a rich and famous city of Italy …' In the second and in the third variant, the story of Cervantes then proceeds with no obstacles. However, with the first possibility, if the Curate read loudly the words, '*Chapter thirty three*', this narration would become a meta-story in which the characters from the history of Don Quixote are reading in the inn the found description of their own peregrinations. Two hundred years later, Jan Potocki in his *The Manuscript Found in Saragossa* will multiply his reality five times, like origami, pioneered by these experiments in *Don Quixote*. In Potocki's story, we are listening in to the history of Commander Toralva, who managed to tell it to Blaise Hérvas, who has shared it with Busqueros, who told it to Chevalier Toledo in the presence of Avadoro, who finally, by writing it down in his diary, could pass it on to us!

9 All authors are indebted. They are hopelessly indebted, yet also quite happily, blithely indebted to Ariosto, Herodotus, Lucian. Shakespeare, and Chaucer before him, borrowed from Boccaccio; Spenser in *The Faerie Queene* takes a whole world from *The Romance of the Rose*; Boccaccio steals from Arabic authors and paraphrases the translations from Sanskrit. Sterne adores Cervantes and is rewriting whole paragraphs from *The Anatomy of Melancholy* by Robert Burton (1621). This is an unbelievable chain of echoes, repetitions, variations, conversions, always surprising, never stopping: Joyce dialogues with Homer, Tolkien reaches for *Beowulf*. The text is a reflection of another text. The author, like the designer at a dress fitting, looks in the mirror of another text and decides – here we add a little, there we shall cut, then pleat a little here, please, and then we raise the hem. So we could say that the text chats with another text, imitates it, mocks it and plays with it. Licentiousness reigns in the kingdom of narration. Books meet one another, they travel together, they even sail together to some island – Kythera – there they become lovers and they have offspring. And afterwards the libraries are full of their illegitimate issue; shelf after shelf, bookcase after bookcase, their origins appear in every second tome. In every department there are mongrels, mixed-heritage beings and hybrids. Think, for example, about poor Jane Austen. Her fate was to be relentlessly copied by hordes for two centuries. Or about Lord Byron, shamelessly imitated by hundreds of pretenders.

And yet it seems to be impossible to write without a bond

with an important predecessor. Could Witkiewicz appear without the previous melodies of Sienkiewicz, without the bombastic expressions of Miciński, without Przybyszewski's manner? Could Gombrowicz find his own voice without the tales of Rzewuski, without the seventeenth-century Polish of Jan Chrysostom Pasek?

All authors are indebted; they pay back however and whenever they can. They are all literary bastards, brought into the world by the same desire for illicit procreation. The ugly offspring pushes away the better-formed. In the deformed, defrauded shape of the latest novelty, the original often cannot be recognised anymore.

The anxiety of influence? That term was made famous by the late Harold Bloom, an American critic. Bloom writes about literary influence as if it were an ancient curse and irresolvable problem (1973). You want to write as a genius, oh, dear poet, because you were infected with geniality by some other poet, earlier than you. Therefore, you are imitating him and, contemporaneously, the last thing you would like is anybody else noticing your theft. According to Bloom, Beckett, for example, keeps manoeuvring in his works, surrounded by the endless fear of the influence of Joyce, while – surprisingly without fear – continuously annexing Shakespeare. The same Shakespeare before whom Joyce is simply trembling like an aspen, as he is before Milton, Austen and Wordsworth.

Bloom also fiercely defended the existence of 'the Western canon' of literature. In a book of the same title (1994), Bloom ravishes, with particular satisfaction, the work of Sigmund Freud: 'Shakespeare is the inventor of psychoanalysis; Freud, its codifier.' And later: 'Hamlet did not have an Oedipus complex, but Freud certainly had a Hamlet complex, and perhaps psychoanalysis is a Shakespeare complex!'

And even more:

Freudian literary criticism of Shakespeare is a celestial joke; Shakespearean criticism of Freud will have a hard birth, but it will come, since Freud as a writer will survive the death of psychoanalysis ... Freud's work, which is the description of the totality of human nature, far transcends the faded Freudian therapy.

With a fierce passion, Bloom defends a certain obviousness: at the end it is evident that every outstanding writer takes freely from his or her predecessors. The more outstanding they were, the more they value them. Acknowledging Shakespeare and Dante as a basis of the Western canon is hardly a revelation. It is as if one might suddenly claim, with much ado, that most of the philosophical dilemmas were formulated by Plato and Aristotle. Well, they were, and so what?

The stubborn conservatism of Bloom can sometimes be tiresome. Nevertheless, he can also be surprisingly convincing and fresh when he invites us to stop using, in the process of reading literature, the prosthetics of ideological or political correctness:

> The Western Canon is Shakespeare and Dante. Beyond them, it is what they absorbed and what absorbs them. Redefining 'literature' is a vain pursuit because you cannot usurp sufficient cognitive strength to encompass Shakespeare and Dante, and they are literature.

At the end, Bloom asks probably the most important question for every critic: why do people keep reading literature? His answer, I dare to think, is worth quoting:

> Traditions tell us that the free and solitary self writes in order to overcome mortality. I think that the self, in its quest to be free and solitary, ultimately reads with one aim only: to confront greatness. That confrontation scarcely masks the desire to join greatness, which is the basis of the aesthetic experience once called the Sublime: the quest for a transcendence of limits. Our common fate is age, sickness, death,

oblivion. Our common hope, tenuous but persistent, is for some version of survival.

10 To find one's own voice. This metaphorical formula refers to singing, not without reason. Creating literature even in the nineteenth century was still commonly connected with the gift of the Muses. Writing is 'singing', the voice of the poet is related to the 'music of the spheres'. Yet even in prose, the subtle sequence of rhythms, the length of phrases, a choice of words, create together a specific kind of music. The phrases are created by the author, who is highly conscious that their words may be spoken publicly one day. Prose, similar to poetry, sings, and each of its authors have their own tone in the choir. One can recognise the characteristic tone of Diderot, let's say, or Dostoevsky, after a few lines – by the middle of the page at the very least.

And yet the 'voice' here is not only a musical matter. The metaphorical voice of the writer is in fact the measure of their originality, of their uniqueness. Once you have heard Miron Białoszewski, you will never confuse his voice with anyone else's. I could even risk saying that the writer creates their own voice and their own language in a similar way to the way the theatre creates a different, new world, with its own idiom in every performance. Finding a 'voice of one's own', for the writer, has a lot in common with the process of an actor perfectly performing his role. A pitch-perfect performance in the theatre delights us with its almost ideal combination of sound, of movement and emotion, evoking the aura of the character. It fascinates us with its effortlessness and the limitless ability of both physical and psychological transformation. To find one's own voice in literature is an analogical blessing. I would dare to say that it is hearing and transferring the seemingly 'natural' expression of words to the page. It is as if some character in the author's head was dictating words and phrases and the author was simply tapping them out on the keyboard. During the process of rehearsals, a moment comes when the actor finds that the character starts to dictate rhythms, gestures and actions. From that moment, these simply cannot be any different from what they are.

Yes, but the role of the actor, once alive, will be revived again many times until the end of the run. It will change slowly from one show to another, it will mature, it will even lead the actor into some unforeseen territories, while the work of literature, once written, stays on the shelf forever, unchanged, like a tomb in the cemetery. It is true to say that sometimes the author decides to change something, to cut, to add or to correct in the next edition. It may happen, but it is not common or usual. We seem to be convinced that the work, which has managed to 'appear in the world' once, should be able to stand on its own.

It is interesting, this invulnerability of the printed, literary text in our culture. Most probably it came from the elevation of the Scriptures, from the not fully conscious sacralisation of anything which is written. This habit may change with time, because why can the written text not be corrected or amended? Yet is also possible that my prophecy is wrong and that it is only my experience of the theatre speaking. In the theatre we keep changing, amending, reviving, reshaping all the time. Any agreement on a non-changeable state would seem to us simply stupid and artificial. Also, the old controversy raises its head: is the literary creation a part of the ancient Greek *arte*, or rather *techne*? Would it be possible to mark any border between one and the other? Well, we would need a whole new chapter for this.

11   Cervantes wants Don Quixote to visit the theatre. To be precise, the theatre visits Don Quixote during one of his escapades. It takes place in the inn, where Don Quixote lodges. Master Pedro arrives, well-known to the landlord.

We should note that Master Pedro 'had his left eye and nearly half his cheek covered with a patch of green taffety, showing that something ailed all that side' and by the end of the chapter we shall learn more about his questionable past as a thief. Meanwhile, Don Quixote asks the landlord who he is. 'This is a famous puppet-showman' answers the landlord:

> who for some time past has been going about this Mancha de Aragon, exhibiting a show of the release of Melisandra by the famous Don Gaiferos, one of the best and best-represented stories that have been seen in this part of the kingdom for many a year; he has also with him an ape with the most extraordinary gift ever seen in an ape or imagined in a human being; for if you ask him anything, he listens attentively to the question, and then jumps on his master's shoulder, and pressing close to his ear tells him the answer which Master Pedro then delivers. He says a great deal more about things past than about things to come; and though he does not always hit the truth in every case, most times he is not far wrong, so that he makes us fancy he has got the devil in him.

The landlord promptly finds a place in the inn for Master Pedro and his infamous ape. Soon afterwards:

> Don Quixote and Sancho went to where the show was already put up and uncovered, set all around with lighted wax tapers which made it look splendid and bright. When they came to it Master Pedro ensconced himself inside it, for it was he who had to work the puppets, and a boy, a servant of his, posted himself outside to act as showman and explain the mysteries of the exhibition, having a wand in his hand to point to the figures as they came out. And so, all who were in the inn being arranged in front of the show, some of them standing, and Don Quixote, Sancho, the page, and cousin, accommodated with the best places, the interpreter began to say what he will hear or see who reads or hears the next chapter.

'The show already put up and uncovered' was most probably a wooden box of a transportable size (two metres by almost a metre? – roughly the proportions of a modern cinema screen), open from above and with one wall absent. The lack of this wall creates a scenic window and this way the spectators can watch a three-dimensional diorama. Inside the box, roughly a metre deep, let's say, various miniaturised sets and painted screens appear (like a forest, the sea, mountains or clouds), while the operator of the marionettes, probably covered with some cloth, moves the marionettes from above and carries on with his colourful, loud narration.

Drums and trumpets were heard to sound inside it and cannon to go off. The noise was soon over, and then the boy lifted up his voice and said:

This true story which is here represented to your worships is taken word for word from the French chronicles and from the Spanish ballads that are in everybody's mouth, and in the mouth of the boys about the streets. Its subject is the release by Señor Don Gaiferos, of his wife Melisandra, when a captive in Spain at the hands of the Moors in the city of Sansueña, for so they called then what is now called Saragossa; and there you may see how Don Gaiferos is playing at the tables, just as they sing it –

I can bet that in this moment Master Pedro was giving, from behind the curtain, his fulsome baritone, singing the well-known ballad about the unfaithful Don Gaiferos:

> At tables playing Don Gaiferos sits,
> For Melisandra is forgotten now

while the marionette impersonating Gaiferos – I imagine – was impatiently scattering the chess figures and was going towards the battlements of the castle of King Marsilio, seen on the horizon, that is, under the walls of Saragossa. One might think that Don Quixote was enjoying the show because he was silent and did not intervene. In that moment, Master Pedro was skilfully changing the backdrop to the interior of some chamber and this way the spectators were transferred from Saragossa to Paris, to the Court of Charlemagne. Master Pedro was inserting the marionette of the King and the boy continued: 'And that personage who appears there with a crown on his head and a sceptre in his hand is the Emperor Charlemagne, the supposed father of Melisandra …'.

The Emperor Charlemagne in Paris worries about his daughter, while in Saragossa Don Gaiferos prepares to free her from the Moors – the show fluently moves on. Don Gaiferos cleverly liberates Melisandra from the tower where she was incarcerated (I can almost hear the joy of Melisandra, that is the efforts of Master Pedro squeaking in falsetto), and the lovers start their escape. Suddenly – the whinnying of a horse, banging on the metal sheet, the alarm of the trumpets! The Moors notice that Melisandra has escaped, and these horrible Mamelukes begin to chase the fugitives. The boy continues: 'word was brought to King Marsilio, who at once gave orders to sound the alarm; and see what a stir there is, and how the city is drowned with the sound of the bells pealing in the towers of all the mosques.'

Here, in the text of Cervantes, an intervention happens, totally unexpectedly, but also not, I think, incidentally:

'Nay, nay,' said Don Quixote at this; 'on that point of the bells Master Pedro is very inaccurate, for bells are not in use among the Moors; only kettledrums, and a kind of small trumpet somewhat like our clarion; to ring bells this way in Sansueña, is unquestionably a great absurdity.'

The intervention is not incidental, I dare to think, because Cervantes wants to show to his readers that in this concrete moment of the performance Don Quixote remains absolutely lucid and completely cognisant of reality. Cervantes knew very well what the Moors would use in such a case from the times of his own Moorish captivity after the Battle of Lepanto. The show of Master Pedro evokes – as we can see – only a distanced and factual comment from the Knight of Rueful Countenance.

On hearing this, Master Pedro stopped ringing, and said, 'Don't look into trifles, Señor Don Quixote, or want to have things up to a pitch of perfection that is out of reach. Are there not almost every day a thousand comedies represented all round us full of thousands of inaccuracies and absurdities, and, for all that, they have a successful run, and are listened to not only with applause, but with admiration and all the rest of it? Go on, boy, and don't mind; for so long as I fill my pouch, no matter if I show as many inaccuracies as there are motes in a sunbeam.'

'True enough,' said Don Quixote; and the boy went on: 'See what a numerous and glittering crowd of horsemen issues from the city in pursuit of the two faithful lovers, what a blowing of trumpets there is, what sounding of horns, what beating of drums and tabors;' …

From the professional point of view, this must have been for Master Pedro a particularly difficult moment: three, maybe even four heavy horses with Mamelukes astride them, then Melisandra and Don Gaiferos on the splendid horse in his second hand, and above of all this the need to mimic the beat of hooves, the tumult, not to mention the sound of the bells (kicked with the left leg?). And suddenly this freak, Don Quixote, in the middle of all this war music, thinking that:

it would be right to aid the fugitives, and standing up, exclaims in a loud voice, 'Never, while I live, will I permit foul play to be practised in my presence on such a famous Knight and fearless lover as Don Gaiferos. Halt! ill-born rabble, follow him not nor pursue him, or ye will have to reckon with me in battle!'

We know roughly what happens next, but despite this I recall the description for the sake of accuracy:

> he drew his sword, and with one bound placed himself close to the show, and with unexampled rapidity and fury began to shower down blows on the puppet troop of the Moors, knocking over some, decapitating others, maiming this one and demolishing that; and among many more he delivered one down stroke which, if Master Pedro had not ducked, made himself small, and got out of the way, would have sliced off his head as easily as if it had been made of almond-paste. Master Pedro kept shouting, 'Hold hard! Señor Don Quixote! can't you see they're not real Moors you're knocking down and killing and destroying, but only little pasteboard figures! Look – sinner that I am! – how you're wrecking and ruining all that I'm worth!' But in spite of this, Don Quixote did not leave off discharging a continuous rain of cuts, slashes, down strokes, and backstrokes, and at length, in less than the space of two credos, he brought the whole show to the ground, with all its fittings and figures shivered and knocked to pieces, King Marsilio badly wounded, and the Emperor Charlemagne with his crown and head split in two. The whole audience was thrown into confusion, the ape fled to the roof of the inn …

This is a key moment for the story itself and for the general dialectics of fiction and reality in the work of Cervantes. Please mind: Don Quixote's jump of consciousness from critical realism to Romantic fiction happens in the blink of an eye. Only a moment ago he was lucidly criticising the director's solutions (those unfortunate bells of Master Pedro), and a moment later he pounces, outraged, and starts to demolish the squadrons of enemies. This does not happen gradually, nor is it any hallucinogenic episode. It is rather as if there is a switch in the brain of Don Quixote between a 'real' state of mind and a 'Romantic' one. It also seems that Don Quixote may have some influence over this switch.

Was the encouragement of Master Pedro ('Go on, boy, and don't mind') the catalyst for this rapid change of perception? That's how it looks, I'm afraid. And, if I am right, this particular moment illustrates that the madness of Don Quixote consists in a wilful pursuit of moral principles, no matter what actually happens in the story. Watching the primitive puppet theatre provokes him not only to the critical comment about the director's faults, but the mention of the priority of Master Pedro's purse over these principles liberates in him an almost superhuman power. Watching a primitive, probably poorly lit puppet theatre in some lice-infested inn is a waste of time but standing with a sword in his hand against the enemies of the marvellous Melisandra equates with choosing a reality 'more enduring than bronze'. Only a moment ago, Don Quixote was a critical spectator in a comfortable chair, and yet in a split second he decides to jump acrobatically from the Vale of Suffering to the Kingdom of Glory.

We can imagine him as he suddenly steps into the middle of the stage and runs towards the puppet box brandishing a sword. There is general panic, fear, shrieks of people, the monkey escapes to the roof. Master Pedro is crying and moaning, but Don Quixote returns to reality only very slowly:

> The complete destruction of the show being thus accomplished, Don Quixote became a little calmer, and said, 'I wish I had here before me now all those who do not or will not believe how useful knights-errant are in the world; just think, if I had not been here present, what would have become of the brave Don Gaiferos and the fair Melisandra! Depend upon it, by this time those dogs would have overtaken them and inflicted some outrage upon them. So, then, long live knight-errantry beyond everything living on earth this day!'

In this moment he is still, with his whole being, on the battleground. Master Pedro will have to moan much longer before

Don Quixote goes quiet, loses confidence and finally feels embarrassed.

Sancho Panza was touched by Master Pedro's words, and said to him:

'Don't weep and lament, Master Pedro; you break my heart; let me tell you my master, Don Quixote, is so Catholic and scrupulous a Christian that, if he can make out that he has done you any wrong, he will own it, and be willing to pay for it and make it good, and something over and above.' ...

'That is true,' said Don Quixote; 'but at present I am not aware that I have got anything of yours, Master Pedro.'

'What!' returned Master Pedro; 'and these relics lying here on the bare hard ground – what scattered and shattered them but the invincible strength of that mighty arm? And whose were the bodies they belonged to but mine? And what did I get my living by but by them?'

'Now am I fully convinced,' said Don Quixote, 'of what I had many a time before believed; that the enchanters who persecute me do nothing more than put figures like these before my eyes, and then change and turn them into what they please. In truth and earnest, I assure you Gentlemen who now hear me, that to me everything that has taken place here seemed to take place literally, that Melisandra was Melisandra, Don Gaiferos Don Gaiferos, Marsilio Marsilio, and Charlemagne Charlemagne. That was why my anger was roused; and to be faithful to my calling as a Knight-errant I sought to give aid and protection to those who fled, and with this good intention I did what you have seen. If the result has been the opposite of what I intended, it is no fault of mine, but of those wicked beings that persecute me; but, for all that, I am willing to condemn myself in costs for this error of mine, though it did not proceed from malice; let Master Pedro see what he wants for the spoiled figures, for I agree to pay it at once in good and current money of Castile.'

This is unheard of: here a person with a strongly distorted sense of reality acknowledges his medical condition and declares

31

that he will cover Master Pedro's material losses. 'I am willing to condemn myself in costs for this error of mine' – there are two Don Quixotes it seems. One, who fights with Mamelukes and another one, who understands – at least to some extent – that he is ill, even if not himself but the 'wicked enchanters' are responsible for his actions. Both the realities which Don Quixote perceives, and in which he lives, exclude one another. By this I mean only one can exist, they cannot exist together. But our patient, somehow desperately, seems to defend the possibility of their paradoxical co-existence:

Master Pedro picked up from the ground King Marsilio of Saragossa with his head off, and said, 'Here you see how impossible it is to restore this King to his former state, so I think, saving your better judgments, that for his death, decease, and demise, four reals and a half may be given me.'

'Proceed,' said Don Quixote.

'Well then, for this cleavage from top to bottom,' continued Master Pedro, taking up the split Emperor Charlemagne, 'it would not be much if I were to ask five reals and a quarter.'

'It's not little,' said Sancho.

'Nor is it much,' said the landlord; 'make it even, and say five reals.'

'Let him have the whole five and a quarter,' said Don Quixote; 'for the sum total of this notable disaster does not stand on a quarter more or less; and make an end of it quickly, Master Pedro, for it's getting on to supper-time, and I have some hints of hunger.'

'For this figure,' said Master Pedro, 'that is without a nose, and wants an eye, and is the fair Melisandra, I ask, and I am reasonable in my charge, two reals and twelve maravedis.'

'The very devil must be in it,' said Don Quixote, 'if Melisandra and her husband are not by this time at least on the French border, for the horse they rode on seemed to me to fly rather than gallop; so you needn't try to sell me the cat for the hare, showing me here a noseless Melisandra when she is now, may be, enjoying herself at her ease with her husband in France. God help everyone to his own, Master Pedro, and let us all proceed fairly and honestly; and now go on.'

Master Pedro, perceiving that Don Quixote was beginning to wander, and return to his original fancy, was not disposed to let him escape, so he said to him, 'This cannot be Melisandra, but must be one of the damsels that waited on her; so if I'm given sixty maravedis for her, I'll be content and sufficiently paid.'

Oh, cruel alternative! Oh, you either-or, never satisfied! Either I have just – unintentionally – minced Melisandra (therefore I am mad), or, while chopping the Mamelukes and their King Marsilio, I have accidentally ripped the bosom of her assisting lady (this is called 'the unplanned losses of our side' in military jargon), while all the time Melisandra flourishes in Paris.

In short, the puppet-show storm passed off, and all supped in peace and good fellowship at Don Quixote's expense, for he was the height of generosity.

12

Is it a game of the 'wilful suspension of disbelief'? The case of Don Quixote, who attacks Don Pedro's marionettes with a sword, is not an experiment in 'suspending disbelief'. Nor is it an experiment in a temporary 'supporting of belief'. It is a complete act of belief, of faith. It is a complete immersion of the subject in the 'world of speculative fiction'. Don Quixote seems to understand, to some extent, that he is ill, as I have written above, and his case touches precisely the ambiguity of the human states of health and of illness. This is not the refined knowledge of a human game, which the dialectical juggling of conventions in the theatre requires. The game in the theatre calls for a state of heightened consciousness, a state of readiness to play for high stakes. Who is not ready to step up to this challenge should better stay at home and should stay away from the theatre. Otherwise, they may risk breaking our marionettes.

The battle of Don Quixote with Don Pedro's marionettes reminds me of the history of my peer from theatre school, Bogusław C. Bogusław was unusually handsome and untouched by too much reading, born in one of the villages near Kraków. He managed, despite some difficulties, to finish the four-year actor's course and started to work in one of the provincial theatres. Some colleagues who witnessed this event told me later what happened. Bogusław played one of the leading roles in the show, which started as usual at quarter past seven. Bogusław appeared in strong, unnatural make up. He played, with some effort, the first three scenes, and then in the fourth, during which he was not supposed to be on stage, he turned up unexpectedly in the first row of the audience, loudly applauding the actors, laughing, tearing his costume and shouting insults. The performance was immediately stopped and poor Bogusław was taken straight to hospital. The doctors diagnosed schizophrenia.

13 It happens regularly in performances for children that they root for certain characters. 'Run away, the wolf is hiding behind a tree!', or 'Don't go in there, there is a witch inside!' – these voices suggest that children are absolutely engaged in the action. Does it mean that children also regularly enter the stage to, for example, protect the hero or heroine from the witch? Or chase the wolf from the bushes? No, it does not, because their engagement does not equate for them with a loss of any sense of reality.

Children are very comfortable with the cognitive land of 'as if' because, from their first beginnings, their parents regularly play with them games which use the concept of 'as if'. I am throwing you into the air, son, to make you believe for a short moment that you will fall, but really we both know very well that such a danger remains only hypothetical, remains only 'as if'. The game 'as if', or 'what would happen if', is the tool for discovering and experimenting with our environment from our earliest years. And therefore, the young audience, loudly warning the character about a danger on stage, absolutely does not destroy the social convention of the performance. The pleasure of adults terrified 'as if' they were in extreme peril, while watching a thriller, is based upon exactly the same principle.

Don Quixote is not 'forgetting himself', nor 'getting totally involved in fiction' like some imagined bourgeois in the arguments of Bertolt Brecht. Simply, in given circumstances, Don Quixote switches on an internal lever and jumps from a 'realistic' mode to a 'Romantic' one. He is also able, though with some difficulty, to travel in the opposite direction. Using today's terminology, we could call him bipolar. He functions in two juxtaposing phases and he is not happy about it at all. He knows that he has a problem with himself, a rather serious problem. Not knowing what to do, he blames 'the wicked enchanters'.

Don Quixote seems to be a man with a serious disability. His cognitive skills are deprived of the sense of play which we call 'as if'; a sense of play elemental for the effective functioning of human society. As such, he is an unhappy, poor man. And the truth may be even worse: he seems to refuse to acknowledge the universal practice of people – to accept the everyday, never-ending game of 'as if'.

14 Is the theatre necessary for redemption? This is a provocative question, no doubt, but our intuition can help us here. The pandemic has closed, daily, thousands of theatres around the world, putting thousands of theatre practitioners into a dystopian situation, which would have been difficult to imagine before. In these extraordinary circumstances, human societies can still flourish without the world of live spectacle. Films and pre-recorded television immediately filled the gap.

Statistically, spectators viewed more digital shows than ever before. But real, live performances have temporarily vanished, not for the first time in history. Yet people continue to be born, love and die as if as if nothing has happened.

Therefore, yes, one can imagine a planet on which the phenomenon of the theatre remains unknown. Such a planet has been imagined and thoroughly described by China Miéville, an English science-fiction author, in his novel *Embassytown* (2011). In some distant future, very far away, a planet named Arieka exists, populated by insect-like, intelligent Hosts, each one of them with a double throat. Humans communicate with them with the help of carefully groomed twin Ambassadors from Earth. The habitants of Arieka have their economy, their cities and society, but their language remains an idiom of sacred, pure names – the Hosts are unable to lie. The Ambassadors from Earth can imitate their idiom thanks to their pairs of twin throats and, thanks to this, the exchange of trade flourishes. The highlight of the Arieka–Earth relationship is a Festival of Lies, celebrated at important occasions. At the festival, in front of the crowds, the ambitious participants from Arieka make, for example, unbelievable efforts to cough – while indicating that some green object – 'is red!' Such a concept simply has no place in the insect-like heads of the Ariekei, but it decidedly intrigues them. In the novel by Miéville, the discovery of the meaning of metaphor by the Ariekei will finally happen, in turbulent circumstances threatening the annihilation of their kind. To be able to start using language which distinguishes between 'truth' and 'fiction' the Hosts will have to revolutionise their culture within one generation. This complicated operation, paid for by numerous losses, will end with success. Arieka will change its status from exploited colony to a full member of the Galactic Federation and the novel will end. Yet we will be left with an anxiety in our souls, an anxiety consciously created by the author: is it true that civilisation and culture cannot exist without the lie?

The word 'lie' weighs heavily in ethical terms and probably because of this Miéville, quite convincingly, prefers to ponder the concept of 'metaphor' – understood as the process of transferring the meaning from one object to another. Let's take a randomly chosen pair of words: the 'ocean roars', for example. Seemingly it makes no sense because it is not water, but animals, which roar. And yet despite this we understand such a mix of meanings in the blink of an eye. The invention of an alphabet would not be possible without such a transfer of meanings. Drawing a map would not be possible, or painting an image which communicates meaning, not to mention musical composition imitating the songs of birds. Sadly, the live theatre in its European, known-to-us, shape, is probably not indispensable for the continuity of human culture. However, the mimetic principle, at its roots, combined with proficiency in the 'what would happen if' game, remains necessary for its existence.

15 In the beginning was the beginning which was *incipit*. And what if one starts from the end? The Book of Genesis, as we know, starts from what was in the beginning but St John starts his Book of Revelations, that is, the Apocalypse, from Alpha and Omega. That is, he starts both from the Beginning *and* the End. He fires from this huge cannon, because, although it is only the beginning of the Revelations, the Revelations are all about The End. St John wants to avoid any accusation of forgetting about The End from the very beginning. From a purely literary point of view, St John knows perfectly well that by elevating the eschatological End (end of the world, end of humanity, end of man) in his prophecy, he is also giving a higher, exceptional sense to the beginning. This is why beside the Omega Alpha also appears, I suspect. But of course, apart from a 'purely literary point of view', other perspectives are possible. For example, the figure of the snake Ouroboros, of

Vedic origin, which bites its own tail, or Plato's mystical insight into the essence of Time, in which both the Beginning and the End unite in One.

No, I am, of course, not mocking St John of Patmos. I am talking about how we got from the circle to the line. I am talking about how Christianity straightened the timeline of history, which was an absolutely crucial action for the way we perceive human experience. Earlier, the ancients usually went in circles with time: there was my grandfather, after him my father, here for some time I am, but then there will be my son after me, and soon also his son will come in time; whatever seems to be new has already been before. Nothing new, complains Marcus Aurelius, nothing new under the Sun, Ecclesiastes moans. Caesar Marcus Aurelius, in his existential tiredness, even risks an observation that whoever has lived for forty years in this vale of sorrows, has already seen everything that was worth seeing. The ancients were like a strange bunch of cranks, a club of white-haired old men, cinema fans, who were watching the same film with satisfaction, for the thirty-ninth time (most probably Fellini's *Amarcord*). Therefore, when somebody like St John appears and proclaims: 'I am Alpha and Omega, the Beginning and the End, says the Lord, who is, who was, and who will come, Omnipotent', their jaws drop and they are silent. Because this game is not about what the grandfather or father of whomever has managed to do. Nor about what the grandson might do in the future; this game is a game of Everything, of the Beginning of the World and of its End, and of your own Redemption. And all of a sudden, the club of old-film fans is faced with a Great Race to the Final Judgement. Time has extended immensely, in both directions, backwards and forwards. Suddenly, the perspective of the future is intellectually changed. New theories are born, theories previously impossible to think about. It was a revolutionary, completely new understanding of time, and of history and of our place within them. St John was probably the first to start the race and others soon followed. In this way the competition of *Those Magnificent Men in Their Flying Machines* was born.

Fine. And if one starts from the end? With this question I am returning to the beginning of the chapter. It is a perversity, I know, but maybe it will pay to go first to the beginning when wanting to talk about the end?

Harold Pinter, for example, starts his play *Betrayal* (1978) from its end. There are three characters, three friends: Emma, her husband Robert and his mate Jerry. Seven years of marital betrayal are told in a series of realistic scenes from the end to the beginning, together with lies, prevarications and all the games of pretence. Pinter was influenced by Proust's *In Search of Lost Time* (1913–27) but the trick with the inverted time of narration was used before him by many other authors. George S. Kaufman and Moss Hart used it in their play *Merrily We Roll Along* (1934), which was adapted into a successful musical by Stephen Sondheim (1981). Science fiction could not renounce it, of course – travels in time are its constant motif. The extreme case is a novel by Philip K. Dick from 1967, *Counter-Clock*, describing a future in which time starts to flow backwards. The dead wake up from their tombs and live their lives in a time juxtaposed with the 'normal' one, until they return to their mother's wombs. The novel was preceded by an earlier story, titled 'Your Visit Will Happen Yesterday' from 1966. My favourite case of the time paradox in sci-fi is the seventh journey of Ion Tichy in *The Star Diaries* by Stanisław Lem (1957) in which the hero meets, on board a spaceship on Saturday, 'himself from Friday', then 'from Thursday', from 'Tuesday' and many other selves.

The reversal of time in narration has probably always been known. Virgil used it in *The Aeneid*. So, yes, it can be done and often it can be quite fascinating, because of the variations of time and the point of view which is moving in time, which does not change the vector of reality and the objective state of things. Even when reading a narration reversed in time in a refined way, usually we do it from the first page to the last.

16 That is no country for old men.
Every lecture about the written text is a process inevitably immersed in time. As well as every story received by us in the theatre. For many thousands of years, we have been measuring the flow of time with the rising and the setting of the Sun: with changeable lengths of shadows cast by trees or rocks, with changes of weather, the travel of birds or with the colour of grass and leaves. For the last few centuries, we have perceived the passing of time often through the sense of hearing. The bell on the tower significantly tolls a quarter or an hour, a clock in the sitting room sends a message with its tick-tock, a watch on the wrist whispers, too. This tick-tock is unstoppable; time runs as fast in silence as when it gallops.

'The King your father ... – Dead, for my life! – Even so; my tale is told.'

That unexpected arrival of Chevalier Marcade at the very end of Act V of *Love's Labour's Lost* is one of the most poignant moments known to me in literature. It makes us aware of our ephemeralness. Marcade arrives at the peak of a mad, crazy festivity which has been cranking up with no breaks for four-and-a-half acts. He arrives in the middle of the characters' outbursts of laughter, as well as those of the audience. His few relatively ordinary words are like the stab of a rapier in the heart, like the fall of the blade of the guillotine. We feel a cold shiver down our spines. The parade of riotous youth, chasing each other with jokes and witty remarks, turns in one second to a dance of death, led by skeletons.

That is no country for old men. The young
In one another's arms, birds in the trees
– Those dying generations – at their song,
The salmon-falls, the mackerel-crowded seas,
Fish, flesh, or fowl, commend all summer long
Whatever is begotten, born, and dies.
Caught in that sensual music all neglect
Monuments of unageing intellect.

An aged man is but a paltry thing,
A tattered coat upon a stick, unless
Soul clap its hands and sing, and louder sing
For every tatter in its mortal dress,
Nor is there singing school but studying
Monuments of its own magnificence;
And therefore I have sailed the seas and come
To the holy city of Byzantium.

The first words of 'Sailing to Byzantium', a poem by William Butler Yeats published in 1928, served Cormac McCarthy as the title of one of his novels. Yet more than that novel, I remember the unusual way in which the poem was referred to by Robert Silverberg, a renowned American sci-fi writer, in his short story 'Sailing to Byzantium' in 1985.

In his story we are on Earth in the fiftieth century, when only a few people still live in reconstructed, historical cities. These cities are Mongolian Chang-an, Scandinavian Asgard, New Chicago, Timbuktu and Alexandria. They are dismantled from time to time (it is not clear by whom) and only then do new cities appear. There are never more than five of them at any one time. Their inhabitants are human-shaped perfect androids – 'temporaries' from the cities' most wonderful, historical periods, created for the comfort of a few 'non-temporary' others who resemble tourists, whom they never interact with directly.

Charles Philips and his partner Gioia stay in Alexandria. They are visiting the famous lighthouse and the library. Charles has landed here straight from New York in 1984, and simply does not know how he has found himself in the fiftieth century. Charles goes with the flow of events. Gioia and all of her 'non-temporary' young and beautiful friends (there are no exceptions) do not work anywhere. They visit places during the day, and have parties in the evening. Then they move to another city.

Charles and Gioia move to Chang-an. They are hosted by an Emperor who – like most of the guests in his court – is 'temporary'. Until now, Charles thought that Gioia and her friends would never grow old. He is surprised that one morning Gioia finds some grey hair on her head, which makes her very anxious. Later that night Charles realises that it is Belilala, Gioia's friend, not Gioia, who lies beside him in bed. Gioia has vanished.

One of the new cities is Mohenjo-Daro. Belilala informs Charles that Gioia has gone there because she is a 'temporary' and therefore gets older. Charles follows Gioia to Mohenjo-Daro but she is no longer there. Charles finally finds Gioia in New Chicago, a city from a later time. However, she soon escapes again, not wanting Charles to see her as an old woman.

After a long search, Charles finally finds his Gioia, only a little older, in their beloved Alexandria. Both of them know by now that Gioia is subject to the passage of time, while Charles is not. They manage to find a way forward despite their situation – but let's omit it here.

Only after some years I realised that Silverberg's story, which I read at the end of the 1980s, was most probably the first book which, for me, fully met the criteria of a postmodern work. The general mood of melancholia and the fading of the human world dominate the story. Despite the technological perfection of its fantastical future, the described world seems only to be able to look backwards. The desired state, the most prized one, is that of immortality, which remains possible only for the very few. Nevertheless, this immortality remains combined with the deep feeling of the loss of any true – because mortal – reality. This state is damned by the curse of its lack of authenticity. The unnatural, eternal youth of Gioia's friends is only a mask. The mask covers the grief of old age and of what has passed. A howl for what once was and will never be again.

17 This little chapter no. 17 (in the original Polish text of my book) discusses four different existing translations of Yeats's 'Sailing to Byzantium' in Polish. The words of Yeats in the fourth stanza: 'a golden bough', are present in Jolanta Kozak's translation, but are missing in other translations. Here is Yeats's full original text:

I
That is no country for old men. The young
In one another's arms, birds in the trees
– Those dying generations – at their song,
The salmon-falls, the mackerel-crowded seas,
Fish, flesh, or fowl, commend all summer long
Whatever is begotten, born, and dies.
Caught in that sensual music all neglect
Monuments of unageing intellect.

II
An aged man is but a paltry thing,
A tattered coat upon a stick, unless
Soul clap its hands and sing, and louder sing
For every tatter in its mortal dress,
Nor is there singing school but studying
Monuments of its own magnificence;

And therefore I have sailed the seas and come
To the holy city of Byzantium.

III

O sages standing in God's holy fire
As in the gold mosaic of a wall,
Come from the holy fire, perne in a gyre,
And be the singing-masters of my soul.
Consume my heart away; sick with desire
And fastened to a dying animal
It knows not what it is; and gather me
Into the artifice of eternity.

IV

Once out of nature I shall never take
My bodily form from any natural thing,
But such a form as Grecian goldsmiths make
Of hammered gold and gold enamelling
To keep a drowsy Emperor awake;
Or set upon a golden bough to sing
To lords and ladies of Byzantium
Of what is past, or passing, or to come.

A 'golden bough' is of course a reference to the sixth book of The Aeneid by Virgil. In Virgil's poem it is the gift of Proserpine to Aeneas, a gift which enables him to enter the underworld. It is also, of course, the title of an important work by James George Fraser, a work which influenced Freud, Jung and Malinowski. Without that book, the discipline of anthropology might not have been born.

Well, this is how it is: the books, even before they tumble into satin to wallow in the sheets, chatter with each other over the centuries; they quarrel, they talk.

18 A vision of man and the world, later called 'modernity', was a conscious and wilfully radical rejection of the humanistic scepticism of authors like Montaigne or Shakespeare by their seventeenth-century successors. A successful attempt upon the life of Henry of Navarre (1610) became a turning point in the fate of European ideas. The stubborn, almost manic question of Cartesius about the basis of every possible certainty, was not the lonely call of some hermit in an ivory tower, but a search for a medicine for the whole continent. A search born straight from the bloody experience of that time, which had found itself 'out of joint'. These are the main points of *Cosmopolis: The Hidden Agenda of Modernity* (1990), a work by renowned British philosopher Stephen Toulmin.

During The Thirty Years' War (1618–48), writes Toulmin:

> ... in a series of brutal and destructive military campaigns, shifting alliances of outside powers used the territory of Germany and Bohemia as a gladiatorial ring in which to fight their political rivalries and doctrinal disagreements, most often by proxy, and turned the Czech and German lands into a charnel house. Just after Henry of Navarre's assassination, it was too easily assumed that his death had proved the policy of religious toleration unviable.

All the forests were already on fire then, and there was no time to cry after the roses. Toulmin:

> The longer the bloodshed continued, the more paradoxical the state of Europe became. Whether for pay or from conviction, there were many who would kill and burn in the name of theological doctrines that no one could give any conclusive reasons for accepting ... Yet, the more brutal the warfare became, the more firmly convinced the proponents of each religious system were that their doctrines must be proved correct, and that their opponents were stupid, malicious, or both. For many of those involved, it ceased to be crucial what their

theological beliefs were, or where they were rooted in experience, as 16th-century theologians would have demanded. All that mattered, by this stage, was for the supporters of Religious Truth to believe, devoutly, in belief itself ...

In this blood-drenched situation, what could good intellectuals do? Toulmin:

> The humanists' readiness to live with uncertainty, ambiguity, and differences of opinion had done nothing (in their view) to prevent religious conflict from getting out of hand ... If scepticism let one down, certainty was more urgent. It might not be obvious what one was supposed to be certain about, but uncertainty had become unacceptable.

Those were, says Toulmin, the circumstances of the birth of the complex beliefs generally called 'modern'.

> 'Tis all in peeces, all coherence gone;
> All just supply, and all Relation:
> Prince, Subject, Father, Son, are things forgot

wrote John Donne in the poem the 'Anatomy of the World' (1611). In the face of the crumbling social world (both medieval and feudal) and the ruins of the cosmology of Ptolemy, destroyed by Galileo and other astronomers, finding a new 'Cosmopolis' became a critical need. Cosmopolis, says Toulmin, is a 'natural' (cosmos) and 'social' (polis) order of the world, already connected into one entity by the ancient stoics. It is an idea deeply rooted in European thought, which claims that the structure of the world of Nature enhances rational social order.

The seventeenth century has indeed found such a new, modern Cosmopolis, writes Toulmin, which consolidated in a new way both cosmic and social structures. First, *Principia Mathe-*

matica by Newton (1687), then soon afterwards the ecumenism of Leibniz and his *Theodicy* (1710) restored – with immaculate elegance – the cosmic edifice of 'natural philosophy'. Hierarchy and stabilisation were brought back, because for both Newton and Leibniz everything in the order of Nature confirms God's power. God is for Nature what the King is for the State. It is just, therefore, that a modern nation bases its state organisation upon structures which God shows us in the world of astronomy. This way, *Le Roi-Soleil*, The Sun-King, maintains his power over his circles of subjects, who all know their place and keep themselves in their proper orbits. What God is for Nature and the King for The State, the husband is for his wife and the father for his family. The natural and social order once again were shown to be governed by a similar set of rules.

The next three centuries of flourishing modernity are contemporaneously a process of gradual and inevitable – as Toulmin calls it – 'dismantling of the scaffolding'.

> ... Certain pillars defended themselves better than others; the dismantling of some less important elements started already in the middle of XVIII century, but the whole task has been finished only in the second half of the XX century.

Stephen Toulmin greets our contemporary end of modernity with evident joy. He sees in it a chance for the return to the Renaissance humanism of Montaigne: the bankruptcy of modern abstraction once again directs man, like in the Renaissance, to concrete experience. Seen from this perspective, Postmodernism seems to be a humanistic reversal of modernity. It calls for the return from the written word to what is said, from the universal to the particular, from the general to the local; back, from timeless modernity, to what is temporal.

19 The eternal youth of golden girls and boys in Silverberg's story seems to cover their suppressed, desperate
grieving for the lost authenticity of their mortal lives. 'Sailing
to Byzantium' is only a fiction, of course, a science fiction; it is
just some postmodern, not fully serious, literature. Nevertheless, the vision of the human condition proposed there opens a
strange, anxious question: what, if there is no end?

Immortality? Yes, we know, it always was the eternal dream
of humanity, a privilege reserved for heroes and for gods.
Human immortality is a possibility, which has never in fact
been seriously analysed by philosophy. And yet every possible
mental image of such a (hypothetical) state would have to start
from a question about the loss of the End.

And here the problem starts, because what is striking in such
a case is the loss of an aim. Let's repeat: the loss of the End is
equal to the loss of an aim. *Telos* (the aim) of the Ancient Greeks
effortlessly found its place in the writings of the Fathers of the
Church. Not because it was Greek – almost all of them were
writing in Greek, that is, in the idiom of the educated, cultural elite of the time. Since the time of the Christian breakthrough in the understanding of Time, *telos* became incredibly
important. Since Eternal Redemption became dominant over
suffering upon this earth, since it became the final settling of
everything that exists, the aim of various enterprises started
to absolve actual, imperfect, human deeds. More precisely:
the aim started to absolve the means, which were leading to it,
while the lack of an aim started to be seen almost as a sin.

The new, Christian, understanding of time and of history
surrendered us to the power of the End of Time and to the
irrevocability of the verdict of the Last Judgement. Human life
became understood as a being-towards-death, a being subdued
to the ultimate end of what will happen after death. In modern
times, that vector has managed to overwhelm not only individuals but whole societies, whole nations. The utopia of Hegel's

Ghost of Time reaching its future self-fulfilment, as well as the Marxist vision of the future, Communist paradise, were both teleological projections, unknowingly repeating the basic construction of a Christian eschatology. The modern, secular versions of these, both were driving the gaze of humanity towards the future, which is a paradise, by definition.

That unstoppable wind of progress pushing us towards paradise, even until recently, made it possible that we were speeding, rushing, racing without a break. 'We shall run into the ground the mare of history!' shouted Mayakovsky. Witkiewicz only laughed and speedily continued to finish the writing of his *Crazy Locomotive*.

And then, suddenly: crash! A speculative question started to exist, most probably uttered in an incredibly shy manner in some Parisian café in the 1960s or 1970s. What if there is no end? It may have been that at the beginning it was not even a question, but only a careful, experimental effort of naming some strange phenomena around us. It was starting slowly, without any certainty, as if the questioning people did not believe it themselves. That attempt at naming tried somehow to evaluate the conclusions of *The Structure of Scientific Revolutions*, a work by Thomas S. Kuhn (1962) with the practice of humanistic sciences. As we know, Kuhn was the first to describe the process of formulating new theories in science in a purely *historical* context. In science, as time goes by, usually a certain 'paradigm' prevails, which is a set of empirically tested opinions about the world and its appearances shared by the majority of scientists. Observations which question the existing paradigm are usually marginalised or not mentioned. Yet the number of 'improper' observations often has a tendency to grow, up to the point where it reaches a 'critical mass'. Then, a tumultuous breakthrough happens, and a new paradigm is formulated which efficiently explains the earlier aberrations. And then the whole cycle is repeated again.

When publishing his work, Kuhn thought mainly about his

own scientific territory, that is, about the history of science, but his readers from various disciplines soon saw the possibilities of using his model on a much larger scale. Suddenly, all the sciences, philosophy, and particularly the humanistic sciences came to be seen as imperfect tools for the description of the world. They became seen as tools immersed in time and, as such, were condemned to be only temporary. Their descriptions, therefore, could never be final. This new understanding of the situation and the role of humanistic sciences very soon accelerated and soon became mainstream: in architecture, in literature, in economics, in philosophy, even in musicology.

The loss of the End in human culture, first imagined, then fully articulated, happened during my life, on a global scale. I cannot exclude that that process – and not the overcoming of Communism – was the most important movement that I have witnessed in my life. Anyway, the farewell to Communism most probably would not have been possible without that deeper and wider breakthrough in the human sciences happening first.

We call that loss of the End in culture 'postmodernism'. It is quite striking that this phenomenon, or even wave, is still going on. As far as I know, nobody has dared to declare that it's ended. It seems there is no end to the point of view proclaiming the lack of an end, at least for now.

20 'We shall run into the ground the mare of history!' The obsessive fascination of twentieth-century intellectuals with Marxism is most accurately presented in the figure of the Professor in *Operetta* by Gombrowicz: 'There is no God!' – shouts the Professor in the critical moment of action – 'There is a situation. I am finding myself in the situation. I am choosing the revolution.'

All these complicated connections are described by Marci

Shore, a professor of history at Indiana University, in her thought-provoking book *Caviar and Ashes: A Warsaw Generation's Life and Death in Marxism, 1918–1968* (2006). Shore consciously explores a topic that is still somehow touchy in Poland:

> Those cosmopolitan intellectualists – many of them were, as Isaac Deutscher has written, the 'non-Jewish Jews' – felt themselves to be Poles. Their Jewish identity was fluid and complex. Some, like Adam Ważyk, Julian Stryjkowski, Jakub Berman, came from families torn between Communism and Zionism, between a Jewish and a Polish background. For example, the father of Aleksander Wat was a Cabalist, who spoke Yiddish every day, but read Nietzsche in German and Tolstoy in Russian.

Apart from Broniewski, Shore mostly does not mention the non-Jewish poets, but she writes about those with a Jewish background with great care. It is undoubtedly a fact, after all, that the most interesting poetry in Polish in the first half of the twentieth century was created by assimilated, cosmopolitan Jews. They were mostly following Leftist views and choosing – in the 'situation' of that time – Marxism.

The titles of the chapters of Shore's book sound like the names of train stations on the route of their epic journey: 'When God died', 'Once Upon a Time in Ziemiańska Café', 'Love and Revolution', 'The Visit of Mayakovsky', 'Terror and the Art of Confessing Guilt', 'The Autumn in Soviet Galicia'. Later we have 'In the Abyss', and also 'Stalinism in the Ruins of Warsaw'. Provocations, arrests, deportations: horror. They were not privileged with a shot in the back of the head, like the officers in Katyń. They were dying in *gulags* (Stande, Jasieński and so many others) like animals, from hunger, incidentally – the human manure of the Stalinist version of history. They were dying after first confessing their non-existing crimes, along with the ideological protocol. Shore quotes the authentic confession of Jasieński, recently found in NKVD archives, but the best literary synthesis of the essence of these documents is still, I think, articulated by Gombrowicz's Professor: 'I hate! But I also hate my hate! / Because it is mine! / From me! Who hates? I hate, I do! I, the bourgeois, the product of the pathological system ... I hate ... and I puke!' We find a similar sentiment in Shore: 'A Marxist intellectualist, imprisoned in the role of a representative of the avant-garde of progress, often suspected a priori because of his bourgeois roots, fully conscious of belonging to the class which is condemned by History to extermination ...'

The grandson of Adolf Warski (the former correspondent of Rosa Luxemburg), Stanisław Krajewski, wrote about Wat and his contemporaries:

> They have found themselves in a void, without any support, because all of them managed to undermine whatever support they had. And yet they could not bear the void, with its anarchy and its lack of any sense. So, they decided to jump from the kingdom of freedom into the kingdom of necessity ...

The Communist involvement of Wat and his friends was a desperate escape from nihilism. At the same time, it was a desperate effort to preserve the exciting state of 'living on the edge', to preserve the desire of constant intoxication. At the end, writes Shore, '... the heroes of this book, both the creators and victims of their tragic fate, lived their lives full of fear and of guilt. In fact, it was Marxism that destroyed them; their decision to accept Marxism. Their history does not leave any aesthetically satisfying end ...'

From beyond the grave, the skull of Witkiewicz (with many teeth missing) grins. He used to be their occasional, much respected interlocutor in Ziemiańska Café. He managed to present many of their histrionic *salti mortali* and dilemmas – connected with their acceptance of the communion of Marxism – in his dramas and in his novels. The Princess, Irina Zbereźnicka-Podbereska, from *The Shoemakers*, for example, is evidently Wanda Wasilewska, the future lover of Stalin. Prosecutor Scurvy could be any of the Berman brothers, in any phase of Marxism's pursuit of its aims. All those intellectuals were telling themselves: 'Who, if not us? When, if not now?' The Train of their History was incessantly hurrying and scurrying ... their locomotive was evidently a lunatic one.

21 It has taken some time for the end of the Tyranny of the End to find its way into common awareness. Time was needed to receive it, to digest it, to understand it. To think about some revolutionary consequences. The 'end of grand narratives' for example. This shortcut of thought has meant, among other things, a radical questioning of Plato's triadic concept of truth–good–beauty. From a purely philosophical point of view, this change of direction is basically against Plato and against Kant. All beings and ideas which are 'above Time' and are detached from history, are being deposited in the museum, in the archive of lost illusions. What matters from now on is what is concrete, placed in a particular time and place. We descend from the abstract level of 'humanity', 'history', the 'progress of history' down to the actual experience of individuals and their multi-layered interactions in a specific historical reality.

The consequences of the 'end of grand narratives' are numerous and wide. For example, one of them is the fact that Europe cannot anymore pretend to dominate the rest of the world. The 'end of grand narratives' means also that the tag 'New' on the shampoo in the market, which uses the automatic, subconscious conviction that the latest product must be *better*, becomes invalid. It also means that the text written later, or an opinion formulated in the most recent discussion is not automatically better than the previous one. In the end, the 'end of grand narratives' also means that every kind of 'progress' in science, in art, in the development of civilisation, remains questionable. The story of 'progress' very often simplifies the complexity of the world because of some ideological or political reasons. Ideological, because it is much easier and more efficient to rule the world when one knows where it comes from and where it is aiming. Political, because as long as one keeps both power and knowledge one remains practically untouchable. The story of the world as a land of non-questionable, never-ending progress becomes unmasked by postmodernism as a thoroughly false, convenient fairy tale used by every cynical power. It has taken some time to understand that no modernistic 'historical mission' or 'forging of a shining future' is possible anymore.

Therefore, in 2000, an American philosopher, Richard Rorty, could publish an important article titled 'The Decline of Redemptive Truth and the Rise of a Literary Culture'. In it he proclaimed the abolition of the main differences between all religious, philosophical or literary descriptions of mankind and its world. He writes:

> Kierkegaard rightly said that philosophy began to set itself up as a rival to religion when Socrates suggested that our self-knowledge was a knowledge of God – that we had no need of help from a non-human person, because the truth was already within us. But literature began to set itself up as a rival to philosophy when people like Cervantes and Shakespeare began to suspect that human beings were, and ought to be, so diverse that there is no point in pretending that they all carry a single truth deep in their bosoms.

There is no final 'redemption' reachable by created texts; all of these are only the various form of literature, said Rorty. We can, of course, quarrel about their content, but – to tell the truth – there is not much to quarrel about.

Roberto Salvadori, an Italian living these days in Poland, a historian of ideas, was a pupil of the late Alexandre Kojève, who was a teacher of many generations of Parisian philosophers (he died in 1968). Salvadori has written a farewell letter to his master and published it in 2010 in the book *Silhouettes and Portraits*. He writes there:

> You cannot even imagine how much both the world (enough, if I tell you that the 'real socialism' has fallen), and the cultural climate have changed during the last hundred years. To put it briefly, we have moved from the ideology of the Totalitarian 'end of History' – that is of Humanity freed from alienation – to the continually refreshed 'beginning of history', understood as an incidental product of many individuals of flesh and blood, who are given freedom of action and remain open to the unpredictable future.

The state of the loss of the End is also a state of the loss of many illusions. We feel slightly strange because our hopes were aroused. And we feel also strangely light, like when one ceases to be ill. We have lost something, and this is sad, but that loss is a gain, in fact, because what we have lost was only a mirage.

22 One can celebrate the arrival of the End while, nevertheless, still holding onto an illusion. Francis Fukuyama, the author of the famous book *The End of History*, was blinded by his immense joy at the fall of the Soviet Union in 1991 and from the earlier fall of the so-called 'socialist system' in 1989. The end of the Cold War (1945–91), observed by Fukuyama, meant, in his words: 'not only the end of a particular period in the history after the war, but the end of history as such'. It meant: 'reaching the endpoint of human ideological evolution and the universalisation of the model of Western liberal democracy as a final form of people's government'.

For Fukuyama, something that in reality was gradual, lasting a few decades, became a political happy end, along with the recipe of The American Dream. The 'final' victory of liberal democracy, claimed by Fukuyama, follows the deep traces set down by Hegel and Marx. For both of them, history was a form of linear progress from one socio-economic epoch to another. This progress was to be crowned with a 'final solution'. Fukuyama managed to notice a singular, political end of the Soviet empire and decided to extrapolate from it a global vision. The attack upon The World Trade Center on 11 September 2001 brought about a brutal end to his illusion about any political 'end of history'.

When we talk about the 'end of the End', it does not mean that time has stopped. It only means that, basically, the Christian, decidedly theological, Western narrative about the nature of time and about its aim, became compromised. It was forced, at least temporarily, to retreat to the very edge of the horizon of discussion.

23 What are these discursions all about, and what are they for? Well, they are about theatre and about literature, and about the numerous connections between them. What for? It was mentioned in the beginning: to not permit the pandemic to win.

Three possible, temporary titles for these notes go around in my head. The first is: *The Unfinished Catalogue of Non-essential Issues*. The second, *An Archive of Lost Illusions*. The third is still *Excrements* ...?

24 Maybe this end of the Tyranny of the End all started from *Marat/Sade* by Peter Weiss (1964)? I mean, the work of Kuhn was chronologically first, no doubt. But, of course, it has not been the only book of this kind. For example, the outspoken work of Paul K. Feyerabend, *Against the Method* (1975), with its 'methodological anarchism' aimed against every possible scientific authority, was a wild attack against any epistemological establishment. 'Away with any method!' and 'Anything goes!' shouted Feyerabend. The revolutionary winds of the Parisian May of 1968 had a lot in common with this attack, no doubt. Nevertheless, let's not forget that Paul K. Feyerabend, the philosophical scandaliser of the English-speaking and scientific world in the 1970s, lived as a young officer of the Wehrmacht through the defeat and the chaotic retreat of his army from Czestochowa (Poland) in 1945. The great turn 'against the method', against the teleological approach leading to various 'final solutions' (*Endlösungen*), has its roots in the *Stunde Null*, in the 'hour zero' of 1945.

This German term describes the apocalyptic, deadly silence over the smoking ruins of the Second World War. This silence resembles one 'after the end of the world'. Such was the silence of Hamburg, levelled to the ground in 1945, so poignantly described by Winfried Georg Sebald in his *On the Natural History of Destruction* (1999). *Stunde Null* also became the basis for the works of both Różewicz and Beckett. What is more, it gave birth to the rhetorical question of Theodor Adorno: How is art still possible after Auschwitz?. The search for the sources of a deep mistrust in any magical final solutions, so strongly apparent in the second half of the twentieth century, starts with the shock created by the Second World War, by Auschwitz and by Hiroshima.

When writing his *Marat/Sade*, Peter Weiss was most probably unable to foresee all the political consequences of his idea. Weiss was a fervent Communist with a complicated past. His parents managed to emigrate from Germany to Sweden just before the start of the war; Weiss grew up in Stockholm and moved back to West Germany only after the war. He originally wrote *Marat/Sade* as a radio play describing episodes of the French Revolution. Within the play, Jean-Paul Marat is somehow an 'eternal' leader of the poorest people and of all the masses starving in the course of history. In the play, the half-naked Marat, borrowed directly from the famous painting by Jacques-Louis David, has all the characteristics of Christ among the poor. The Marquis de Sade, his antagonist in the imagined dispute about human nature and the nature of the world, embodies all the worst, abominable attributes of the enemy of every revolution: the stuffy egotism, the contempt for the average man, inherited sadism and cruelty.

The dispute between the two historical antagonists is surprisingly ambitious. Many important questions are asked: who is man, what is his nature, what organisation of human society would be optimal, and – in the end – how to 'move the block of the world' from its immobility? The main opponents are surrounded by the poor masses, who sing this recurring refrain:

> Marat, what has happened to our revolution?
> Marat, we do not want to wait for tomorrow anymore
> Marat, we are still the poorest class
> And we want to see the promised change today!

The honest, well-schooled Communist Weiss addresses some of the urgent questions and problems of the acute reality of 1964 through this historical context; his literary intention is easy to see. In his contemporary world, the so-called 'real socialism' is stuck in poverty. The Communist paradise, promised by Marx, still remains an infinitely distant promise. Meanwhile, the hedonistic triumphs of the capitalist system, together with the audacity of the open markets, provoke and offend our decency. It seems that in his play Weiss wanted to present an honest, deep analysis of the failures and defeats of the Marxist idea in its factual, twentieth-century edition. Weiss presents the discussion between two antagonistic, philosophical positions in an incredibly refined form, borrowed from Bertolt Brecht and supported by the author's exquisite familiarity with historical dialectics. The action of the play, based upon historical truth, is a play-within-a-play. De Sade is its director and the choristers and actors are the patients of a mental institution in Charenton (Paris) in 1808, under the reign of the Emperor Napoleon. The Brechtian *Verfremdungseffekt*, the so-called alienation effect, is used in an extremely sophisticated way. All the actions and speeches are given a particular, ambiguous colour. The spoken lines, answers and commentaries get their second and even third nuances, and these ironic meanings, not always foreseen by the author, reflect one within the other as if in some distorted looking glass. I can only imagine the joy of Konrad Swinarski, who directed the world premiere of *Marat/Sade* at the Schiller Theatre in Berlin. In the end, Marat, this Christ-like eulogist of a redemptive, final revolution, suffers a total defeat; while the cynical, pessimistic views of the Marquis about human nature and history triumph over Marat with no possibility of an appeal.

All the reviews of the play were, in Berlin, as well as, soon after, in London and many other places, enthusiastic and strongly underline the bell tolling for Communism in the play. After reading them, Weiss kept trying to correct the meaning of the play in some interviews. He even started to write the text anew, but it was already too late. Weiss's play, although intellectually wonderful and theatrically marvellous, presented the Leninist project of a Communist, earthly paradise as a totally doomed disaster.

Therefore, one cannot exclude that it could have been that, indeed, everything started from *Marat/Sade*.

25 In *Marat/Sade*, Peter Weiss reached the fullest possible acme of the play-within-the-play formula. This is an operation analogous to the story-within-a-story. Whenever one uses it in the theatre, some new, exciting possibilities always open. But let's start with prose.

In literary prose, in a shorter or longer story, usually the narrator is key. For example, with 'The hounds streamed into the woods' the author starts his story, putting a full stop after the 'woods', immediately proposing a convention for him/herself and the reader. In this case, *Ashes* by Stefan Żeromski (1902), the narrator, possibly Żeromski himself, writes in the third person. He creates a particular world and describes it in the past tense.

Let us note: the narrator–storyteller remains apparently anonymous. Let's skip at this moment the presence of the author's name on the front page. The narrator–storyteller is also omniscient. From the beginning they know what has happened in this story and they know the order of the events. They know how all of it started and how all of this will end, and the rhythm, colour, content and the scale of detail in their story will decide the quality of their writing. In continental studies of literature, this convention is usually called 'The Marquise went out at 5 o'clock'. Let's also note that both Żeromski, with his herd of hounds, and André Breton, the author of the line about the Marquise, with their first sentences, bring us into the world of realism, a world very similar to ours. Since the Marquise 'went out', he probably left some house or flat. Usually, we have also heard about hunting parties happening in some country village. Altogether, in such a convention, contact with the world of the anonymous narrator happens in the blink of an eye.

Things are different when the novel starts, let's say, from: 'Someone must have been telling tales about Josef K., for one morning, without having done anything wrong, he was arrested' (translator Mike Mitchell). On the one hand, the first line of *The Trial* supports the conventional 'Marquise at 5 o'clock' but, on the other hand, we learn that, in the world of this novel, innocent people get arrested! The practice of denunciations seems to be common here. It is a dangerous, unpleasant environment and because of that, who knows, maybe it is not fully real.

Things are different again when the text of the story starts like this:

> At 19.00 hours, ship's time, I made my way to the launching bay. The men around the shaft stood aside to let me pass, and I climbed down into the capsule. Inside the narrow cockpit, there was scarcely room to move. I attached the hose to the valve on my space suit and it inflated rapidly. From then on I was incapable of making the smallest movement.
>
> (Trans. Joanna Kilmartin and Steve Cox)

Well, this is yet again decently close to the realistic convention of the 'Marquise at 5 o'clock', but these nouns (capsule, hose, valve, space suit) are not typical – could it be some plumber's report? The mention of 'ship's time' suggests that, if it is not a case of a malfunctioning submarine, we must be in a spaceship. And if we are in a spaceship, then most probably we are starting a journey into the land of science fiction. Well, we might already know it when reading the title and the author's name: *Solaris* by Stanisław Lem.

Over the centuries, the prearrangement of the voice of the narrator in prose went through every sort of imaginable experiment. Thumbing through hundreds and thousands of books – and there are millions of them, maybe even tens or hundreds of millions – one can encounter a story told by a ghost or by somebody who died a long time ago. There are stories told by an electronic brain, or by a malfunctioning computer, or even by some extra-terrestrial from a distant galaxy. Below, I bring you a random example of the creative manipulation of the identity of the narrator. It is an incidental example; I simply have this recently published novel to hand: it is Bernhard Schlink's *Olga*.

Schlink is a contemporary German author, whose internationally successful book, *The Reader*, was published in 1995. In *Olga*, he starts with a line from the mother of the girl in the title. She leaves her daughter in the care of a neighbour when the little girl is just one year old: 'She does not make any trouble, she simply loves to stand and to look.' In the first part of the novel, we learn from the narrator about Olga's life and her rather unhappy relationship with her beloved Herbert in Eastern Prussia. It is set sometime between the end of the nineteenth century and the Second World War.

In the second part, we learn with surprise that the narration of the first part was in fact recounted sometime after the Second World War by the son of a certain family in West Germany, where Olga was temporarily working as a seamstress. Herbert, meanwhile, has vanished, before the war, in some crazy expedition to the North Pole.

The third part of the book consists of a large collection of Olga's letters to Herbert which Olga has been sending for many years to an address in Norway, the last *Poste-Restante* she had for Herbert. The narrator has found this collection after many years and presents it to us. The end of the novel is a bit like a *deus ex machina*: the narrator befriends a lady who, unbeknownst to him, turns out to be the granddaughter of Olga. We learn only incidentally that her father was a Nazi and an illegitimate son of Olga and Herbert. At the very end, the narrator and Olga's granddaughter Adelheide decide to live together.

The narrative construction of this extraordinary novel exemplifies many of the possibilities of the game of playing with the narrator's voice. Who is the narrator in the first part of the novel *Olga*? We learn this only in its very last line, and it is a huge surprise for us. No less a surprise is the authorship of the lost letters. In their light, Olga becomes a much more complex character than we thought before. The structure of the whole novel is based upon the constantly changing, alternating perspectives of narration. The re-evaluations of particular characters, and of many events in their lives, which must be made by the reader, become, therefore, somehow inevitable. These changes of perspective, meaning and sense remain the ambitious and deliberate aims of the author. The author wants to draw us in, to woo us, to delight us. The effect of surprise and of bewilderment, created by him, is very effective. He wants to compel us to read the whole book after the first page. The decisions of the author about who narrates, when they narrate, or whose mask the narrator is hiding behind, are the most important actions of the writer.

Among the multiple possibilities for the prearrangement of the voice of the narrator, quite often authors chose, somehow, the most simple and most courageous: here I am, dear readers, the author, speaking to you, in my own person. Such a seemingly simple decision is fraught with many perils. First of all, if the author is making this decision in an honest way, the work can turn very quickly into reportage, or a letter, or some variant of a diary. It turns into some form of relation from a witness, who was present at the events he/she describes. This is a problem, because here, where a novel was supposed to be written, it suddenly becomes testimony. Authors do not usually like such solutions. In Polish literature, one needed Miron Białoszewski to make some scraps, off-cuts, fragments of a child's memory come together in a consciously chosen, incredibly artful form in *The Diary of the Warsaw Uprising*. Apart from such rare exceptions, the literary works of the type 'I am telling you' roughly divide into two kinds. The first kind is composed of 'the story about past events, worthy of being told by a witness'. This is how most types of memoirs, with various levels of credibility, and all autobiographies and diaries, are composed. In the second kind, the identity of the author is in fact hidden behind the identity of a fictional character, often constructed in a laborious and refined way. Let's look at two examples. The first one is the beginning of *Three by Three* by Count Aleksander Fredro (1877):

On the eighteenth of February, in the year 1814, there was a man in his middle age, slightly corpulent, riding his white horse in a frock coat buttoned under his chin, in a hat with no insignia apart from a little tricolour cotillion. Behind him, in the distance, there was another one, much younger, also in a frock coat, a dark-green one, also in a hat with no insignia, also hunched like the first man, sitting this time on a grey horse. The grey horse was …, well, was a grey horse, there is not much more one could say about him. The horse was often stumbling, not being burdened by thoroughbred lineage, nor by his own gait. The first of the riders was Napoleon, and I was the second one.

Fredro's narration is exactly like the narration of Beckett's *Krapp's Last Tape*. Krapp (and Fredro), both being old, are searching through their memories and looking at much younger versions of themselves with a mixture of pity and tenderness.

The example below exemplifies the second kind:

I wish to state quite definitely that it is by no means out of any wish to bring my own personality into the foreground, that I preface with a few words about myself and my own affairs, this report on the life of the departed Adrian Leverkühn. What I here set down is the first and assuredly very premature biography of that beloved fellow-creature and musician of genius, so afflicted by fate, lifted up so high, only to be so frightfully cast down.

This is obviously *Doctor Faustus* by Thomas Mann (translated by Martin Secker), its first paragraph allegedly written by a certain Doctor Zeitblum. The fictional character of Zeitblum permits the author to tell the story in the first person. It also gives him a chance to write, apart from the relation about the life of Adrian Leverkühn, a bitter commentary upon art and German political affairs of the first half of the twentieth century. Thomas Mann plays here, like a *virtuoso*, on a few instruments at once.

When talking about the *incipit*, which opens the novel, and about the arrangement of the narration, we have to notice that much more subtle, much more perverse games are possible. There are shameless provocations which pretend to remain innocent. There are even some openings cloaking themselves in Dante:

> Tuesday morning I awoke at that pale and lifeless hour when night is almost gone but dawn has not yet come into its own. Awakened suddenly, I wanted to take a taxi and dash to the railroad station, thinking I was due to leave, when, in the next minute, I realised to my chagrin that no train was waiting for me at the station, that no hour had struck. I lay in the murky light while my body, unbearably frightened, crushed my spirit with fear, and my spirit crushed my body, whose tiniest fibres cringed in apprehension that nothing would ever happen, nothing ever change, that nothing would ever come to pass, and whatever I undertook, nothing, but nothing, would ever come of it. ... Half-way along the path of my life, I found myself in a dark forest; and the worst of it was that the forest was green.
> (Trans. Danuta Borchardt)

This beginning, of Gombrowicz's *Ferdydurke*, is told by a thirty-something-year-old narrator, Józio, who will be returned, in an unexplained way, to the reality of his secondary-school years. Nevertheless, Józio has all the intellectual characteristics of Witold Gombrowicz himself. The author plays a perverse game with the character of the narrator he has created. The author is mocking himself and at the same time experimenting audaciously with his reader's tolerance. The author knows very well that the borderland of dream and reality, the state of half-awareness, is ideal material for the beginning of an ambitious novel. Here is the beginning of another work, from which Gombrowicz openly borrows his first paragraph of *Ferdydurke*:

For a long time I would go to bed early. Sometimes, the candle barely out, my eyes closed so quickly that I did not have time to tell myself: 'I'm falling asleep'. And half an hour later the thought that it was time to look for sleep would awaken me; I would make as if to put away the book which I imagined was still in my hands, and to blow out the light; I had gone on thinking, while I was asleep, about what I had just been reading, but these thoughts had taken a rather peculiar turn; it seemed to me that I myself was the immediate subject of my book: a church, a quartet, the rivalry between François I and Charles V. This impression would persist for some moments after I awoke; it did not offend my reason, but lay like scales upon my eyes and prevented them from registering the fact that the candle was no longer burning. Then it would begin to seem unintelligible, as the thoughts of a previous existence must be after reincarnation; the subject of my book would separate itself from me, leaving me free to apply myself to it or not; and at the same time my sight would return and I would be astonished to find myself in a state of darkness, pleasant and restful enough for my eyes, but even more, perhaps, for my mind, to which it appeared incomprehensible, without a cause, something dark indeed. I would ask myself what time it could be; I could hear the whistling of trains, which, now nearer and now further, punctuating the distance like the note of a bird in a forest, showed me in perspective the deserted countryside through which a traveller is hurrying towards the nearby station; and the path he is taking will be engraved in his memory by the excitement induced by strange surroundings, by unaccustomed activities, by the conversation he has had and the farewells exchanged beneath an unfamiliar lamp that still echo in his ears amid the silence of the night, and by the happy prospect of being home again.

(Trans. C. K. Scott Moncrieff and T. Kilmartin, revised by D. J. Enright)

There is no Józio, no substituting figure of a friend or another Doctor Zeitblum. On the first page of the novel, along with its title, *Swann's Way*, is the name of the author: Marcel Proust. There are no obstacles, therefore, to treating Proust as a narrator. And yet the problem seems to be even more complicated with him. Richard Rorty has written about it in his article 'Redemption from Egotism: James and Proust as Spiritual Exercises':

> There is only one character whose career is followed by the reader of *In Remembrance of Things Past* [*In Search of Lost Time*]. This is Marcel the narrator, the person whom all of Proust's readers take to be identical to the novelist, and with whose hopes and guilt and hesitations they themselves identify. So when the narrator, in the last volume, realises that he is now in a position to write his novel, it is their triumph, as well as his. They share both his confidence and his exaltation. By writing a novel about a man who keeps hoping to write the novel that the reader is reading, and who finally succeeds, Proust brings about the same sense of intimacy that Bayley describes as felt by the readers of James. By his success, Proust gives the idea that one's life can be a work of art – an idea previously familiar from Pater, Wilde and Nietzsche – the idea that substance and plausibility of a sort could not have acquired otherwise.

26 In the theatre, the possible presence of a narrator is usually much less complicated than in literature. The narrator, in the theatre, is often not needed at all. I mean, he is unnecessary from the moment that the action starts. Earlier, yes,

we sometimes have the Chorus borrowed straight from ancient tragedy, or here and there a pompously dressed Prologue. All of them are there, first of all, to bring to our attention the frequently still-chatting, or even still-consuming-something, spectators. All of them are there to impose upon the spectators a certain convention of social behaviour: Ladies and Gentlemen, we are in Thebes, or in Verona, or in Elsinore, and therefore we need to finish our *souvlaki*, or our drinks, please; attention, please, now the play begins. The possible presence of the narrator on stage – which sometimes happens – seems evidently to be borrowed from the convention of the novel. An immediate, surprising engagement of the spectators, starting with the very first moments of the show, is simply natural in the theatre. There is darkness, let's say, and the loud pounding of some iron thunder-sheets, a blast of strong wind, some flying pieces of canvas, and a desperate shout: 'Ahoy! Captain, we are drowning!' – and we know, immediately, that we are in the middle of the ocean and that *The Tempest* has just started. Or: 'Are you, Father, going to the High Castle?' a teenage girl asks a gentleman with a bowler hat and an umbrella who is walking around the table in a bourgeois dining room – and we know, immediately, that we are in Lvov at the Dulskis' family house in *The Morality of Mrs Dulska* (Gabriel Zapolska, 1906). Or: 'Now is the winter of our discontent / Made glorious summer by this son of York' says a suspicious hunchback looking straight into our eyes – and we immediately know that this is the Duke of Gloucester, presenting himself to us even before he becomes Richard the III. Action is the natural element of the theatre. It creates the course of dramatic events and our participation in the ongoing narrative. Who is telling us this story? Usually, we do not ask this question during the show. After the show we may answer such a question with the impatient: 'It's obvious, the actors. And probably some director. Oh, and probably some author, too. Or isn't it mainly the author?'

The connection with a novel, with a book, is individual and very intimate. It is extended in time and one can always return to the details of the plot after many days, or even after weeks. One can postpone finishing the reading until later. By contrast, an evening in the theatre is always the participation in an intense public event. It is always an experience shared with hundreds of other spectators and the resolution of the dramatic process usually happens the same evening.

In modern theatre, the performance-within-the performance is a conscious act of doubling the perspective from which spectators perceive the reality which is presented to them. It is an act of placing an additional layer of theatre. The world which we have accepted as credible during the first fifteen minutes of the show is the first level. We willingly suspended our disbelief in this world, and we willingly agreed that this other world exists 'as if for real'. And now the moment comes when the characters from that first level of scenic reality decide to watch some theatre, or to participate in some theatre, or to do both things. Claudius and Gertrude take their places to watch *The Murder of Gonzago*. Theseus and Hippolyta and their court take their places to enjoy 'A tedious brief scene of young Pyramus and his love Thisbe'. The Court of Navarre is dying of laughter when watching *Nine Famous Men* while we, the real spectators in the real world, find ourselves the 'cheated' ones. But, being the 'cheated ones', we nevertheless remain 'wiser than the ones who cheat'. The exact translation of Plato's line from his dialogue *Gorgias* is taken from Plutarch: 'Tragedy is a deceit, where he who is being cheated, is more just than he who is not, and the cheated one is wiser than he who cheats.' We find ourselves being the spectators who can observe and judge the actions of another audience, that is, the audience watching the plot on stage, as well as the actions of the characters, which are being judged by that audience.

27 All the entangled plots and complicated intrigues in the comedies of Shakespeare inevitably lead to a final scene which ends the show. In that scene, numerous masks are removed from the faces of numerous characters, and many disguises are stripped away. Dark schemes of wrongdoers end with failure, fathers find their long-lost children again and star-crossed lovers overcome all obstacles and fall into each other's arms. 'At last, though long, our jarring notes agree,' proclaims Lucentio, starting the final scene of *The Taming of the Shrew*. It is a particularly 'final' scene because it is a second finale. The laboriously constructed pyramid of appearances, which was the work of Tranio, has already been exposed in the previous scene, together with the discovery of the secret marriage of Bianca and Lucentio. That final accord of 'agreeing notes' in comedy brings back order and common sense to the world in which the accumulation of disguises and swapped identities was threatening everybody with madness only a moment ago. The world returns to normal and – because this is comedy – this return is usually cheerful and optimistic. But because this is Shakespeare, this 'agreeing note' also screeches with some worrying dissonance.

No, not everybody will have their deeds measured evenly in *Measure for Measure*, and not everything will end well for everyone in *All's Well That Ends Well*. The challenging, derisive ending of *As You Like It* will not please everybody and the final duel between Winter and Spring will remain unsettled at the end of *Love's Labour's Lost*.

One could say that comedy exists only to make all possible bravura useful in the playing out of its ending. The first four acts of *Measure for Measure* are like an exceptionally long prologue which prepares us for the mind-blowing last act. In *Measure for Measure*, as in *All's Well That Ends Well*, this final scene is a court session. The Prince of Vienna and, accordingly, the King of France, celebrate the Act of Justice. This is a human and therefore strongly imperfect justice and celebrating it as a comic finale seems like an open provocation by Shakespeare. The Law turns into a farce in front of our eyes, and the Judge into its main manipulator, its director. If the world is a theatre, and if people are actors, this director will always be useful pulling the strings in the finale.

Sometimes, surprisingly, the role of the director can be secretly fulfilled by one of the characters. Rosalind, disguised as a boy, directs the final scene of *As You Like It* with an extraordinary tenderness. She postpones the key moment of the exposure of her identity for as long as possible. Most probably Shakespeare, an admirer of paradoxes, must have been giggling at that moment: Rosalind, who has been pretending to be a boy for three acts, enters the stage in female dress. A moment later she will say farewell to the audience as a woman and she will carefully underline this fact. But on the stage of the Globe Theatre, in that moment, a boy was standing there all the time, a boy disguised as a girl! The Prince, the hidden director of *Measure for Measure*, achieves their final unmasking with a highly refined theatrical sense. He organises his court to arrive at the gates of Vienna, encouraging his subjects to perform a strange kind of theatre. All the characters lack the full knowledge of the intricate plot and will be shown up as fools, marionettes dancing to the rhythm of his commands. In *All's Well That Ends Well*, Helena is the hidden director of the final scene. She has the King of France as her helper and at the decisive moment she will appear, from her tomb, and also pregnant, to dispose the final graces and gifts. Two more hidden directors are Puck in *A Midsummer Night's Dream*, bidding goodbye to the audience with his menacing monologue at the end of the play, and Prospero at the end of *The Tempest*, who breaks his wand in front of the audience's eyes and asks for their prayers.

That ending is probably most spooky in *The Tempest* and most poetic in *Love's Labour's Lost*: four weddings were to happen; the funeral will take place instead. Nice comedy, with such a perverse ending.

'La commedia é finita' – this is the end, Ladies and Gentlemen, this scenic world has lived for a certain time, has existed, but in a moment it will disappear, it will vanish and dissolve … Shakespeare cherishes this final moment. He adores it, celebrates it, holds on to it for as long as he can. It is as if he wants to underline the uniqueness of this moment, the moment when theatre and life look into each other's eyes. It is as if he wants not just to allow this 'final accord' to resound but is, rather, asking us all about the end of the plot of life: every spectator and all of society.

28 Twice, in *Love's Labour's Lost* and in *A Midsummer Night's Dream,* the final scene of a Shakespearean comedy is preceded by another comedy. Both *The Parade of Famous Men* and 'A tedious brief scene of young Pyramus and his love Thisbe' remain, in the intentions of the players at least, serious works. But both these examples of crazy theatre-within-theatre raise the level of comedy up to the highest point. Both are theatrical extravaganzas, displays of the art of juggling the sheerly absurd. Both are a game of pure game, a meta-theatre. In both cases, the author's intention underlines the strong ambivalence of the finale of the main comedy. The *happy end*, so much adored by spectators of every epoch, is not something Shakespeare really seems to like. He proposes something more: he proposes to look together into the magical crevice between reality and fiction, between what endures and what passes, between fantasy and truth.

Italian comedians in the sixteenth century in London performed this kind of additional comedy as if it were a well-rehearsed dessert at the end of a dinner. It was from them that

Shakespeare learned this trick, and their half-improvised stories suggested the hidden possibilities of that form to him.

The Italian *Commedia dell'Arte* is a natural successor to the Roman *Atellanae*, the shows for which the ancient city of Atella in Campagna was famous. The forebears of that time of Arlecchino and Pulcinella were, among others, Bucco and a sensual Maccus. The latter's thin figure and cowardly nature will be reborn in the character of Pulcinella. Beside them, the militant Manducus was known and, in fact, Miles Gloriosus from the plays of Plautus will be transformed over time into the braggart Captain. Also, the character of Lamia, a patroness of all plotting widows and midwives, originates there.

Atellanae consisted of comedies and short farces, parodies and political satires. Particular roles kept the same characteristics, whichever play the actor appeared in, and this was underlined by the wearing of the proper mask. The dialogue was improvised from the sketch of an action. The farces were often quite simple but close to everyday life, as many preserved frescos and reliefs document. The actors were freely taking inspiration from the life of all classes and social groups.

The term *Commedia dell'Arte* means – according to the Italian scholar, Dottore Scherillo – 'a form of comedy, which unlike the written comedies, never was and never could be staged otherwise than by professional actors'. His article appeared in the third number of *The Mask* in 1911, a periodical published by Gordon Craig. Dottore Scherillo's definition fascinates me. The line dividing amateurs from professionals is drawn sharply and relentlessly. And these professionals evidently know all the secrets of comedy of the highest sort and all its techniques, which cannot be imitated.

In the sixteenth century, the Italian companies were already present in most of the big European cities. Their names were widely recognised, well-known trademarks: Gelosi, Confidenti, Uniti. Soon the character of Beltram appeared from

Milan, as well as the characters of Scapino, the Brighella brothers and Menenghino. Pulcinella arrived from Naples, later Scaramuccio and Tartaglia, Meo-Patacca and Marco-Pepe came from Rome, and even later Cassandrino. Gianduja was from Turin, and Coviello from Calabria. The seventeenth century saw a real Italian invasion of Paris, where the Italian Commédie a l'Impromptu is elevated to the impressive name of Commédie Italienne, with its own building. The next two centuries see the continuous process of 'Frenchifying' this Italian material. Jean-Gaspard Debourau appears with his Pierrot, a French, lyrical version of Arlecchino in love. Just to think, how long and winding a road Pierrot had to travel before he showed up in *The Booth at the Fair* by Alexander Blok (1906).

I have written above about Shakespeare's intentions: about the crevice between enduring and passing, between phantasy and truth. Would the Italian comedians discover the European recipe for an empathic story about life, love and death?

Carlo Goldoni struggled with the mad, multi-layered ideas of the *Commedia dell'Arte* during his proposed reform of the Italian stage. Just let us imagine: it is the middle of the eighteenth century, the Enlightenment is burgeoning, while Goldoni forbids (it was only an attempt, never a formal action) various groups of *dell'Arte* their often vulgar, uncontrolled improvisation. At the same time, he is writing down all the wonderful dialogue of *dell'Arte* in his perfectly constructed, exquisitely expressed comedies. In his *Il teatro comico* (1750), we find ourselves at the morning rehearsal in a Venetian theatre (where else?), and in between many other, incidental occupations, the actors also try to rehearse the farce, *A Father Rivalling his Son. Il teatro comico* presents a full-blown, unbelievably comical, theatre-within-a-theatre. Buster Keaton, Charlie Chaplin and others will exploit this tradition shamelessly.

Also, Luigi Pirandello will decide to borrow from it in 1921, and he will do it in a surprisingly innovative way. At the beginning of his *Six Characters in Search of an Author* we are at the rehearsal in an Italian theatre (where else?) in which some horrible, unfunny comedy, by a certain Pirandello, is being rehearsed. Suddenly, six mysterious 'characters' enter this rehearsal. They enter as a whole family – father, mother, niece and younger children, to demand from the actors that they perform their allegedly 'real', very tragic drama, which has not yet had the chance to be shown on stage. The characters are very agitated, the actors are in a panic. In front of our eyes, an experiment takes place in the time-honoured convention of the theatre-within-a-theatre. This particular experiment is unique, unheard of before, because it involves not only a distinction between the first and second levels of scenic reality, but also a confrontation between characters and actors, face to face.

Pirandello's play is one of the first global hits after World War One. Consecutive openings of this play happen literally week after week in theatres all over the world. The next hit of this kind will be *The Threepenny Opera* of Brecht and Weill.

Six Characters was a refreshingly innovative play because the text had picked up – in a new, provocative manner – the topic of the relationship between a living being and a dead 'doll', a mannequin, a marionette. It also touched on the ancient mystery of theatre, in which people often talk pleasurably with ghosts. Nevertheless, Pirandello basically refreshed the idea of Goldoni who, by the way, loved to reach for much older scenarios than those of *dell'Arte*. Plays, like novels, love to talk to each other, to steal from each other, to mock each other notoriously and to quote, eagerly, one another.

29 I would like to understand better 'the passage' which Salvadori wrote in his *Silhouettes and Portraits*. I would like to understand better the re-directing of our visions of a possible future from:

the ideology of the totalitarian 'end of History' to the culture of a continually refreshed 'beginning of history', understood as an incidental product of many individuals of flesh and blood, blessed with a freedom of action and remaining open to the unpredictable future.

The future deprived of an expected 'End' becomes, indeed, unpredictable. Such a state brings – there is no need to hide it – great relief. It feels like taking off a painfully tight pair of shoes or undoing some buttons. Finally, we are 'blessed with a freedom of action' and this is a joyful feeling. But the unpredictability of the future, which liberates some people, also seems to terrify others. 'Am I supposed to continually refresh some 'beginning of history', not knowing where it is aiming?' people ask. 'Oh, never!' they answer, and they vote Trump, or the PiS Party or Orbán. To be brief, a large part of the population votes for the restrictions of tight shoes and buttons, confirming the beliefs of The Grand Inquisitor from the work of Ivan Karamazov.

The future, even a sad future, remains acceptable for such people for as long as it also remains predictable. This is because the unknown, unfamiliar future can be synonymous with danger, extreme risk and even pure evil. We are afraid of the unknown, we are afraid of the incomprehensible, the unnamed fills us with fear. This is why people usually choose paths already well-known to them. They prefer to choose the familiarity of oppression, rather than the freedom of unlimited choice.

Anxiety also arises from Salvadori's continually refreshed beginning of history understood as 'an incidental product of many individuals of flesh and blood'. The everlastingly refreshed 'incidental' beginning may be quite exciting as a formula for a choreographic composition, but as a social formula it threatens our way of life with total chaos. Salvadori, it seems, has somehow exaggerated a little with that 'incidental product'. The loss of the End – the end understood as the aim of culture

– does not bring us back to a state of innocence, of course. The abandonment of the dictates of teleology does not eliminate the existing laws, principles, habits or traditions. In our new situation of the End of the End, it is the future that has to be shaped in a new way and not the bygone, unchangeable past.

The loss of the End, therefore, reminds us about the lack of any clearly drawn direction from the middle of history, in which we find ourselves. This direction, it seems, needs to be created by ourselves, although not necessarily in a random way. Common sense tells us that the best method would probably be trial and error, although some mistakes may be costly.

Well, maybe errors of direction are inevitable, but the Captain from *Jacques the Fatalist* was wrong when he maniacally insisted that 'Everything is written up there'. The loss of the End, about which we are talking here, clearly confirms the lack of any determination in the course of events. We are alone with our contingency and which star we are drawn to depends only on us. This is true, no doubt, but equally true is another fact: apart from our will, there are also biological and cultural genes at work which will decide upon the direction of our future journey. One can risk saying (paraphrasing Professor Janion): 'Towards the future, yes, but together with our ancestors'.

Writing about *Jacques the Fatalist and His Master*, Milan Kundera noted a certain paradox. On the one hand, all the issues and histories in that book, allegedly previously 'written up there', find their solutions absolutely free from any deterministic faith. Human free will and the freedom of human choices are fully confirmed in Diderot's book and the Captain can go hang himself. On the other hand, Diderot seems to notice a completely unexpected, thought-provoking predictability in human fate. You get born, you finish your education, you fall in love (or not), then you have a career (or not) and usually you produce some children. Then your health starts to fail, the world starts to seem worse and worse, and your fellow human beings disappoint you more and more. And in the end you simply die and that's it.

That positive and joyful gift of the '*blessed freedom of action*' of Salvadori still has, it seems, at least for now, some limits.

30 The state of remaining in the not fully precise 'middle', without a clearly charted aim of the journey, is not a completely new situation, previously unknown to us in history. Over two thousand years, Christian teleology tried many times to reconcile somehow the dogma of the inevitability of the End, with teaching about free will and the full freedom of ethical choice.

There were many efforts of this kind, with various results, usually underlining the illusion of contradiction between these two spheres. The depressing shortness of human life has often been very helpful in such reasoning. Life is as brief as a dream (Calderón de la Barca, *Life Is a Dream*, 1630):

> if this is a dream
> if everything is changeable and ephemeral
> and everything is useless
> who
> would want to take this nothing
> knowing that he will lose
> what is unchangeable and eternal
> heaven
>
> the same with everything
> our beautiful past time
> is it not a dream
> is there anybody
> who remembering past triumphs
> past happiness

would not say
I was dreaming no doubt

yet I know
desire is a high flame
but a whisper of wind is enough
from wherever
to turn it into
ashes

let us then move to the eternity
to this that is
and let my name be repeated
through ages
by the lips of generations
who do not sleep
(Trans. Jarosław Marek Rymkiewicz)

Segismundo from *Life Is a Dream* chooses, following Plato's example, the 'real' eternity. Eternity which lasts, as opposed to 'the temporary' of today, ephemeral as a dream. Well, Segismundo, as his father Don Basilio has assured us, 'is a Christian and has received a fine education'. Segismundo makes a kind of classic Pascal's bet: by desiring to join the 'generations who do not sleep', he does not want to risk erasing this possibility by some stupid, impulsively committed sin. When proclaiming this monologue, he has Rosaura, a lady making a huge impression upon him, lying at his feet, a very enticing and lovable lady ...

Certainly, it is not easy to remain a Christian believer in times of irony and doubt, in times which I have called 'the times of the loss of the End'. The dismantling of grand narratives and the rejection of artificial hierarchies and divisions inherited from the Enlightenment can be seen by such a person as a Godless attack against the pillars of Western civilisation. And there is also the fluidity of classes and sexes, the fluidity of social roles and ways of communication joining that wave, not to mention the ongoing climate apocalypse.

The incarnation of the Christian God into history was an epochal event, which changed the shape of two millennia. Remaining under the influence of that event, at the end of the second millennium, Hegel elevated his Ghost of Time to the form of History-Which-Is-the-Sense-of-the-World. The time of the loss of the End is as far as possible from such ideas. Simply, this time does not believe in any of those effusive, grandiloquent expressions, which smack of totalitarianism. Even more, our time fears them. The loss of the End discreetly moves God away from historical time. It moves God to the individual sphere, to the intimate zone. It moves God to this sphere, which remains very respected by a majority, but only for as long as it does not threaten their social peace. No, the time of the loss of the End does not fight actively with the followers of God, nor does it fight with the Flat-Earthers. For all of them, there is a separate space in the wide, multicultural panorama of societies. Just as there is for cyclists, mushroom-pickers, fans of cricket and stamp collectors. Under the condition, of course, that all of them will get vaccinated in the proper way.

Let's be honest: it is not easy to remain a Christian believer in present times.

31 These discursions are about theatre and about literature, and about the numerous connections between them, as I have written above. Let us be precise, therefore, in what this unfinished catalogue of non-essential issues is not about. Well, it is not a novel, or a cookbook or a telephone book. It is not a catalogue of characters, it is not a dream dictionary, or a Baedeker. It is not a diary, a memoir, a manifest, a report or a memorandum. It is not travel writing, reportage or a list of intentions. It is not an announcement, advertisement,

proclamation, a planned argument, proof, evidence or pledge. This catalogue basically does not defend anything and does not demand anything. It does not try to take any side, it does not hold any position, it does not offer any decision. Altogether, it is much easier to enumerate what this catalogue does not do than to indicate what it actually does.

Well, this catalogue is basically full of doubts. Very often, therefore, it questions. It researches and asks, speculates and hesitates. Not being strong in anything, this catalogue is a thin stream of thought or of pondering. The pondering, whose aim – as we have known for a long time:

> both at the first and now, was and is, to hold, as 'twere, the mirror up
> to nature, to show virtue her own feature, scorn her own image, and
> the very age and body of the time his form and pressure.
> (Shakespeare, *Hamlet*)

32 The postmodern search for 'weak thought' is connected with the works of Gianni Vattimo, an Italian philosopher, author of many books, among them *The End of Modernity* (1985). Vattimo is an influential philosopher, a former European MP, who declares himself to be both gay and a Catholic. The 'weakening' of philosophical thought means for Vattimo, and for his followers, the relinquishment of categorical judgements. It means for him, the movement away from high, Kierkegaardian choices of 'either/or', from the universal laws and common axioms of Kant, and the movement towards careful, modest sketches of uncertain, individual cognition.

Pondering upon the arguments of 'strong thought', as opposed to 'weak thought', is a task for professional philosophers. Nevertheless, I remember – paradoxically – how strongly I was struck by Vattimo's idea when I read about it for the first time, many years ago.

For somebody who has spent their life in the theatre, 'weak thought' almost automatically coincides with *Via Negativa*. That is, with a consciously passive attitude towards the actors' process and every form of creation in the theatre. This idea was borrowed from the physical martial arts of the Far East and propagated by theatre revolutionaries of the 1970s, among them Jerzy Grotowski. In 1975, Peter Brook expressed this idea in the briefest way in Wrocław (I was there): the *Via Negativa* approach is not about – he said – 'how to do good' but about what not to do for the sake of permitting good to show up by itself.

The comparison of both these postulated 'weaknesses', of the philosophical one and that of the actors' process, opens unexpected horizons in human self-awareness. To forbear from doing 'good' and instead to await for 'good' to appear by itself, means, for the actor, a willing suspension of consciousness, previously seen as dominating over a subdued body. It practically means a willing rejection of the brain–body dichotomy of Descartes and relying – along with the Buddhist teaching of Tao – upon the primordial, pre-intellectual sensitivity of the whole body.

In a surprisingly similar way, this pushing against the 'strong' theory, propagated by structuralists and imitating the model of exact sciences, became the main task for Vattimo and for all followers of postmodern 'weak thought'. Their aim was the resignation from any general, objective, universal and autonomous theory. This means the resignation from any theory that is unsusceptible to historical or cultural changes, any theory that stays away from ethnic, racial or gender issues. Specificity becomes everything for 'weak thought', in complete contrast to any general law or rule.

The simultaneousness of both these anti-Enlightenment reactions – taking place at the same time in philosophy and in the theatre – surprises and 'makes one think'. And in the most natural way it coincides with the new 'culture of constantly refreshed "beginning of history"' so welcomed by Salvadori.

33 So, what could this wild garden of literature, this fragmentary catalogue of various issues be? If it was a novel, it might start like this:

§ Someone must have been telling tales about Umberto Enea, for early one morning, when he was returning on wobbly legs from a party at Paola's, he could not find the entrance to his house. He jingled his keys a couple of times, then walked down Via Vespucci to both the left and the right. The street was empty at this hour but everything was as usual: the grey apartment block, number 15, closed as usual; on the other side, that strange house number 19, with a glass entrance and a corridor with green tiles, and only the house of Umberto, number 17, was not where it always was. It was not where it should have been.

I shall phone Paola, he thought, and for almost a quarter of an hour he turned all his pockets out. In one of them he found his bank card and his identity card in the lining, but no telephone. I can't lose the keys, he thought. Resigned, he put them into the pocket of his jacket and shouted very loudly: 'Fuck!' The echo responded resoundingly but no window opened at Via Vespucci.

'Fuck, fuck!' he repeated, not fully convinced, and then he checked the entrances once more. The grey apartment block was in its usual place and, right beside it, number 19 with the glass entrance was visible as always. Only the apartment block number 17, which he used to enter at various times of night and day, for the last nine years, was missing.

On the little green towards Piazza Saffi, apart from a few bushes and a little olive tree twisted like a cripple, there were two benches made from dark metal. Showered many times by the nearby dogs, they stank. Somebody had sprayed them with pink paint. Umberto slid down onto the nearest one, hit his elbow with his head and was immediately asleep.

34 At midday today, I received the first dose of an anti-Covid vaccine. The morning began and was, for London, surprisingly cold. Maybe minus two, and a rare snow was swirling on the wind. The vaccine station was only two streets from my flat. There were people in yellow vests showing the way, people identifying newcomers, people directing you to the right room. Everything was wonderfully organised and it all lasted just a few minutes. I was vaccinated with the British vaccine, Astra Zeneca. Two hours earlier I had read in some paper that its effectiveness with the South African variant is surprisingly low, something like only ten percent. I would only receive the next dose of the vaccine twelve weeks later and I would get an SMS about a concrete date.

Anyone who believes that the vaccination programme will eliminate the threat of getting infected is totally wrong. The vaccine is an incredibly important, maybe even deciding factor, lowering the probability of infection, but nothing more. All right then, today's jab has decidedly lowered the probability that I will get infected but one still has to remain very careful and one should not lose hope that everything will be all right.

35 If one wanted to develop the caprice of a novel for longer, the next episode might go like this:

§ He was woken by the freezing cold, his head was exploding and his bladder was bursting. He crawled under a tree and looked at the crossroads while relieving himself. It was still dark, the lamps still glowed yellow with sodium light. He was surprised to see the whirling, blinking flakes in this light. Was it snow? Snow, he thought, this is extraordinary. Wet flakes were dancing in the piercing wind and were melting fast when touching the tarmac. But it was already settling, there were little heaps of snow along the kerb.

The day was slowly beginning. A car, with its lights on, flashed by, then a lorry behind it. The driver in a Volkswagen, coming from the opposite direction, pressed his brakes instinctively. His car slowly turned around on itself, then landed helplessly at the kerb on the left. The snow was getting more dense, it was already a blizzard.

Umberto was cold and wet, and because of that he decided to return to Via Vespucci. He crossed, sliding on the cobbles, to the other side of the street. But there was no Via Vespucci there. There were other streets, other lamps and trees, and a few shops with neon lights in their windows, but none of them were familiar. This city did not look like Forlí. It looked similar; it was no doubt some Italian city. The torn poster of the Medrano Circus on the wall and the sign 'Macelleria' over the corner shop left no doubt, but it was most definitely not Forlí.

More cars were sliding on the tarmac now; their numbers were growing. All of them were spinning and swaying from left to right. Younger drivers were discovering the joy of controlled skidding, while the older ones slowly slid through the snowy slush, terrified. There was growing panic on the street, the snow created a level of extraordinary, paralysing cataclysm.

I am getting old, thought Umberto. He was shivering. It was probably only a few degrees above zero, but his corduroy jacket did not protect him from the chilling cold. He strolled slowly down the wide street with planted acacias. At the third crossroads he read the plaque on the wall: Via Vittorio Emanuelle. He was struck by a thought: I was here, I was here once before in my life, I was walking this same street, it was summer, some time ago, some time ago I was in this town – the question is when?

The morning, with its still-failing, heavy snow gradually revealed signs of life. He was passing the greengrocer shop; its rising blind screeched. A woman with two children enchanted by the snow exited from a side alley. She pulled them violently towards some school or kindergarten. At the next corner, behind a steamy window, lights flared: a bar. He entered, trembling. It was warm inside, it smelled of coffee, the coffee machine was hissing. Four men commented on the latest misfortune – the weather. They were talking one over the other, in a not-easily understandable southern dialect. They looked at him: he was an alien, not easy to categorise, not easy to pigeonhole.

'Cappuccino and a brioche,' he said to the barman, pulling his card from his pocket. The barman brought the card machine, the card worked. Umberto swallowed a sip of coffee and felt the warmth slowly seeping through his body. He bit into the croissant.

'I am very sorry, would you mind telling me which city this is?' he said. There was silence in the bar.

'Constantinople!' snorted one of the guests; the others whinnied in response.

'I know, this does not happen every day,' he continued, 'but I snoozed on the train, you understand ...'

'You are in Palermo,' said the barman, 'but you might not believe me. There was no snow in Palermo for forty years. Where are you from?'

'From Emilia Romagna,' responded Umberto. He finished his coffee and thanked the barman. On the sidewalk there were some people who were going to their work or maybe to the shop. An older gentleman with an umbrella in his hand was trying to clean the snow from his parked Lancia.

Palermo? How can I be in Palermo, why Palermo? he was asking himself. If it is Palermo, I need to find Rafaella. She was a friend of his, whom he had visited maybe ten years ago when going to a conference in Syracuse. Via Vittorio Emanuelle now made more sense in his eyes. He knew, therefore, that he was going towards the port. The snow had ceased to fall, and it was getting brighter. There was some shop with sports clothes at the corner; he was their first client that day. After twenty minutes he exited the shop in a burgundy-coloured, waterproof Gore-Tex coat. Luckily, his card worked once more. He checked his account at the ATM: he had almost five thousand Euros; temporarily, he was fine.

He started to ask the passers-by where the nearest telephone was; somebody pointed out the Post Office. He found the name of Raffaella Pizzol in the telephone book, with her address and number. Her voicemail responded. He left a message: he has found himself in Palermo unexpectedly, he hopes that they can see each other, he will phone again later.

Afterwards, he wandered through the city. The snow was slowly thawing, and in the afternoon the Sun showed itself from behind the clouds. Water from melted snow was flowing everywhere, the temperature had risen from zero to nine degrees. He ate ravioli in some self-service café, with a quarter of red wine. There were only a few clients, but at least they were there. The city was slowly returning to the normal rhythm, although the atmosphere of a natural disaster could still be felt. He phoned Raffaella once more. It went to voicemail again. He hung up. There was a handmade poster at the corner of the street. He had time, therefore he wandered slowly to the address two streets away.

There were not many spectators in the puppet theatre of the Mancuso brothers at Via Collegio de Maria. Two families with small children and a few incidental, half-frozen tourists were there. A red-haired girl, tightly buttoned up, held some English tourist guide in her hand. The theatre was a little room on the ground floor, the entrance fee five Euro per person. After a long wait – maybe for latecomers? – the older brother, Francesco, finally hit the gong. The puppets were not very tall, sixty, maybe seventy centimetres, but they were heavy. The armour of the knights weighed a lot, not to mention the jewellery, earrings and the costumes of the oppressed ladies and their noble attendants. The metal wings of the monsters and dragons were particularly heavy. Francesco and his younger brother Lorenzo worked hard. During each one-hour show they carried a few hundred kilograms each. Apart from this, they had to change the tone of their voices constantly because ladies speak with thin voices, while knights speak with thick and rough voices. The monsters squawk, the dragons roar, the attendants sway, moaning, and when morning rises upon the stage, the actors are supposed to trill like a blackbird or some other bird. The proscenium arch was roughly one metre by three; these are the measurements of the cinema screen, invented long before cinema existed.

Ruggiero, a Christian Knight in love with Bradamant, a Christian lady, was raging on the stage. He was able to save her from the charmed castle of the magician Atlantes. Rinaldo, one of the Twelve Paladins of Charlemagne, famous for performing incredible deeds in fights with dragons, was beside him, as well as Orlando, the most important Paladin, the King's nephew. Orlando's beloved was Angelica, the Princess of Cathay, with whom all the knights were in love, particularly Rinaldo, Ferrau and Ruggiero. But Angelica did not want to marry any of them because her heart was conquered by a Saracen fighter, Medoro.

Umberto understood: this was Ariosto. This was *Orlando Furioso* in a simplified version, still carefully rhymed and practically unchanged from the times when Cervantes was enslaved by the Moors. During his peregrinations, his Don Quixote attends a similar performance and because of that he meditates on the fate of every possible hero, himself included. The marionettes of the knights, with their red skirts, silver breast plates and their helmets, could have been bought in Palermo in every shop with souvenirs, beside miniatures of the Greek temple in Segesta, of the amphitheatre in Taormina and the volcano of Etna.

Most of the scenes performed by the Mancuso brothers ended with ferocious fights. Knights were getting even with the armies of their opponents, with monsters sent by malicious magicians, or with both at once. Armour clashed with armour, sword with sword. The clang of metal obscured warlike shouts emitted by invisible actors. The army of enemies, with which a Christian warrior was fighting, usually consisted of the dark-skinned Mamelukes with colourful cloths on their heads. Among them were giants with enormous arms but they were powerless against Orlando or Ruggiero who were chopping them into pieces with their swords. In the midst of the furious shouts and clatter of metal, the marionettes were losing their heads, their hands and legs were falling off, clickety-clack. A body with no limbs was thrown into a corner like a wet rag. The dragons and monsters were disintegrating, losing their wings and legs. Their tails were being systematically sliced into tranches. It was a bloody, relentless, Sicilian slaughterhouse.

'You are wonderful, Lorenzo, Francesco, you are simply wonderful,' mumbled Umberto after the show, putting into the hands of both sweaty actors a few rumpled notes. 'Is it possible to phone from here?' It was.

'Is it you, Umberto?' – this time Rafaella picked up the phone – 'Get into a taxi and come immediately, we are waiting!'

36 § 'You must have been totally hammered,' said Raffa after dinner. 'You got drunk like a pig, you lost consciousness, and then somebody, just for fun, put you on a train to the south.' Antonio, Raffa's husband, a fluffy bear with a red beard, kept smiling, nodded his head as he ravished his plate of cannelloni and stayed silent.

'This is true, I was drunk,' Umberto said, 'but not so drunk as to not remember what was happening. The house where my flat is was simply not there. It had vanished. I fell asleep on a bench and I woke up in Palermo on Via Vittorio Emanuelle.' He reached for Raffa's phone.

'I shall call again.' He had called Paola in Forlí for the fourth time, asking if she had found his phone. But Paola's number did not answer; she could have been at her shift at the hospital, perhaps. 'You will sleep soundly in the guest room,' said Raffa, pouring them both a farewell noggin of grappa, 'and in the morning we shall see what we can do.'

The next day, after saying goodbye to his hosts, Umberto took a taxi to the airport. An Alitalia flight to Bologna was departing a few minutes after eleven. He reached Forlí by the local train; it was not very far from the station to Via Vespucci. The last hundred metres he almost ran. Number 17, his house, was still not there. He grabbed the elbow of an old man exiting from number 19.

'Please, signor, explain to me what has happened here,' he asked.

'Well, it was always like this,' the old man smiled, 'ever since I remember, always. Are you looking for anyone?'

'I am looking for number 17.'

'There is no such building, and there never was. They must have missed it 150 years ago, when they were building these houses,' said the old man happily, swinging his Co-op bag.

Paola's flat at Via Silvestrini was on the second floor. The card on the door said: 'U. A. Cangione'. He did not remember that card. A white-haired, well-kept women in a florid dress opened the door.

'There must be some misunderstanding,' she answered, 'no Paola Sergione has ever lived here. I have been living here for over twenty years, so I think I would know.'

How was it possible? It was inexplicable, some elaborate joke. 'I am not Alice,' he mumbled to himself when exiting to the pavement. It was already dusk and suddenly he felt very tired.

He slept in the Hotel Masini. After breakfast, he stayed in his room. The number of the printing house in Bologna – for which he worked regularly, editing works about the history of art and the visual arts – was not responding. He checked in the telephone book, but Pagine Verdi, his printing house number, was not listed. He went downstairs and asked for access to a computer. He checked, one after another, the names of every person known to him. None of them were there. What was more, he was not able to find a single name he recognised. For example, Gianpiero Palmieri, with whom he sometimes played tennis, did not answer when he phoned; instead, an unknown person responded.

Umberto paid for his hotel and went to the Medical Centre at Via Guardiola. The girl at reception could not understand what he wanted. Then, looking dubious, she started to check the computer system. Finally, she got up, exasperated: 'I am very sorry but, as you can see, there is no Umberto Enea in our catalogues.'

He went to the Ronaldini café and found a solution while he was paying. At Piazza Saffi he went to the Post Office. The telephone number was in the book. After a few transfers, the service department of his bank responded. He gave his name, date of birth, the number of his identity card and, after some time, he got a confirmation that, indeed, he had an account at Unicredito Bank.

'It is about my address. I have found myself in a very strange situation and I need to know whether the address which you hold for me in your system is the correct one.' The lady he spoke to did not know what to do and decided to ask her boss. The boss, a baritone with a strong Venetian accent, joined the conversation and once again checked all the data, with a key password (his mother's name) included.

'This is what we shall do,' said the boss, 'you will give me the address first and I shall tell you whether it is the same one or not.' Umberto took a deep breath.

'Forlí, Via Amerigo Vespucci 17,' he said.

The boss laughed. 'You see, no need to worry. The address is correct, have a good day.'

37 Should I leave him like this, a man without a home, or any work, with no family or friends in an unfamiliar and hostile town? Should I abandon an intriguing story for the sake of more speculation about the end of the End? Or should I forget him and leave his history with no beginning and no end?

The passing of time and the habits we develop make us tell stories, including beginnings and endings, even if they do not appear in this order. What has started must end. Unfinished, ruptured, unresolved stories make us nervous because they shatter the hope – deeply coded in our genes – for an explanation, for a resolution, no matter how many difficulties and obstacles occur. This resolution may be tragic and final, as, for example, the final entrance of Fortinbras's army in *Hamlet*. After Fortinbras's last words, it is not possible to continue this story; the Wheel of Fortune is come full circle. That's even without mentioning the hope for resolution in lighter, comical plots. An expectation for a *happy end* dominates the majority of literary and film scenarios.

The Austrian writer, Peter Handke, has managed, despite all the circumstances mentioned above, to create a history (even a tangled handful of histories), which has no beginning, nor an end. He did it in his work *The Hour We Knew Nothing of Each Other* (1992), which can only disputably be called a drama, although it remains a record of scenic action. He managed to invent a story, in which so much is happening that, in fact, nothing really happens. The director can start or end this history at any random moment. Storytelling – Handke asks us – what is it really all about? Are various narratives, with their beginnings, middles and endings, objectively happening in the world? Maybe they are only invented and told by their authors, directors, storytellers and playwrights? Or maybe all the beginnings and ends of every possible story are being told in the theatre by us, the audience. And not only in the theatre, but also in so-called 'Life'. Maybe all possible stories gain an understandable structure only thanks to us, a species of addicted story-tellers?

To be able to see, live, an exquisite production of Handke's play is a profound and enriching experience. So much ado about so little nothing. In a town, individuals and some groups of random people cross a piazza. Some of them seem to be in a hurry, some of them not. Some of them return and some do not. It seems that every one of these anonymous characters carry their own individual, separate story, which we can start to imagine from their clothes or their behaviour. Yet none of them are talking with anyone else. There is no plot, no intrigue starts, and there is no dialogue. It is exactly as in the title: the characters (and the audience) do not know anything about themselves. The author and the director simply have to start the action some-where, but sooner or later the spectator will understand that the middle part of the action might be similar to its incidental beginning. Because of this, the potential end of the story in this situation doesn't really matter. There will be no fifth act. There is no gun, hanging on the wall, that will be fired in the finale. One does not need to wrack one's brains to ask, 'Who is the cul-prit?' or 'Who will inherit the crown?' What a relief! It may be, like in some mathematical equation, that many trains with many different velocities start contemporaneously from many different stations, and it may be that they will all meet one day, somewhere, sometime, but the calculation is not our responsi-bility. Whoever wants to worry over the fate of the world, let him do it; like the pensioners in a small town, we feel free from the need to do anything, and free from guilt, while looking through the window on a sunny afternoon.

Inventing stories, which absolutely do not want to be sto-ries, probably started from an excess of all the stories that have already been told. Because, although there is, indeed, an infin-ity of stories and an infinity of ways of telling them, strangely, most of them have already been told, at least once, before.

Therefore, some malcontents say that in the theatre everything has already been seen. And also, say such killjoys, whatever is written has already been written before ...

So, should I simply leave Umberto Enea – forty-three years old, shoe size 42, two missing teeth in his upper jaw and a scar from a ski incident on the left knee – there, in the middle of Piazza Saffi, in a hostile Forlí? Or maybe I should save him, at least for now?

38 § The very same evening, Umberto got on the express train to Milan. Faenza, Imola, Bologna; stations were passing fast. He was going to Milan because this was where he had spent his childhood. An older man with a moustache sitting in front of him in the compartment seemed somehow familiar. Umberto was going to Milan because someone who loses his flat, his neighbours and his acquaintances in one day, with no explanation, should be doing something with himself. Therefore, he was doing something.

At Reggio Emilia station, the moustachioed man suddenly got up, pointed two fingers towards Umberto, like a gun, and said: 'K-pow!' Then he babbled something inaudible and left quickly. The train was already approaching San Donato Milanese when, finally, recognition flashed through Umberto's brain: the moustachioed man was the same man, who, two days earlier in Palermo, was cleaning a dark-green Lancia, while holding an umbrella, on Via Vittorio Emanuelle.

39 Is this a thriller, then? One of the possibilities. Perhaps somebody is running away because somebody else is stalking him? The possible combinations are innumerable. For example, this one:

§ The very same evening, Umberto got on the express train to Milan. Faenza, Imola, Bologna; stations were passing fast. He was going to Milan because this was where he had spent his childhood. A young woman sitting in front of him in the compartment, well-dressed, seemed somehow familiar. Umberto was going to Milan because someone who loses his flat, his neighbours and his acquaintances in one day, with no explanation, should be doing something with himself. Therefore, he was doing something. The woman sitting across from him was reading the *Financial Times*. 'Where do I know her from?' thought Umberto. The train was already reaching the suburbs of Milan, when recognition dawned upon him: the woman sitting across from him was a tourist with an English guide in her hand, the red-haired girl seen by him two days earlier on Via Collegio di Maria in the theatre of the Brothers Mancuso.

40 Instinctively, I prefer the version where Umberto recognises the unknown woman. Let it be a mysterious romance, rather than car chases and shooting. Let them fall madly fall in love and let them break their hearts afterwards. Even later, let them get together again; then he will have to leave her, then she will have to leave him. Let the history of their love be complicated, full of dramatic turns, gripping us and moving us to tears. Like *Doctor Zhivago*, with the great history of the world in the background.

Play, oh beloved imagination: she is, let's say, the daughter of an American media mogul. She is travelling through Italy incognito, hiding from a shockingly handsome, brutal and shamelessly rich Arab prince. The prince saw her once on the street; his name is Hassan, let's say, and he decided immediately that this red-haired beauty with emerald eyes would be his. Ever since then he has been chasing after her and he threatens to kidnap her and take her to his harem in the palace at

21 Northern Ring in Riyadh. Because of that, Umberto does not have any choice. He must help her, and he must save her. Her name is Jessica, or Phyllida, or Naomi and she falls in love with Umberto very fast. He remains chivalrous and tender, naturally.

Meanwhile, Hassan acts like a madman. His henchmen, disguised as clowns, pester Jessica and Umberto in Cinecittà in Rome. But Umberto manages to deflect them with the help of a supersonic gun, and innumerable enemy corpses lie still in the courtyards. Behind the scenes, the Italian–Moscow mafia is blackmailing them, hoping to gain concessions for oil in the Al-Jamal province. So, they sometimes support Hassan, but when he annoys them they change sides and support Umberto and Jessica. However, they plan to feed them to the tigers when they've got what they want, and worst of all, one never knows where they are hiding. And that's exactly what the poet intended:

> Of lovers and Ladies, Knights and Arms, I sing,
> Of Courtesies, and many a daring feat;
> And from those ancient days my story ring,
> When Moors from Afric passed in hostile fleet,
> And ravaged France, with Agramant their king,
> Flushed with his youthful rage and furious heat,
> Who on King Charles', the Roman emperor's head
> Had vowed due vengeance for Troyano dead …
> (Trans. William Stewart Rose)

The Polish translation of Ariosto's *Orlando Furioso* by Piotr Kochanowski is over four hundred years old. It is an unbelievable translation. It transfers faithfully the rhythm and colour of the Italian original, but first of all it is done in wonderfully juicy Polish, which Piotr mastered like his uncle Jan Kochanowski, the greatest Polish Renaissance poet. 'Lovers and

Ladies, Knights and Arms' have entered the canon of Polish literature — without his translation we would not have *Beniowski* (a Romantic poem by J. Słowacki) and maybe not even Miłosz.

Yes, but today's students, if ever asked about Ariosto at the seminar, open their eyes wide and look discombobulated. They have never heard of Orlando. Which does not stop them from enjoying *Game of Thrones*. I get frustrated and overwhelmed by the wish to vow due vengeance upon their heads. How is it possible to praise *Game of Thrones* or *Star Wars* without being conscious of their literary sources? How is it possible to praise them and be unaware of Tasso, or Ariosto?

C. S. Lewis (a close friend of J. R. R. Tolkien) writes very beautifully about Ariosto in his *The Allegory of Love: A Study of Medieval Traditions* (1936), one of his most important works. Lewis leads the reader through the allegorical poetry of the French troubadours, meticulously analysing the versions of the *Roman de la Rose*: of Guillame de Lorris and of Jean de Meun. He tracks the influence of these works upon Chaucer and other contemporary English authors and ends the whole thing with a bravura evaluation of *The Faerie Queene* by Edmund Spenser.

Lewis dedicates a separate chapter to the lyric poetry of the Italian Renaissance, which has him in raptures:

Ariosto is admittedly the greatest of Italian poets after Dante ... He is a master of irony and of comic construction ... The power in which Ariosto excels above all poets that I have read, is the one which he shares with Boiardo – invention. The fertility of his fancy is 'beyond expectation, beyond hope'. His actors range from archangels to horses, his scene from Cathay to the Hebrides. In every stanza there is something new: battles in all their detail, strange lands with their laws, customs, history and geography, storm and sunshine, mountains, islands, rivers, monsters, anecdotes, conversations – there seems no end to it. He tells us what his people ate; he describes the architecture of their palaces. It is 'God's plenty': you can no more exhaust it than you can exhaust nature itself. When you are tired of Ariosto, you must be tired of the world. If ever you come near to feeling that you can read no more adventures, at that very moment he begins another with something so ludicrous, so piquant, or so questionable, in its exordium, that you decide to read at least this one more. And then you are lost: you must go on till bedtime, and next morning you must begin again … The *Orlando Furioso* in its own peculiar way, is as great a masterpiece of construction as *Oedipus Rex*.

Lewis writes about Ariosto with admiration because books and their authors adore talking among themselves. Lewis, a historian of literature and Tolkien, a philologist, through the 1930s and 1940s met in an Oxford pub *The Eagle and Child* (nicknamed 'The Bird and Baby') or in Lewis's rooms in Magdalen College. They read, with a group of their followers and fans, fragments of their latest works and shared with them their fascination with medieval times and their literary passions (a provocative slogan of Lewis's was: 'The Renaissance never happened!').

Without many years of encouragement from Lewis, the author of *The Lord of the Rings* would never have been able to finish his work. Tolkien admitted it many times afterwards. As we know, he created his fantastic world of Middle-earth because of his fascination with the Old English poem *Beowulf* from the seventh or eighth century. He was enchanted by griffons, dragons, magicians, curses and war escapades, and the eternal fight between Good and Evil. For both professors, that fabulous, cultural universe, lost in the gloom of history, remained the land of artistic and human fulfilment.

When, wanting to learn more about the Lannisters, Starks or Daenerys Targaryen, we begin a new episode of *Game of Thrones*, in the background Beowulf (who was fighting with Grendel) strolls. Also, Ruggiero with his Bradamante, the amorous Angelica from Cathay and valorous Orlando 'who went mad from incredible love'.

41　Precisely because books and authors talk intensely outside the confines of time, a particular department of literature, a peculiar one, called the *Dialogues of the Dead* was born. The author of the oldest existing fragments of this kind was, of course, Lucian of Samosata, but one can bet that others must have already composed them before him. In his *Dialogues of the Dead*, Lucian describes famous kings, heroes and leaders long after their deaths, as they meet in the netherworld and compare their achievements and conquests. They evaluate their war strategies and the contents of their treasuries.

The work of Lucian inspired a whole bunch of imitators in modern times. Among them were Bernard de Fontenelle (1683) and François Fenelon (1712). In Fontenelle's work, Julius Caesar chats with Alexander the Great, while Montaigne, walking on the Elysian meadows of *asphodel*, discourses with Seneca. Bishop Ignacy Krasicki decided to imitate the French, and his *Conversations of the Dead* were published in Polish in 1798.

'So now, when all of us are dead, could we return yet one more time to that evening in Copenhagen?' Margrethe Bohr asks, opening with this line the play *Copenhagen* by Michael Frayn (1998). This play is a fascinating attempt to recreate the real events of 1941. In particular, the quarrel of Niels Bohr and Werner Heisenberg, a source of historical consequences which influenced the fate of World War Two. Frayn's text remains, somehow, an exemplary 'dialogue of the dead', created for the theatre.

The dead also talk with themselves – even more, they disagree sharply and ferociously – in an atmospheric short story by Dostoevsky, titled 'Bobok'. These dead bodies, deceased at various times, rest one beside another in the same cemetery. Yet after sunset, their voices regain their full life-energy. They start to shout at and mock each other, and to curse. No, they are not the noble North American corpses from the *Spoon River* anthology by Edgar Lee Masters, who communicate with the living through short, poetical epitaphs. On the contrary, the dead from 'Bobok' are a herd of poorly educated simpletons, full of envy and violence, a bunch of malicious rascals, of dead souls borrowed from Gogol and then procreated in the imagination of Dostoevsky.

It was always an incredibly tempting operation for literature, to be able to talk with the dead. It happens to all of us in life, yes, it does, even during the day, usually after the death of some close person, or, less frequently, after the death of more distant people. The dead also appear in our dreams, usually unexpectedly, but peacefully. 'Is it you, Uncle?' or 'Mum, what are you doing here?' we ask those familiar to us and yet profoundly changed, in our dreams. They appear either unnaturally young, or unexpectedly silent, and even when they talk to us it is difficult to hear them and understand them.

The first ghost of a formerly deceased person saved in the archives of literature was, most probably, King Darius in *The Persians* by Aeschylus (BC 472). Atossa, his widow, calls her husband from his grave. She wants him to give advice to the Persians, who were devastated by their fresh loss at the battle of Salamina. The ghost of Darius praises the victorious Athenians and warns the Persians of their next impending losses.

Aeschylus uses the ghost of Darius to emphasise the superiority of the Athenian democracy as opposed to the Persian dictatorship – in the democracy the citizens are much more eager to defend their state. When, at the end of the play, Xerxes, the son and heir of the late Darius, enters the stage on a chariot, in a torn robe, and despairs over the death of Persian soldiers, the power of the victorious Athenian state shines like never before. '*Kommos*', the final song of the tragedy, may begin.

It was always understood that Seneca the Younger, in the first century after Christ, was next – after Aeschylus – the ancient author of tragedies who liked to introduce ghosts to the stage. The influence of Seneca's tragedies upon the English authors of the Elizabethan age, and afterwards upon French authors like Corneille and Racine, was immense. Thomas Kyd was proclaimed a specialist of the 'revenge tragedy', a genre in which the role of the deceased, most often maliciously murdered, was crucial. In the revenge tragedy, the ghost, usually called from the underworld to demand retribution for murders and offences, left without recourse. The ghost was like a moral alibi for the deeds committed on stage by the characters. Nevertheless, quite recently it became evident, after checking all preserved tragedies of Seneca, that in his works only three ghosts appear. More precisely, only two, because the authorship of the tragedy *Octavia*, in which the ghost of Agrippina appears, is very dubious and most probably Seneca did not write it. The other two cases are: the ghost of Tantalus in *Tyestes* and the ghost of the same Tyestes in *Agamemnon*. Both ghosts exist like inauspicious prologues and predict a negative turn of events, not so much for the heroes of both plays but rather for the audience. *Tyestes* begins with the speech of the ghost of Tantalus ,who appears on stage against his will, being brought from his terrible suffering in Hell.

It is obvious what should come next. Nothing else can be next, apart from the ghost of old Hamlet, who appears on the walls of Elsinore to his terrified son. He is the most famous ghost in the history of European drama. He would not be there if Kyd had not started, a little earlier, with his ghosts on the stage. Kyd in turn would not have done it if Seneca had not dealt with ghosts at the beginning of the first millennium. Kyd wanted to be on a par with Seneca. Before Seneca there was Aeschylus and supposedly many others, whose names we do not know. Therefore, because of the respect for this procession of authors, what should come next has to be about the ghost of the old Hamlet, no excuses.

Yes, but everything that could be written about the ghost scene from *Hamlet* has already been written. Bloom, in his

The Western Canon (1994) makes fun of Sigmund Freud. Bloom laughs that Freud's whole theory and the school of psychoanalysis was derived from that single scene. Just to think: the discipline of psychoanalysis, all those doctors and professors, all those cranky gurus (those Jungs, Fromms and Lacans), their numerous institutes, thousands of books, hundreds of thousands of articles about 'the Oedipus complex' and the complex of 'the lack of a penis', and all of this from one scene. Just to think, a whole century of laborious work, usually referring to itself, praising itself (or not) and fearlessly self-engaging in the psychic problems created by itself. Just think that without 'Who's there?', without the question which opens the text of Shakespeare, all that psychoanalytical industry would not exist.

Therefore, even if *Hamlet*'s ghost scene *should* come next, even if my text *should* be about that scene, it will not be. No pondering whether the ghost of old Hamlet is from Hell, or maybe rather from Purgatory. Nothing about the hesitations of the prince or his dilemmas, nor anything about his Mummy, mad as a box of frogs. Nothing about his attitude to women, which is, by the way, absolutely outrageous. Nor about his attitudes towards religion, war, knowledge or power. It will be instead, for some time at least, about Hecuba:

> Is it not monstrous that this player here,
> But in a fiction, in a dream of passion,
> Could force his soul so to his own conceit
> That from her working all his visage waned,
> Tears in his eyes, distraction in his aspect,
> A broken voice, and his whole function suiting
> With forms to his conceit – and all for nothing!
> For Hecuba!
> What's Hecuba to him, or he to Hecuba,
> That he should weep for her?

This moment in the play makes us think. 'But in a fiction, in a dream of passion?' Who dares to speak like this? Is it the same person who only in the next scene will confess during the rehearsal with the actors, that:

O, it offends me to the soul to hear a robustious, periwig-pated fellow tear a passion to tatters, to very rags, to split the ears of the ground-lings, who for the most part are capable of nothing but inexplicable dumb shows and noise?

How can such a person speak in such words about the actors' process? That second Prince Hamlet, whose words, 'it offends me to the soul' sound like a rather experienced director, immediately capable of making a clear distinction between obstreperous amateurism and seasoned, professional acting. By contrast, that first Prince Hamlet from the previous scene, that of 'in a fiction' and 'a dream of passion', speaks like someone who does not know much about the nature of the actors' art. That first Hamlet basically sees the actors almost as some cheap merchants of fake feelings. According to the first Hamlet, an actor:

What would he do
Had he the motive and the cue for passion
That I have? He would drown the stage with tears
And cleave the general ear with horrid speech,
Make mad the guilty and appall the free,
Confound the ignorant and amaze indeed
The very faculties of eyes and ears.

While the second Hamlet, he from the rehearsal, absolutely justly warns the actors about playing in an over-the-top way and at the same time respects them and treats them as self-conscious, skilled creators: 'Be not too tame neither, but let your own discretion be your tutor. Suit the action to the word, the word to the action, with this special observance, that you o'erstep not the modesty of nature.'

Which of these two Hamlets is the 'true' one? Whom should we believe?

Let's look at it step by step. The theatre is a place in which the spectators play the game of temporary participation in an openly fictional world. Scenes other than 'imaginary' scenes do not exist in the professional European theatre, and it was no different in the time of Shakespeare. The audience plays the 'game of what if', or the game of 'what would happen if', using the willing suspension of their disbelief. The first Prince Hamlet, the one who accuses the theatre of using a 'fiction' (as opposed to the truth) seems to be some amateur who does not understand the rules of the game. 'A dream of passion?' The so-called feelings or emotions of the actor are always 'untrue' in the theatre – I mean, the professional actor never feels them 'truly'. The professional actor relies upon their occupational, technical abilities to create an impression of their feelings in the minds of the audience. This is what their skill is about. It is not until Denis Diderot's dialogue, *The Paradox of an Actor* (1773–78) that a clear description of the relation between the theatrical fiction and the so-called 'real' truth in the theatre appears.

Yet already, earlier, other authors were writing about the paradoxical relationship between truth and non-truth in the theatre. For example, Antoine-François Riccoboni, a pillar of the Parisian *Commédie Italienne*, wrote about it in his *Art of Theatre* (1750):

One should walk using a firm, even step, possibly with some grandeur and without skipping. Some tragic actors want to look more mightily and therefore they walk using a step so heavy, that all their body trembles and their head simply jumps. This way of moving not only does not add any nobility, but it mocks the illusion, because we discover a pompous actor in the place of a bold hero.

For Riccoboni – and for the second of our Prince Hamlets – the credibility of the illusion remains the highest value in the theatre. Shakespeare, let's agree, knows practically everything about the dialectics of truth and fiction in the theatre. Therefore, where does that double standard come from in the opinions of Hamlet about an actor who is moved by the fate of Hecuba? That inconsistency, where does it come from?

There are, I think, two possible explanations. One of them is the conviction, shared also by Wyspiański in his *Study of Hamlet*, that the version of the play's text known to us is a combination of the two different, earlier versions of the play. The inconsistency in Hamlet's reasoning about the nature of theatre would be, in this case, a result of this synthesis.

The second possible explanation is somehow more simple. Independently of any differences between the text printed in the Folio and the Quarto, Hamlet remains somewhat incoherent in his opinions about the theatre because this is exactly how the author wanted to present him – as an erratic aristocrat. In this version, Hamlet could remain a close friend of the actors and their director, without losing his aristocratic perspective which makes him distrustful of their social status and their questionable craft.

42 It was about Hecuba, as promised, and not about the ghost, although it should have been about the ghost. It should have been, because the conversation of Hamlet with the ghost of his deceased father radiates throughout drama and literature with a force that is rarely surpassed by any other dramatic scene. The dead and ghosts, as we already know, always interested theatre, and eerie stories were always present there. Two of the most vivid threads in European modern culture, the history of Doctor Faustus and the history of Don Juan, repeated over time in innumerable versions, would be

inconceivable without elements of the supernatural, without the diabolical illusions of Mephistopheles or without the statue of the Commodore magically returning to life. And also without the final images of fiery Hell, intended to freeze the blood of the spectators.

Nevertheless, in the middle of the eighteenth century, a phenomenon called 'the Gothic novel' is born in England with *The Castle of Otranto* in 1764. Contemporaneously, the ruined castles, hidden dungeons, dark curses and ghosts – generally, the spooky elements of the medieval dark ages become fashionable. At the same time, the Germans join this trend with their genre of the *Schauerroman* – a type of a novel where ruins, ghosts, spectres, necromancy and secret sects appear in abundance.

This trend in Germany soon evolves into *Geisterroman* (a novel about ghosts) and also into *Räuberroman* (a novel about brigands), born from Schiller's drama, *Die Räuber* or, finally, into *Ritterroman* (a novel about knights). In short, Romanticism explodes across the whole of Europe and from then on Romantic heroes will be talking with ghosts around the clock.

The rapid eruption of this wave was something deeper than yet another change of fashion in the arts. This eruption was not about another superficial change in the ruling aesthetics, it was about an elementary revolution in the understanding of human nature and human history. New, Romantic topics demanded radically new garments, new musical chords, and emotional images of wholly new proportions. In the world of art, glaring exoticism, extreme individualism, and cosmic panache became more desired than ever before.

In the dramatic poem by Lord Byron, *Manfred* (1816), the potent necromancer Manfred, a distant grandson of Doctor Faustus, conjures at midnight the figure of Ahriman, a malicious spirit who reigns over the whole world. We are in a sinister castle, high in the Alps. Byron has borrowed Ahriman from Zoroastrianism of the Ancient Persians. Ahriman comes from their holy book, Zend-Avesta, and also straight from the teachings of their master and the founder of their religion, Zarathustra. Byron's knowledge of Zoroastrianism was at best sketchy, but such a background seemed for him to be the best one for his story. Upon Manfred's orders, the obedient elements appear, as well as whole regiments of flying creatures, invisible to the human eye – the whole menagerie of the Underworld listens to his commands. And yet already in his first, dark monologue we learn that:

> The lamp must be replenish'd, but even then
> It will not burn so long as I must watch.
> My slumbers – if I slumber – are not sleep,
> But a continuance of enduring thought,
> Which then I can resist not: in my heart
> There is a vigil, and these eyes but close
> To look within; and yet I live, and bear
> The aspect and the form of breathing men.
> But grief should be the instructor of the wise;
> Sorrow is knowledge: they who know the most
> Must mourn the deepest o'er the fatal truth,
> The Tree of Knowledge is not that of Life.

The black arts cannot, as we learn, soothe Manfred's aching state of mind. This penitent villain is condemned to incurable suffering by his remorse. *Manfred* and its landscape of heroic human battle with the forces of Good and Evil asks for an operatic version, written by, who knows, Rossini or Charles Gounod. Well, Gounod composed a lyrical opera about Faust (in 1859), while *Manfred* was transposed in the compositions of Schuman and Tchaikovsky.

Luckily, a new form appears together with Romanticism – a puckish, even perverse 'digressive poem'. A new form, but with many references to the past. Byron's 'Childe Harold's

Pilgrimage', *Deutschland, Ein Wintermärchen* by Heine, *Evgeni Onegin* by Pushkin, 'El estudiante de Salamanca' by José de Espronceda, Słowacki's *Beniowski* – all these poetic works with a free, fragmentary composition owe a lot to Sterne, no doubt. Their episodic plots (very often descriptions of journeys) are only a pretext for numerous reflections, records, observations, ponderings and anecdotes by their authors. The narrator very often uses irony and jest. He is mischievous and subjective, maintaining a distance towards the work and its characters. In these digressive poems, the artificiality and literariness of the story are consciously accented, which underlines creativity as a basic attribute of art.

The operatic bombast and exotic background of this new trend paradoxically coexisted among the Romantics with the most holy desire: with the turn towards the 'simplicity of the heart'. Along with Rousseau, and later Chateaubriand, *'le bon sauvage'*, 'the noble savage' embodied the original goodness of man, who remains free from primordial sin. The most precious values of Plato: truth, goodness and beauty, were presented as preserved in the innocent heart of a simple man, a heart untouched by the poison of any 'culture'. This is why, not very long after the pompous exclamations of Manfred from the heights of the Alps, a certain country girl named Karusia, from some tiny Lithuanian village at the other end of Europe, could address her late beloved in 1822 with these words:

> Was it you by night? It's you, Johnny!
> Ah! Loves even after death!
> Here, there, go step by step,
> Stepmother may hear by chance!
>
> Oh, let her hear, there's no more you!
> They've buried you in a grave!
> You're already dead? Ah, I'm so scared!

Why do I fear of my Johnny?
Ah, it's him! Your cheeks, sweet eyes!
Your white cloth on the body!

And you in the flesh, so white,
Cold, your hands so ice-cold are!
Let lay them down, here on my lap,
Hold me, just mouth to mouth!
(Adam Mickiewicz, 'Romanticism', Internet translation)

The late Johnny, let us observe, is in a 'white cloth', already completely cold and 'so white'. It is not fully clear whether an 'autonomous' ghost of Johnny, endowed with full freedom of movement has appeared to Karusia or if Karusia sees only the dead corpse of Johnny, covered with a white shroud. This is probably the way she saw him the last time in his coffin. It is not clear whether Johnny, in this poem, is some weightless emanation of pure, otherworldly energy, able to permeate the walls, or is materially touchable, possibly even with already decomposing flesh.

Ah, it must be freezing in a grave!
It's been two years since you died!
Take me, I'll die with you, Johnny,
I don't like the world and that life.

In any case, Johnny has not appeared after his death to call for vengeance, like some Tantalus from Seneca, oh no. Our hair stands up on our heads: Johnny has appeared to Karusia to take her with him into the grave! A ghoul, he does not speak, not even a word; he only stands there. As he stands there, a mute apparition, he may be the reason why the half-mad Karusia, after two years of grief and woe, will be ready, at the end, who knows, to commit suicide. A blood-curdling ghost, a ghost who brings death. There will be, in Polish literature, many, many more ghosts like this.

> Come to me by day ... Or by night, dreamy ...
> Don't go ... I hold you in my hand.
> Where do you vanish, where, my Johnny!
> It's too soon, too early, wait!

Some incredible fallout happened, as we can see, as a result of the meeting of the Danish prince with the ghost of his father on the walls of Elsinore. The ballad 'Romanticism' by Adam Mickiewicz (1822), which remains a distant echo of that other scene, introduces – it is widely agreed – the period of Polish Romanticism. The suffering of poor Karusia characterises that important moment when the incurable wish for oblivion begins. Polish Romanticism is in love with death.

43 § Audrey happened to be a charming phenomenon, with red hair and dark-brown eyes. She had finished history of art at York University and she loved theatre. She could speak Italian quite fluently, although with a strong foreign accent. Umberto was doing his best to show off his English. They were jumping from one idiom to another, laughing at their various misunderstandings. They talked about everything.

Audrey adored the band Stars and Stripes, Joni Mitchell, the poetry of Emily Dickinson and the films of Jarmusch. She went to Palermo specially to see the puppet art of the Brothers Mancuso. After half an hour spent with her over a portion of *linguine con gamberi*, *zucchini e fiori* in the *trattoria* at Via Brera, Umberto realised that he was head over heels in love with her. He was telling her about his work at Pagine Verdi, about his studies in Bologna, about his journey to India a few years ago, about the book he was writing about it, the first in his life. They ordered an additional bottle of bubbly, giggling like a pair of teenagers. An hour later they landed in the little hotel where Audrey was staying. They found themselves in bed in a most natural way, like children who needed finally to rest after an exciting day.

In the morning they both happily restarted the process of getting to know themselves a little better. They had time; studying the line of Audrey's shoulder was no less important than Audrey's tale about the shocking circumstances of the death of her mother. They discovered the possibility of a subtle disagreement over some preferences. Audrey did not know Leopardi, while Umberto hated Dickens.

In the afternoon they strolled through the city. In the evening they went to see the legendary *Servant of Two Masters* in Teatro Strehler at Foro Bonaparte. This was the reason for Audrey's visit to Milan. Sorrentini played that evening, the fifth or sixth Arlecchino in the last half a century of the history of that show. There was a full audience, many families with little children, grandfathers and grandmothers; the accent of Milan was dominant. The celebrated Sorrentini was throwing plates with mastery. In the last scene, the inevitable exposure of Arlecchino as a trickster serving contemporaneously two masters in front of all the other characters, happened.

'You served two masters at once?' the bewildered Florindo, a candidate for a husband of Dottore Lombardo's daughter, asked. Arlecchino transformed himself from a simpleton from Bergamo into a proud artist in the blink of an eye:

'Yes, sir, I have embraced that challenge. I have done it with no hesitation because I wanted to set myself a challenge. And I can claim that I would not have been compromised if I had not revealed myself through my hidden love. I had great difficulty doing it but I hope that, at the end, all of you will forgive me my madness.'

The applause was frenetic and the actors, still in their masks, running to the front of the stage at the curtain call, were visibly moved. When, finally, they formed one single row for the curtain call, Sorrentini, as *capocomico*, gave a discreet sign and slowly the actors started to reveal their faces from behind their masks. They were sweaty, tired and very happy faces. Audrey, who was clapping her hands intensely, jumped to her feet and over seven hundred spectators did exactly the same.

'Look, Umberto, Strehler is not with us anymore, and yet this miracle is being repeated every evening,' the excited Audrey kept talking loudly and practically with no pauses. 'It doesn't matter that he has managed to build this great theatre. No one will remember that in a hundred years. And this is because all these palaces, monuments, towers do not matter much. Pyramids do not matter. And yet that gesture, with which Sorrentini took off his mask, remains in eternity. It lasts beyond time, it lasts in spite of time, it triumphs over time.'

She was looking thoughtfully into the dark window of the restaurant in which they sat after the show. A buzz of voices surrounded them, the guests were quite numerous.

'Maybe it is something different,' continued Audrey, 'maybe it is not the gesture which lasts – that would be absurd, gestures do not last – but maybe it is something within us. Something in our psyche, which transfers in such moments into a different dimension and stays there.'

Umberto was listening and looking into her eyes, enchanted. She was for him a miraculous – because impossible – turn of fate. She was the statistically improbable jackpot in the lottery of the universe, a gift from heaven. He was afraid that she might be only his desperate hallucination.

'Audrey, I need to tell you something,' he coughed.

She smiled. 'I know what you want to tell me, Umberto. We have happened to each other by chance. We have met' – she hesitated – 'like an umbrella and a sewing machine on the table in the dissecting room. We are both surreal and unexpected. We are both still overwhelmed by our encounter. It will settle down; all we need is some time. We need to do something with it, and we shall do. You want to tell me that you are in love with me, and I am telling you that it is wonderful and that this is how it should stay. You want to tell me that tomorrow you are going to take me to your Forlí and that soon we shall go for a longer time to Kerala or to Kathmandu. And this is fine. I would like a tiramisu' – she has turned to the waiter.

I need to tell her about Via Vespucci 17, he thought. I need to tell her about everything. I will tell her. Tomorrow.

44 § 'You too?' she asked quietly, after a silence. It was already midday the next day. They were sitting on a bench in Castello Sforzesco park. The September Sun was shining brightly through the plane tree's leaves. Ten minutes earlier, regaining his courage, Umberto started to confess the absurd, incomprehensible situation, in which he found himself:

'It is not that I could not find the entrance. There was no entrance. The whole house was not there. Everything had vanished, the neighbours included. And I still do not know what happened to them. Where are the Calendras, where is the Palomini family? And first of all, how is anything like this possible? Why Palermo all of a sudden? I returned to Forlí as fast as I could. I checked everything, even the registers in the health centre. Nothing. Everything has vanished.'

A cyclist in a helmet and a bright yellow shirt flashed by their bench. The relentless noise of the traffic reached them from Via Dante.

'In London, over two years ago,' said Audrey, 'I was staying with friends in Hammersmith. I had fallen asleep. I woke up in a hotel in Kirkwall. On the Orkney Islands, do you understand? Nearly a thousand miles from London. It was idiotic, I couldn't contact anyone by phone. I was alone, with no money, with no driving licence. In the end, the local branch of the Halifax Bank said that they would give me a new card.'

What she had just said slowly dawned on Umberto. He needed to be sure whether he had misheard. 'You too?' he asked. 'So, I'm not the only one this has happened to?'

'The second time, the jump was short, only for four days, to Edinburgh,' Audrey continued. 'I had some friends there. But soon afterwards, the third time, I found myself in Pittsburgh, in Pennsylvania. Their theatre is not bad, by the way. Afterwards, it happened many times. To various places. I landed in Australia, for example. For almost two months. I was in Africa too, in Dar-es-Salaam. Also in Seoul.'

Umberto held his head in his hands and slowly made a circle around the bench. He stopped in the middle of the third circumnavigation.

'We should go to the police,' he said.

'It's useless,' said Audrey. 'They would think you are bonkers, and no wonder. I landed in Rome, when flying from Cairo. They gave me a new passport at the embassy. I told them that I had lost the previous one. The official was nice. I have been travelling throughout Italy for the past six months because I love Italy and one has to live somewhere. I feel happy when I wake up in the morning in the same place.'

Unexpectedly, she started to cry. He kneeled beside her, taking hold of her hands. She became quieter.

'I waited, Umberto. Subconsciously I knew that I would meet somebody in my situation, earlier or later. I knew that I was not mad and I knew that it must also involve other people. And that there must be some solution. Umberto, you and I, we have to find a solution.'

'Yes, Audrey,' he responded, 'we shall find a solution, surely we shall. And we shall be together till that time.'

45 § For two days they kept conferring intensely. Finally, they decided to go to the Julian Alps. They bought rucksacks and sleeping bags and they started their trek from Tolmezzo. September was petering out with all its colours. The slow walk through meadows full of flowers and through shady spruce woods was a sheer joy. They slept in a tent or in refuges. They said 'Ciao!' or 'Salve!' to the other tourists on their route. In the evenings the stars burned brightly, somebody usually crooned with a guitar while the bonfire smouldered. They wanted to live, and they wanted to travel like this forever. He told her about his treks in the Pyrenees, and about his adventures in the Bulgarian mountains. He told her about his book, soon to be finished. He wanted to embellish his documentary material from the Maharashtra province with carefully chosen excerpts from the *Mahabharata*. She was responding, recalling some fragments from Peter Brook's production, which she knew off by heart.

One morning, at the end of the second week, Umberto woke up in the tent well before daybreak. It was strangely warm and quiet. Audrey was still asleep in her sleeping bag. Careful not to wake her up, he slowly got out of the tent. In the twilight, there was sand everywhere. Greyish, sometimes yellow sandy mounds were stretching in every direction. The air was sultry, not very clear, the sky was covered with clouds. On one of the hills, in the distance, some twisted metal ruins could be seen. They looked like a steel construction of a petrol station, destroyed by a tornado.

'Umberto!' Audrey was standing in front of the tent. He returned to her.

'Audrey, we have a problem,' he said quietly. 'We are not in the mountains anymore.'

They rolled up the tent, packed their rucksacks and walked towards the hills. All the windows in the destroyed petrol station were broken, the glass crunched under their feet. They found a few plastic bottles of Texaco oil on the deformed shelves. Umberto took one of them, just in case. The counter with demolished cash machines showed some traces of fire.

They turned downhill. The next hill was in front of them, maybe a kilometre away. A ribbon of hard-packed sand was leading to it. It could have been, a long time ago, a road. They left the Sun, more and more blistering, behind their backs.

It was a desert. Some big, grey stones were randomly scattered on the sand. They found a dwarfish, twisted tree in a ditch. A dark, rusted maze of metal sheets beside it could have been a car once, maybe even two cars. Umberto bent down and pulled from this maze a piece of metal. Two melted, blackened letters.

'GM,' he said.

After three hours, they reached a line of low hills. In the middle of the plain, maybe two kilometres away, a debris of bricks, fallen walls and some metal constructions were visible. They sat in the shadow, leaning against a tall stone the size of a house.

They shared some water; it was warm. In front of them, the image of the deserted, ruined settlement trembled in the heat haze – broken roofs, half-covered in sand. There were no trees. At the edge of the ruins, one could see the crushed balloon of the water tower, its metal supports bent and rusted. It looked like a giant spider on very long, telescopic legs, suddenly stopped in the middle of its movement. Beside the spider a particularly tall, metal mast had a giant letter K at the top.

'This is America,' said Audrey, 'we are in the States. Look, all these streets form an east–west grid. Those were low family houses or some factories or warehouses.'

'Something has happened here,' said Umberto, 'some catastrophe. Everything was destroyed and anyone who could ran away. They left everything. A long time ago, maybe twenty, maybe fifty years ago.'

On the far edge of the ruined settlement something moved. From between the crushed bricks, a plume of black smoke appeared. The wind was slowly dissipating the smog. She touched his arm.

'People. There must be some people. Look there, there, beyond that large field. Can you see?'

From behind a ruined building a caravan appeared. The distance was huge, but Umberto managed to recognise three or four camels in the train. A few loaded donkeys or mules were following them closely. The riders, wrapped in grey shawls, swayed in their saddles. The caravan was moving through a large free space, which could have been a parking lot or a shopping centre decades ago.

'Shall we go and meet them?' asked Audrey.

The distant sound of a rifle shot was suddenly heard. Then another, and yet another. The caravan rapidly accelerated, aiming at the break in some windowless building. The galloping animals and their riders were almost hidden behind a pile of rubbish when machine-gun fire exploded in the distance.

'Hide!' shouted Umberto. They hid behind a rock, crouching in the sand. It was silent around them. A huge bird flew above them, soundlessly. After some time, Audrey moved closer and burrowed her face into his breast. He embraced her and this was how they stayed. Dusk was falling. They waited.

46 § They dared to enter the ruins only after dark fell. They kept moving very slowly from one building to another, carefully stopping at every corner and trying not to make any noise. They stopped for a while in one of the deserted houses. The main door was off its hinges, the kitchen was half-immersed in sand. In the corner, inside the fridge thrown onto the ground, a whitish skeleton of a cat or a coyote was visible. Umberto found what he was looking for in the kitchen,

in one of the dirty cupboards – a tin of canned pears in syrup. They left their rucksacks; Umberto took out a torch and they sneaked out to search for more.

All the windows in the long, low building on the other side of the former street were broken. The light from Umberto's torch revealed the entrance. They entered the corridor. They kept moving forward along the tainted, greenish walls. A hospital? A school? The entrance to the left opened towards some huge abyss; the light from the torch could not reach the opposite wall. Their steps sounded with an echo in the darkness. Umberto directed the torch downwards. It was a big swimming pool, with its sloped base covered in sand. At the edge of the pool a burned wreck of something, which could have been a pick-up once, glimmered in the torch beam.

They returned to the corridor and turned in the opposite direction. They passed a long row of tables, covered with metal – a kitchen? a canteen? – aiming to get to one of the rooms at the upper floor when suddenly they heard a sound of scratching. They froze. The sound was coming from below, from the stairs leading to the basement. An irregular knocking, combined with screeching. A squeak, a pause, silence, one more squeak. Umberto switched off the torch, took off his shoes, left them on the step of the stairs and slowly started to descend. Audrey followed him closely. After the third turn of the stairs, they felt that the source of the sound was in front of them, inside the room. A squeak. Some knocking, some screeching, a pause. A squeak. A wet sound. A squeak.

Without any warning, Umberto switched on the torch. In the spotlight, a raggedy, unshaven man in a military coat was eating straight from a tin with the help of a metal spoon. Caught by the light, he froze. Audrey stepped forward.

'Mike?' she said.

47 I experienced the end of history in person, some time ago, at the Oregon Shakespeare Festival in Ashland. I was watching *Henry V*, very well directed by Libby Appel. An almost empty, large thrust stage, slightly stylised, yet non-contemporary, costumes, with a very high level of work by the ensemble of actors. The performance was going on efficiently and jauntily, the monarchs were crossing the stage vividly, leading their armies, the patter of the war drums was warming up the atmosphere. The whole action – in accordance with Shakespeare, of course – was conducted by the Prologue. She was also a single-person Chorus, played by a strikingly good-looking actress with long, curled, blonde hair, dressed in a snow-white frock and pantaloons.

> Think, when we talk of horses, that you see them
> Printing their proud hoofs i'th' receiving earth

The Prologue was eagerly painting the visions of galloping horses in the battle. The Prologue, very visible because of the whiteness of her costume, was transferring us from Dover to Calais in the blink of an eye, from the Port of Harfleur to the palace in Rouen. In the mayhem of the final battle of Agincourt, between eruptions of smoke, loud shouts and the footfall of running soldiers, suddenly a single shot was heard, everything froze on stage – and, unexpectedly, the Prologue slid to the ground. Everybody and everything was silent. The actors – there were maybe twenty of them – at first helplessly and very privately looked at each other. Then they turned – in silence – their glances towards the audience. We were sitting in front of them, tense, as helpless and shocked as they were. We looked into their eyes for a long time, and this was the kind of silence one does not forget. Suddenly the Prologue rose from the ground, informed the audience that she was fine and healthy and that the show, of course, must go on. There was huge applause, as big, in fact, as for the final curtain. And yet that moment of the unexpected, dramatic break in the narration, that perfectly used Brechtian 'V-effect', will stay with me forever.

'The future appears in the shape of ruins,' summarises Gianni Vattimo, when investigating the twentieth-century dystopias and counter-utopias. The quotation comes from his work *The Transparent Society*, in which he describes the sand overwhelming the skyscrapers and highways, the rusted wrecks of vehicles and machines. Among this debris, only a very few people are crossing the desert on horses or camels – this catastrophic landscape is nevertheless still a utopia. This is because:

> the post-apocalyptic state described by similar works is, paradoxically, a positive condition. It is positive in the sense that a nuclear catastrophe hanging over us is something, which has already happened, and which means some sort of liberation for the survivors.

In this context, the landscapes from the stories and novels of J. G. Ballard (his *Hello America*, 1981, for example) or *A Canticle for Leibowitz* by Walter M. Miller (1959) come to mind. Also, the black and white, spine-tingling landscape of *The Road* by Cormac McCarthy (2006). 'An event, which has found an expression in counter-utopia,' writes Vattimo, 'can be described as an emergence of the counter-finality of Reason.' He does not only think about the negative experiences of humanity (like the two world wars, the multitude of local ones, the general slaughterhouse and mass murder), but he indicates the fundamental:

> discovery, that the rationalisation of the world turns against Reason and against its aims. And that it happens not as a result of some mistake, of some incidental circumstances or of some incidental deformation, but exactly along the way on which Reason more and more perfectly accomplishes its programme.

Vattimo recalls that Georg Wilhelm Friedrich Hegel still believed that 'the truth is whole'. Today, evidently, 'the whole is not true', because, as Vattimo writes: 'during a century and a half, which divides us from Hegel, a rational totalisation of the world has happened'. He adds: 'The historical events do not constitute a progress, nor a regress. Nor are they the return of the same. They are an interpretation, [which remains] more or less falsified by the promises and legacy of the past.'

Well, the future appears in the shape of ruins because the result of the past two millennia of a continuous European campaign under the banner of a redemptive final aim is a global battlefield. Let us quote the Ninth Thesis (from eighteen of them) of Walter Benjamin's 'Theses on the Philosophy of History' (1940) [Please note that the philosopher considered himself a Marxist!] Benjamin writes about the Angel of History, a patron of the unimaginable destruction caused by the progress of time. Walter Benjamin's Angel:

> His face is turned toward the past. Where we perceive a chain of events, he sees one single catastrophe which keeps piling wreckage upon wreckage and hurls it in front of his feet. The angel would like to stay, awaken the dead, and make whole what has been smashed. But a storm is blowing from Paradise; it has caught in his wings with such violence that the angel can no longer close them. This storm irresistibly propels him into the future to which his back is turned, while the pile of debris before him grows skyward. This storm is what we call progress.
> (Trans. Harry Zorn).

Benjamin's Angel of History is an unstoppably creative destructor who does not know even a moment's rest. He is a constructor of ruins. And yet, historically speaking, its paradoxical name was given for the first time to somebody else.

His name was Arthur Evans. He finished history at Oxford

and after some complicated journalistic trials and tribulations, in 1884 he became the Chief Custodian of the Ashmolean collection. Within a few years, he managed to turn it into one of the most important archaeological museums in Europe. He was passionate about excavations on Crete. In 1899, he managed to buy a decent lot in Kephala near Heraclion, known as the most probable location of Knossos, the legendary palace of King Minos. A year later he started the excavations, and, after only a few weeks, a 'throne' was found in the ruins of the room immediately named 'The Throne Hall' by Evans. Also, a 'Bathing Room' was unearthed and some fragments of frescos. Evans's imagination was racing: could it be the figure of Ariadne? Or maybe of the Minotaur? Evans was inventing the names for the successive heaps of stones: this is 'The Double Axes Hall' and that 'The Megaron of the Queen'. Despite their arbitrary character, the names – this is interesting – were accepted in the same way as the name of the discovered civilisation: Evans called it 'Minoan'. Soon, an ensemble of painters and architects brought from London started 'a completion' of the destroyed frescos, contemporaneously rebuilding the ruins according to Evans's instructions. The restored frescos – as Evans's contemporaries already observed – were surprisingly similar to the style of the front pages of *Vogue* magazine. The reconstruction was done in the fashionable style of Art Deco (Evans himself compared Minoan decorative art to the wall papers of William Morris). The Minoan frescos titled 'The Blue Monkey' or 'The Prince of the Lilies', still admired today by millions of tourists, are a historical palimpsest, born from Evans's ambition and ignorance. A French newspaper had already named him 'an architect of ruins' a hundred years before.

When correcting the existing state of things in the name of a return to their 'natural' shape, Evans was following – possibly unconsciously – the mainstream of English aesthetics of the past two centuries. That trend came into being in the theory and practice of a new type of garden called, indeed, the English garden. Lancelot Brown, aka Capability Brown, the most influential gardener of the eighteenth century, was irreversibly eliminating geometrical avenues, topiary and rigid flowerbeds borrowed earlier from Italy and France – so-called formal gardens. In their place, he was introducing artificial 'natural' hills, similar cascades and lakes, as well as rolling carpets of grass, 'naturally' unfolding before the windows of stately homes. Romanticism, born soon after, added to this landscape the indispensable, picturesque ruins (of course!), shrines of meditation, islands, grottos and other follies. That 'natural' English garden is very well-known to Countess Respect from *Fantazy* by Słowacki:

> Gaetano! Order to be brought the flocks
> On the little meadow in the garden! Let the old
> Anton throw his net into the water
> And sit under the willow. Beside him in pairs
> Boys entwining the baskets – like in Tasso.
> Put nearby a huddle of harvesters
> And tell them to sing! Let Anna bring to graze
> The goats on the rocks ... Ah, start the cascade!
> Remember to start the cascade this evening ... This wild
> English garden is a complete nightmare ...

The Architect of Ruins (*Der Ruinenbaumeister*) is also the title of a novel by the Austrian writer Herbert Rosendorfer (1969). The novel was inspired by *The Manuscript Found in Saragossa* and by its bravado in the use of the embedded-story convention. In reference to Boccaccio, instead of the Plague, from which the characters of *The Decameron* are hiding, here we have war, the end of the world and a giant cigar as a refuge. The number of women telling the stories is the same (eight), the stories flourish within stories, irony is mixed with horror, apocalypse with burlesque. Yet that story is not happening 'in reality', it is only the dream of the narrator. The ruin of the underground tower filled with tales seems to be an unknown figure who looks into himself and finds successive dreams and costumes, fragments of strange set designs and frightening abysses. There are presentiments, fears, memories, crazy theories, incidental patterns. In the afterword to the book, Adam Lipszyc wrote:

> A theory, or rather a theology of storytelling is being, quite seriously, developed here. It may be that for Rosendorfer in '*The Architect of Ruins*' the reference is also a future 'hecatomb', as the catastrophe which has already happened. It may be – as Rosendorfer seems to suggest – that, starting from the last World War, we do not exist anymore and whatever is happening happens only 'as if'. We are only a long, extended Epilogue of the novel titled The World.

For Rosendorfer, it seems, the Armageddon of World War Two and the mortal silence of *Stunde Null* were the catastrophe 'which had already happened'. Widening the debate, the loss of the status of undisputable Truth by every philosophical Whole, described by Vattimo, also seems to be this catastrophe, with a religious Whole included. I am using here both these terms, 'Whole' and 'Truth' as all-encompassing metaphors, but the process I am trying to describe – with their help – is real. Its consequences are serious and still not fully understood.

48 A theology of storytelling? It means 'a study of the supernatural', the dictionary suggests. 'Super-natural' meaning what? – one might logically ask. Well, one asks driven by habit rather than by conviction – already in the nineteenth century it was agreed that both discourses, the theological and the rational, were incompatible. 'Gentlemen, gentlemen, really, we are not going to burn one another on

pyres in the age of steam and electricity!' some prototype of Phineas Fogg must have shouted at some fiery gathering at the Reform Club. And, most probably, this would be the end, as Gombrowicz writes.

What is this treatise decidedly not about? It is not a theory of storytelling. Nor is it any 'theology' of storytelling. It is an effort to reflect a little upon the never simple, often intertwined, paths in the 'land of stories'. It is an attempt, an experiment, a *reconnaissance* in unchartered territory. It is a short, non-committal, Sunday expedition into the Hundred Mile Forest of fiction.

It is not a textbook. It is not a manual, a dictionary, a dream dictionary, a confession. Therefore, what is it? Well, to be 'this' means that whatever we are talking about cannot be anything other than 'this'. Just look, everybody is calling for boundaries, for barriers, for gates and for demarcation. While we would prefer, during our wanderings, to be able to traverse the unfathomable jungles and wastelands without passports.

49

§ 'These are two chronologically independent groups of envoys,' Mike was explaining. 'The latter ones seem to know about the earlier ones, but they prefer to avoid them. The earlier ones don't seem to know about the latter ones.'

They were sitting in a deep air-raid shelter, built in the middle of the twentieth century. It was Mike's base. It was hidden twelve metres below the ground. One descended narrow steps, passing three times through metal bulkheads with ciphered locks. Mike had everything here: a well-equipped kitchen, numerous gas cylinders, comfortable beds, a stash of food in a working fridge. He had electricity (the bulbs in the ceiling shone quite strongly) and he had water in the taps. The concrete walls were painted in military, khaki colours.

'The earlier ones are seeking print. The Great Boom ten

years ago erased everything from the world. Therefore, any scraps of paper notation are priceless for them. Tiny fragments of knowledge are hidden in such scraps. They are reconstructing any possible science, any possible technology, from whatever they are able to find. They are reconstructing whatever they can. They are evolving pretty fast. They already have weaponry. Those shots, which you have heard, that machine-gun fire was theirs. They are a hundred, a hundred and twenty years after us, is my guess.'

'What was the Great Boom?' asked Umberto. Mike looked at him with distrust.

'You pretend not to know? Ten years ago, when it happened, the two of you, where have you been?'

'I was finishing studying in Bologna,' answered Umberto.

'I was still in York, and you know it, Mike,' said Audrey. Then she turned towards Umberto, to explain to him. 'Mike was in the year above me. We were all in love with him, but in the middle of the term he escaped to his California.'

'I escaped because I had to,' said Mike, 'my dad had an accident and I had to return. And soon afterwards the Great Boom happened.'

'Was it a war?' Umberto dared to ask, after a pause.

Mike looked at him askance for a long time. 'Ninety-six percent of the population died, across all the continents. Sorry, Umberto, are we talking seriously or are we joking? How is it possible that you do not know about it?'

He got up and positioned himself with his back towards the exit. He let his hands hang loosely. 'Who are you and where do you come from?' he asked.

'Mike, we must be from the world in which the Great Boom has not yet happened,' Audrey said quickly. 'This is the only possible answer. In the world of Umberto and myself, Umberto is still patiently working in his publishing house in Emilia Romagna and I am still travelling. I met him, purely incidentally, on the train to Milan. It is the world in which you have inherited a small fortune, so I heard.'

Mike kept shifting his gaze from Audrey to Umberto and back again.

'Audrey, if you and I come from different worlds, they must differ in a very significant way. In my world, eleven years have passed since my return from England. And you can see this passage of time by looking at me. While you have not changed at all.'

'Thank you, Mike, you old flatterer.' Audrey got up and started to pace. 'A question: what are you doing here, in this ruined settlement, in some bunker from the time of the Cold War, four floors below the ground? What is going on here, Mike?'

'Audrey, you are in Utah. On the border with Nevada, in the most forgotten and most distant pisshole one can imagine. Its name is not relevant. Nevertheless, it was officially called Stove-pipe Wells Airport in the so-called Death Valley.' Mike opened a fridge in the corner and took out three cans of Budweiser. He came back to the table and took a gulp. 'What am I doing here? I am defending, excuse me, the honour of humanity. We are saving books, maps, plans, archives, everything on paper. We are transporting it in pieces through the desert – small amounts, some couriers with rucksacks, caravans of camels, sometimes balloons. Whatever works, the situation is volatile, it changes from day to day. We take it to San Diego. The New Library is there, heavily guarded. The rudiments of a new state are there. It is all strongly defended, obviously: rockets, tanks, we even have a neutron bomb.'

'And those other seekers of print?' asked Umberto.

'The sonofabitches somehow know that the mine of printed paper must be nearby. Because there is one. A kind of Eldorado for a print hunter. Because very near to here, I will not tell you where of course, NORAD was here for decades. The military headquarters for the whole Western hemisphere. It is a huge underground city, thirty-two levels deep, each level four kilometres wide, plus storage, aggregates, fuel tanks. All of it two kilometres under the ground. Impossible to destroy from the air. And everything is there, machines and weapons, also thousands of useless computers, of course. Also, the libraries, warehouses, reports and hundreds of millions of printed pages. The print hunters know about it, and that's what they are after. But the other group are worse.'

'These are the ones that come later?' asked Umberto.

'I think that they are from roughly four centuries after us. I mean, after my world, after the world in which we are talking now. They come from the future, which evidently must be a kind of nightmare. They do not shoot us, they are kidnapping us. Biologically, they are still humans and they seem to be lacking spare parts. They take everything: organs, skin and bones. I suspect that some horrendous disease is decimating them in their world. But for some reason they are avoiding the hunters, the hunters may be biologically of no use to them. Or maybe they do not want to show the hunters the way to their world. So, they hunt us, like we were hunting, some time ago, bison or game.'

Audrey started to shake her head.

'No,' she said, 'no, excuse me, Mike, but all this is impossible. Travels in time? Body snatchers? You are using some jargon from bad science fiction. Umberto and myself, only yesterday, were in the Italian mountains, it was September. It was all so beautiful that one could not believe it, but it was all real, one could touch it. Do you understand, Mike?'

They sat for another hour, drinking beer. Then Mike showed them a room with metal beds at the end of the corridor.

'You can sleep here. I am departing with a transport in the morning, I will take you with me. There are people in San Diego, I shall introduce you to some of them.'

They wrapped themselves in blankets. It was quite warm; the air conditioning was working. Audrey could not sleep for a long time.

'Umberto, tell me that you will not leave me,' she whispered, 'tell me that we are dreaming all this and that we will always be together.'

He embraced her and touched her face. 'I love you, little one. And we shall always remain together.'

When she fell asleep, he sneaked away, with bare feet, to the bathroom. There was a small mirror hanging over the sink. He looked into it and froze. He saw that he was ten years older.

50   In most stories the natural time is the past. The oldest and absolutely natural formula seems to be: 'Because something important has happened, or something extremely interesting, I shall tell you about it, because I was there.'

> Rage-Goddess, sing the rage of Peleus' son Achilles,
> Murderous, doomed, that cost the Achaeans countless losses,
> hurling down to the House of Death so many sturdy souls.
> Great fighters' souls, but made their bodies carrion
> feasts for the dogs and birds.
> And the will of Zeus was moving toward its end.
> Begin, Muse, when the two first broke and clashed.
> Agamemnon lord of men and brilliant Achilles.
> (*The Iliad*. Trans. Robert Fagles)

Homer tells us this story in the first person and tells it in the past tense. It is not important whether he was present personally in Troy. What is important is the fact that he knows very well, with all the details, what happened there. In his invocation, he is calling the goddess – most probably Calliope, the Muse of epic poetry – to take care of him in his noble attempt to tell the course of the Trojan War, the war which 'cost the Achaeans countless losses'. We can see that Homer's aim is to explain to 'today's' listeners the events of the past which have significantly influenced the present.

Virgil's *The Aeneid* starts very similarly:

> Arms and the man I sing, who first made way,
> predestined exile, from the Trojan shore
> to Italy, the blest Lavinian strand.
> Smitten of storms he was on land and sea
> by violence of Heaven, to satisfy
> stern Juno's sleepless wrath; and much in war
> he suffered, seeking at the last to found
> the city, and bring o'er his fathers' gods
> to safe abode in Latium; whence arose
> the Latin race, old Alba's reverend lords,
> and from her hills wide-walled, imperial Rome.
> (Trans. Theodore C. Williams, 1910)

Hereby, I, Virgil, on the day you are listening to this relation, dear audience, here I am 'singing' the deeds of Aeneas. I am telling you about his achievements, which happened in the past.

This bond between the epic and the past tense of the story is somehow obvious. In this case, poetry serves the act of preservation, of past deeds and persons, which the author wants future generations not to forget. Epic poetry serves memory, like the pyramids.

The past is also a favoured territory for every kind of tale-teller: 'Once upon a time, behind seven forests, behind seven mountains ...' – the tale starts and we, the listeners, are immediately ready to listen. No matter how many dragons the brave son of the shoemaker, a prince or a bold knight has to kill, and no matter how many bad magicians will be plotting against him, sending horrible curses and horrible monsters, we know, from the very beginning, that everything will end well. And that the princess and the hero will 'live happily ever after'. This is because from the very beginning we know that the story-teller was figuratively 'present' at their wedding and 'has drunk wine and mead, and whatever he has seen there, he tells us'.

Without the past, that inexhaustible mine of events, lives, wars, loves, defeats and triumphs, literature most probably would go round in circles or would never get started. The past does not exist without the memory of it, without a relation (a diary, a record) of past events. The past is inevitably always connected with its reconstruction or a variation upon it. *In Search of Lost Time* by Proust – its title already advertises the aim of the author's enterprise. It is no different from so many passionately written tales by older people. The tales of the 'This is how it was/I remember' type. Notes, letters written a long time ago, preserved depositions, reports, protocols, and all other, similarly authentic testimonies of the past, whenever they are used as literary forms, 'confirm' the credibility of the story being told.

The present time of a literary story was truly born – I suspect – no earlier than the invention of the telephone and of the wireless. I mean, one can find a present time much earlier, of course, most often in the moments of narration when the narrator tries to accelerate the course of events or to bring closer the details of an event. An example? In his *Three by Three*, already quoted earlier, old Fredro remembers how a long time ago he played, at some prince's manor, the popular game Blind Man's Buff:

> Being chased, once upon a time, by my rival, a determined opponent, whose enormous nose was allowing the blindfold almost to slip, I found myself trapped in a corner, like Princess Berry in the chimney. Already I could smell the breath of my opponent upon my face ... It is time to submit myself ... Nevertheless ... I bend my body, I spin it into a ball of wool, and – taking a strong, crazy jump – I launch myself into the centre of the room ... 'Nice one!' and 'Good call!' are

heard, but before these exclamations have finished, I land under the piano hitting it with an enormous bang and seeing a hundred candles in my mind. There I am, lying, not standing up ... because I can feel that my trousers have given up ...

Such a fragment remains nevertheless an exception in the whole memoir, which is composed – like most memoirs – in the past tense.

51   And what if, all of a sudden, this were to happen?
         If I was kept, let's say a week ago, in Charing Cross Hospital, for example, for more tests. It could have been, for example, because of the problematic pain flowing into my body from my upper vertebra and causing aches in my bones and numbness in my right hand. I could have thought, earlier, quite rationally, that it must be due to some damaged bone in my spine. I might have chosen, earlier, to have three useless sessions with an osteopath. I could have finally arrived at A&E a second time – not easy during a pandemic. Only after this, a doctor might have ordered an immediate MRI scan, some other scans (CT) and blood analysis. My first diagnosis: yes, we have a problem, decidedly in the lungs and also in the fifth vertebra. There is also a trace on the liver. The ongoing procedures would have continued: more scans, painkillers, steroids, more analysis all the time, and good afternoon Ivan Ilyich. Perhaps a biopsy of the liver would be needed and, immediately, radiotherapy for the spine. Maybe they would let me go home after two radiotherapies, let's say, and they would permit me to come to the hospital as an outpatient on my own. They might say: after a week, or maybe two, we shall gather all the information and only then will we decide about the kind of treatment we recommend. In any case, there would be chemotherapy afterwards, very strong, and composed individually for my particu-

lar situation. The surgeon's intervention would also become possible but, rather, at the end. First, they would have to see what other methods could achieve. Any surgical intervention might mean a very difficult, complicated operation lasting eight hours.

My K would have behaved wonderfully, given the circumstances. She would have been brave and fantastic; I know it for sure; I would feel more strongly than any time before how much I love her.

No, I do not want to write about it.

I would not like – if all of a sudden what I described above actually happened – to have to write about the illness, about the shock and the fear. I wouldn't like to write any 'diary of my illness'. I would not like to, and therefore I shall not write about the imagined progress of the disease or the progress of therapy; no. I prefer to return to the nature of the story and the theatre, to the beginnings and the endings in fiction of every kind.

Nevertheless, I feel bound to say that such a new, existential situation for an author could open some new, possible perspectives for this narrative journey. It seems to be important – I think – in whichever moment of their life the author finds themself. The author, that is, who decides to speak publicly, in the first person. It is important, whether their child or grandchild has only just been born, or maybe their father or mother has just died. And whether their story happened during war or during peacetime. We all know that our point of view keeps changing, depending on our perspective. So, most probably, change is also inevitable when one's life situation changes. When applying, let's say, for a position in some institution for many years, we write our application in a fundamentally different way than when we write our will.

There is a possible, corrective solution, which could be added as a narrative frame to this treatise. For example:

Dear reader, the author most probably did not know why he started these notes in the middle of December. His body – it seems – already knew. Nevertheless, he started to feel the first pains in his spine only a month later. The notes, which we are presenting here, were found – no, not in the bathtub of an underground shelter, like in Stanisław Lem, and no, not in a deserted house during a siege of Saragossa, like in Jan Potocki, but on the personal laptop of the author.

And so on. And somewhere there, near the end:

The spelling has been checked and unified, the font Arial 12 was chosen for the printed version. Editor: Eveline Lewada. Main Editor: Zeno Eleacki.

52 The Land of the Future, as well as those of the Past and Present, could not have stayed undiscovered as a way of telling a story. But let us first make a distinction: there is the Land of the Future and there is the Land of Fantasy, and they are not the same.

Lucian of Samosata, when he describes his journey to the Moon in the second century AD, represents unlimited, creative fantasy. Plato does the same when he writes about the island of Utopia. Campanella also, when he describes the City of the Sun, and Baron Munchausen, when he boasts about his crazy adventures. The journey of Dante and Beatrice in the netherworld of *The Divine Comedy*, is fantastical, as is Cyrano de Bergerac's *Visit to the States and Empires of the Moon* (1657), a conscious travesty of the epos of Lucian. Over many centuries, expeditions into unknown lands, full of unlimited fantasy, are surprisingly numerous. *Gulliver's Travels* by Jonathan Swift, as well as *Alice in Wonderland* by Lewis Carroll both belong to this genre, of course.

Things were also similar in the theatre. Both *The Birds* and

The Frogs of Aristophanes explore the land of pure fantasy. It is no different in *The Tempest* or in *A Midsummer Night's Dream*. Wizardry, spells and charms, and unexpected transformations are possible because both the island of Prospero and the forest of Athens are creations of fantasy. The fairy-tale-like, fantastical ideas always were and still are the motors of thousands of theatre shows for children and young people: animals sing, flowers dance, pencils, toys, even fruits gain a personality. Everything is possible because in a fairy tale there are no limits to the imagination. The more the imagination frolics, or even goes crazy, the more interesting things are on stage.

But for the Land of the Future to appear in the Land of Stories required a radically long and different process. It would not be possible for the Land of the Future to appear without the future previously being discovered as a territory of events which can be foreseen to some extent. Earlier, for centuries, the future was a kind of black hole. The future of the world was its end, that is, the *Parousia* (Christ's Second Coming) and the Final Judgement, and it did not depend upon man as to when it would happen. In the Middle Ages, the end of the world was expected pretty soon and prophecies of its coming appeared with surprising regularity. Only the Renaissance and the rediscovery of antiquity made it possible for people to look differently upon the nature of historical time. On the one hand, generally, the Christian world was continuing a journey from the known beginning to the known end. But on the other hand, the growing autonomy of human free will started slowly to permit choice along the road of that journey. The geographical discoveries of the fifteenth and sixteenth centuries, the new astronomy of Copernicus, the invention of printing, the Protestant schism, the development of a banking system, the accumulation of capital – all the revolutions of modern times, revealed the future as a territory adaptable for a profitable industry.

The beginnings of globalisation go back to the Treaty of

Tordesillas (1494), dividing the whole globe between the influence of Spain and Portugal and completed by the Treaty of Saragossa (1529). The European empires, which were already shaking the world, were rapidly changing themselves, from continental to global. The stake in that race was the future, which could pay back with gold. Apart from the new model of the universe declared by Newton, the seventeenth-century European religious massacres also added much to the new understanding of time and space. The universe seen from the perspective of the next, eighteenth century, turned out to be managed by the great, perfect clockmaker, the *Primus Motor* (Prime Mover), who – after creating the world – does not interfere with its successive course. Planned, long-time interventions into this reality, in a natural way, were becoming the destiny of man. In his hands, these interventions were becoming bolder and broader: mines, sailing, colonies, the slave trade, and, finally, more and more machines. A historically victorious combination was formulated: economical machines plus the knowledge of how they function as a set of effective tools for controlling the world.

The rollout of these changes was forcing (in full accord with the observations of Kuhn, let's note) a change to the whole paradigm of understanding of our presence in the world. The skeletons of dinosaurs and mammoths were dug out of the ground, and the authority of the Bible, with regard to the age of the planet, was overthrown. The Earth moved from the centre to the peripheries of an enlarged universe. The time of man's life, irreversibly limited, was becoming the natural territory of human actions. Thus, also history started to be a natural object of these actions – 'History', written now more frequently with a capital letter. History as a name for the Stage of Time (*die Weltbühne*) on which human masses fulfil their self-realisation under the command of outstanding individuals in the roles of protagonists (like Napoleon). Human masses act on this stage, or, more precisely, whole nations do.

Those were the times of 'Storm and Stress', of *'Sturm und Drang'*, the times of a 'historical pass' as, many years later, the German philosopher Odo Marquard would call them. A relatively static world which, for the thinkers of the Enlightenment, resembled the precise mechanism of a clock, started to transform itself into a live, pulsating process, perhaps even almost into a live being. Romanticism was spreading like a fire in the Australian bush. What was 'without heart' till now, was gaining now a 'soul', and new, emotional 'feeling and faith' were chasing away the half-dead, cold-hearted 'glass and eye of the wise man' (Adam Mickiewicz).

Hegel was finishing his ground-breaking *Phenomenology of Spirit* (*Geist*/Ghost) under the thunder of Napoleon's cannons at Jena (the Battle of Jena, 1806). The heroic, unstoppable progress of human history was sounding in his ears as the sound of a cosmic symphony from a divine ghost. A ghost battling through the paroxysms of a Napoleonic epic to the final, ultimate 'cadence of spiritual fulfilment' (embodied in the state of Prussia, by the way). In the year 1815, the year of the Congress of Vienna, which drew the map of Europe and the world for the whole forthcoming century, nothing resembled the previous state of things. Nothing was like it was before the French Revolution.

How did, soon afterwards, Georg Büchner, in *Woyzeck* (1837), cruelly mock that Hegelian idealism?

Doctor: Gentlemen, we have reached the important question of the subject's relations to the object. Let us take a creature in which the divine's organic self-affirmation reaches one of its higher manifestations and examine its relationship to space, the earth, the universe. Gentlemen, if I throw this cat out of the window, how will this creature, in accordance with its instinct, maintain its centre of gravity? (Trans. Gregory Motton)

Büchner might have been joking but the old story of Doctor Faustus, a necromantic magician who deals with the Devil, was supplanted by the story of Doctor Victor Frankenstein, an experimentalist, a scientist, the creator of a man-resembling monster (1818). The full title is: *Frankenstein; or, The Modern Prometheus*. Mary Shelley was consciously writing about the Promethean myth, about human creations turning against man. A new kind of fiction was being born, a kind of speculative fiction, full of fantastic ideas, but a fiction remaining on the border of probability. This is how modernism was born. Stories like *The Time Machine* (1895) or *The Island of Doctor Moreau* (1896) or *The War of the Worlds* (1898) by H. G. Wells simply – according to the stream of time – had to appear; they were unavoidable. Soon, the First World War, with its mighty, totalitarian, military and industrial machine, accelerated the birth of a new literary genre, fully dedicated to the future: 'science fiction' was born.

One could talk about utopias and dystopias forever. In the giant library of twentieth-century science fiction, we can find some relatively optimistic, therefore utopian, visions of the planetary or intergalactic future of humanity. They form the minority. The opposite, the pessimistic versions, anti-utopias, represent the majority. There is also a third, cosmic kind: surprisingly numerous bastards of the swashbuckling type; a kind of penny dreadful, of picaresque and general hotchpotch, named 'space-operas'. Anyway, the very name 'science fiction' contains a proud and conscious victory over the past. A modern victory of a 'better', scientifically planned future over the 'worse', incidental, ordinary past.

The invention of science fiction was an expression of this victory of modernity. Gianni Vattimo writes about modernity in his *End of Modernity* (1985) where he proposes his own definition: 'Modernity is an epoch, for which to be modern becomes a value, even more, becomes the only fundamental value. It becomes a value, to which all other values refer.' Which is also complimentary – notes Vattimo – with an even more popular vision of modernity, understood in the terms of secularisation: 'One should simply identify the faith in the progress, understood as a faith in the historical process, a faith gradually deprived of providential and non-historical references, with a faith in the value of what is new.'

And to think that such an incredibly ambitious, Promethean and creative programme has crashed before our eyes. Its elements have fallen out of sync, the time axis has bent and broken, and here we are, before it, scattered. Isn't it a beautiful catastrophe?

53 In the theatre, the Land of the Future, unlike the Land of Fantasy, does not look good. Various 'scientifically' devised worlds of some – let's say – robots (*R.U.R.* by Karel Capek) or some extra-terrestrials, when presented on stage, are simply horrible. They are usually horrendous and unbelievable.

Theatres happen to stage, infrequently, adaptations of Orwell's *1984* or Huxley's *Brave New World* or Lem's *Solaris* but the human factor dominates in these shows. The human factor, that is, mankind's loss, its fear, its ambitions, its dilemmas. The set design is deemed insignificant. Inventing the set of a possible future is a curse for designers. The World of the Future in the theatre is unbearably artificial. And therefore unbelievable.

Trying to perform the future in the theatre, it seems, is in deep conflict with the theatre's own nature. 'Who's there?' – asks Bernardo at the very beginning of *Hamlet* and for as long as every answer remains practically possible, the course of events intrigues us and engages us. Yet, in the case where the answer is 'already' given and known, it is somehow useless to follow the action. It would be better to read a short synopsis. Theatre is a vehicle which – as many have observed in the past – serves us by asking disturbing questions rather than by giving final answers.

The theatre doesn't function well in the role of Pythia, the ancient Oracle, through which Apollo wept cloudy verdicts concerning eventual, future events. But in the role of a mirror, reflecting the present moment, it acquits itself perfectly well.

54 'You're so quiet all of a sudden, Charles,' said Gioia, who could not abide silence for very long. 'Will you talk to me? I want you to talk to me. Tell me what you're looking for out there.'

He shrugged. 'Nothing.'

'Nothing?'

'Nothing in particular.'

'I could see you seeing something.'

'Byzantium,' he said. 'I was imagining that I could look straight across the water to Byzantium. I was trying to get a glimpse of the walls of Constantinople.'

'Oh, but you wouldn't be able to see as far as that from here. Not really.'

'I know.'

'And anyway, Byzantium doesn't exist.'

'Not yet. But it will. Its time comes later on.'

'Does it?' she said. 'Do you know that for a fact?'

'On good authority. I heard it in Asgard,' he told her. 'But even if I hadn't, Byzantium would be inevitable, don't you think? Its time would have to come. How could we not do Byzantium, Gioia? We certainly will do Byzantium, sooner or later. I know we will. It's only a matter of time. And we have all the time in the world.'

A shadow crossed her face. 'Do we? Do we?'

The lines of dialogue above create a scene. A scene is usually a part of a dramatic work, or of a screenplay. Let's say Charles and Gioia are slowly catching their breath, they have just been madly making love in their room. Finally, she couldn't hold it in anymore and she asked. They are, let's agree, in the ancient replica of Alexandria and it is early on a hot afternoon. We are right in the middle of *Sailing to Byzantium* by Robert Silverberg (1985).

Why have I thought about them, all of a sudden? Why am I reminded of them?

55 § Mike wakes up early. Audrey and Umberto get up, helped by mugs of hot fluid resembling coffee in taste. They pack their rucksacks. At the exit they meet two strangers, Kevin and Marla. He is very silent, unshaven, and elderly, she is much younger, armed with a machine gun. They put heavy, metal boxes on the backs of two camels. 'These are parts of the technical drawings of a large transformer,' explains Mike. He gives a sign from the head of the caravan, the others move in a row behind him, also leading two donkeys with canisters full of water and provisions.

Day is breaking. The yellowish dunes are slowly vanishing behind them. They are walking on compacted glass like sand, which, many years ago, could have been the tarmac of a road. From time to time, they pass rusted car wheels and pieces of twisted, black metal sheets on the sides of their path. The Sun shows up, pale, blurry, but strong, dark-brown hills loom on the horizon. The leather harnesses of the animals creak, the camels are spitting.

They stop for a break in the middle of the day in the shadow of a high, almost vertical rock. They throw themselves onto the sand and voraciously drink warm water from plastic containers.

'The worst part of the journey will be behind us,' says Mike, 'if we manage to reach the hills before the sunset. There are canyons in the mountains, it is easier to hide there.'

After the break, they start to move again and this is when the Hunters appear. A misty cloud emerges from the other side of the hills. It is the size of a large house and starts a slow traverse from right to left, maybe two kilometres in front of them. A quiet, electric buzz can be heard in the immobile air. Mike gives a sign and they crouch in a ditch. The animals are wheezing, reluctantly bending their knees. They all wait.

After half an hour, a dark blue vehicle on wide tyres emerges from the cloud. It is a dull metal mass without windows and with no signs. Something silver is blinking at its head. The vehicle moves slowly forward, directed a little to the right from where they are. It stops from time to time, as if hesitating upon its next possible movement, then it continues. In the ditch, Marla nervously holds her gun.

Unexpectedly, one of the donkeys kicks the other one, jerks upwards and, while remaining tied to the rest of the animals, and braying, starts to scramble up onto the slope. Marla rapidly directs her gun towards it. The shot is quiet, but immediate. The donkey squeals and collapses to the ground. There is silence. The vehicle stands immobile but the silver antennae turn towards them. After a few minutes, four humanoid figures spill out from the vehicle. They are dressed in dark uniforms, like soldiers, and have helmets on their heads. There are heavy, anti-tank rifles in their hands. Three of them form an extended line and squat in the sand. The fourth one starts slowly to approach the low-lying caravan. Marla shouts and fires a single shot at him. There is no reaction, she misses. The figure in uniform is slowly approaching the animals. Soon he reaches, with a gloved hand, the boxes on the back of the first camel.

A sudden hit of high temperature is accompanied by an unbearable noise like a thunderbolt. An acoustic blast emerges from nowhere and grows in seconds to the level of a hurricane, denting everything and forcing everyone to the ground. It gets much darker. A roaring, metal ceiling covers the sky at the height of ten metres. Night falls suddenly. Flares and star shells blind people, animals, and armed soldiers. The darkness is boiling. It is spitting blinding laser rays and micro-explosions. Umberto feels as if he is under the giant, fiery undercarriage of an air-transporter, landing without warning on the incidental strip. He pulls Audrey's arm and, half-blinded, rushes to the right.

'It's them!' shouts Mike, pulling Kevin and Marla in the same direction. They are all running. Smoke starts to emerge from the roaring darkness above them. They are running straight ahead, faltering on the uneven ground. A hundred metres, maybe two hundred, and finally they collapse heavily on the ground.

Breathing loudly, they look backwards. A giant spaceship hangs above the desert, standing on pillars of quivering gases. Below it, in a swirl of orange smoke, the four humanoid figures are fighting a lost battle. A tangle of thick, arm-like stems emerges from the ship above the soldiers. The stems, like whitish, elastic snakes, entwine around them. The squirming arms are choking their four bodies, detaching them from the ground. They are pulled upwards to the cargo bay. The soldiers vanish inside, one after the other. The last of them hangs for a moment in the air like some deplumed, immobile, bird before a black hook from the cargo bay mercifully comes down and cuts his head off.

Audrey screams and puts her head between her knees. Umberto wants to embrace her, and he moves towards her. In the same moment, the darkness and the noise grow to an unbearable level. Their brains are stunned; the darkness and noise become pulsating, painful, continuous. Then there is silence.

56 § It took him a long time to wake up. He was struggling, half-conscious, with his coat. It was cold; he was lying on the wet, cold grass. He heard the noise of sea gulls

143

and, a moment later, the sound of the sea. He opened his eyes and saw a blue, morning sky with some little clouds above him.

The ocean was below the grassy cliff on which he was sitting, the crests of the waves were white, at least thirty metres below. A little higher up, he saw a low wall made of stones. There were no trees. No house. A narrow path led along the coast. Higher, there were only grassy fields and stubble.

He was shivering, the wind was strong, so he tied his coat around his waist. The coast stretched for kilometres, up to a small town seen far away on his right. A grey, pointed clock tower signalled the entrance to the well-hidden port among the rocks. He turned to the opposite, northern side. The path was visible on the cliffs, yet there were no people to be seen. He saw the line of a distant, immobile ship very far away, on the horizon, and a moment later, yet another one slowly moving to the left. Trawlers or tankers, he thought, and started to walk. Suddenly he thought that at the very end of the path, maybe half a mile to the front, he could see a receding, red-haired figure. 'Audrey!' he called. 'Audrey! Wait!'

He ran after her, but after few hundred metres it seemed her silhouette was only an illusion. He stopped in the middle of the path, breathing heavily. A dozen dirty sheep's heads chewing grass were looking at him from behind a wooden gate.

After a few kilometres of walking, some roofs and chimneys appeared in the distance, above a group of trees. He climbed there on the steep, cobbled track and reached a road. There was a small board on the shed of the bus stop. 'Gunwalloe', he read. A newspaper, the *Daily Mail*, was in the bin. I am somewhere in England, he thought. Further, beside the road, he found a low, stone building among some farm buildings for cattle. It was a pub named *Hellzephron*, and it was open. He found there a single, bored waitress with blonde hair, and nobody else. There was a fire in the fireplace. He asked for a coffee and went to the bathroom. He saw his face in the mirror; he resembled a sixty-year-old man. He returned to the main room and – awkwardly explaining in English – he asked where he was. He was told that he was few miles from Helston and that the little port to the right was called Porthleven. He was told that there were regular bus connections from Helston to Truro. He was in Cornwall, on its farthest, south-western peninsula, on The Lizard.

57 As we observed before, the role of Oracle is not entirely suited to the theatre. However, among the infinity of stories it is possible to tell in the theatre, there are stories which try to explain history. Not just this or that, or even the most dramatic events in somebody's biography, but the very basic, historical sense of all events and lives – History, with a capital H.

> Rage-Goddess, sing the rage of Peleus' son Achilles,
> Murderous, doomed, that cost the Achaeans countless losses,
> hurling down to the House of Death so many sturdy souls

Homer is explaining History, of course. A History in which human ambitions and passions are the playthings of vindictive gods. Gods no less vindictive and emotional than humans are, and gods competing intensely among themselves. The result of that divine rivalry is pretty frightening: countless sturdy souls, hurled down to the House of Death, but apart from such a miserable end, human values, such as fidelity, courage, cleverness and decency are somehow saved in this story, despite the vengeful gods.

Nativity plays, mystery plays and passion pageants tell a completely different 'History'. They tell a history in which 'In the beginning God created the Heaven and the Earth' and which one day will end with the Apocalypse and the coming of God's kingdom. History, in such a version, still lingers and is happening before our eyes. All smaller histories, events and lives will find at their end their deepest sense. Therefore, no single human deed is unimportant in this finale of history.

As for the histories of Shakespeare, half a century ago, Jan Kott gave them capital letters. He called them 'a Great Mechanism' and compared them to a great staircase. He meant that those standing at the top inevitably must fall into oblivion, while those at their base must incessantly climb up. Shakespeare preferred to call this mechanism, without unnecessary bombast, the 'Wheel of Fortune'. Fortune, like a mill wheel, simply cannot help throwing some characters down while bringing others up. Such is the nature of a mill wheel. And because of that there will be a Richard the Third after Richard the Second and after him a number of Henrys, and so on: 'For some must watch, while some must sleep: Thus runs the world away.'

Georg Wilhelm Friedrich Hegel, in Jena in 1807, was deeply afraid of the thundering canons of Napoleon. The battle happening around him enthused him to such an extent that he got a spiritual fever and quickly finished his *Phenomenology of Spirit*. This way, History squared the circle, for a long time. Hegel was bitten by the daemon of historical progress. The Hegelian story about History – as we know – imitated Christian teleology but gave the reins of history to History's Spirit, written with a capital S. To the Spirit, and not into the hands of actual people. Also, the Hegelian story about History dramatised it incredibly by dialectically using all possible theses, antitheses and syntheses. The 'historical' or 'political' stage, a 'theatre of events' – all these operatic terms come from the vision of Hegel. Man, a single one, or, preferably, people in massed numbers, become now the actor(s) in the Hegelian mega-drama of the Spirit.

This is why, for example, somebody like Danton from Georg Büchner's drama *Danton's Death* (1835) knows that he is 'a historical character'. Even more, he consciously plays such a character, while contemporaneously maintaining – in a fully

Romantic fashion – a proud, ironic distance towards 'historical events'. Although he is a tragic and important actor of the drama of History, he is also its spectator. He looks at the bloody cruelty of the French Revolution as at some undivine, terrifying comedy.

Our Polish Romantics could not permit themselves such bitter self-reflection. Hegel's Spirit was galloping, accelerating and winning, while the Motherland lay, oh God, in the grave. That century was difficult for our Romantic Prophets. How was it possible to doubt the Spirit? If it was a Spirit, it had to be a holy one! Meanwhile, their Motherland was erased from the map. Therefore, Polish Romantic, national, poetic prophets had to rebound, insanely, between epiphany and the asylum.

Anyone whom Hegel had not managed to bite inevitably got bitten later by Marx. The reins of History were taken by the proletariat, which was the Party in fact. The 'scientific' theory of Marxist history was an inspiration for hordes of playwrights. We do not even need to bring in Brecht. In her *Danton's Case*, Stanisława Przybyszewska deeply hates the bourgeois traitor Danton while she raises that virtuous butcher Robespierre to heroic, tragic greatness. His will be the victory at the end of a classless History, because he wanted to do good 'for the masses'.

It was probably Alfred Jarry, in his *Ubu Roi* (1888), who first openly mocked the story of any great History. Afterwards, this idea got picked up almost by itself: Witold Gombrowicz showed history his bare foot ('cocked a snook') in his *History*, a text from his youth. Soon, anyone speaking about History after the battles of two world wars could only provoke disgust. The ghosts have vanished, first the Hegelian one and later also the ghost of the battle between the classes. In the end, in the year 1965, Peter Weiss's text demonstrated (completely unexpectedly for Weiss) that Marat, the revolutionist, is not a patron of contemporaneity anymore. It showed that this role is being taken by the Marquis de Sade, an egoist, a brute and a rapist.

Pure evil, I mean the ugliest sort of evil, has crawled from the tapestry of history, an evil that is now incarnated in man. Something surprisingly similar to the Drunkard in *The Marriage* by Gombrowicz.

Practically, it is not possible to explain History in the theatre today. One can only tell various single stories about this or that event. One can talk about somebody's life, about somebody's experience, or one can inquire (like Frayn in *Copenhagen*) if, what and when anything 'really' happened in history. But a History? The general sense of all the events and all lives? Any author aiming so ambitiously would be courageous indeed.

But of course, the little histories deprived of the support of any big History inevitably become unimportant, insubstantial. And in the end, how many stories about the impossibility of explaining history can one see? Therefore, people willingly return – I have the feeling – and will return in the future, to other stories; stories different from today's story, which we are hanging in the middle of. They will return to those in which the 'gods kill us like flies'. To those in which every crime will receive its rightful punishment. And to those in which changeable fortune continues to spin around. Man is an animal who adores to tell stories.

58 It should be a relief to us to renounce omniscience, to recognise that every generation, our own included, will, must inevitably, understand the past and anticipate the future in the light of its own restricted experience, must inevitably play on the dead whatever tricks it finds necessary for its own peace of mind.

Here is a historian radically distancing himself from the idea of history as a hard science, postulated by so many of his predecessors. His opinion does not seem particularly new today and therefore it is not so much this opinion, but rather its date which surprises us: the year is 1931 at the Congress of the American Historical Association. The author, Carl L. Becker, an outstanding American historian, expressed this opinion in his paper titled 'Everyman His Own Historian'.

In *The Heavenly City of the Eighteenth-Century Philosophers* (1932), the best remembered of his works, Becker's reasoning remains impressively clear and quick-witted while underlined with bitter irony. Becker shows the illusionary nature of the opinion, popular in the 1930s (but also still today), about the eighteenth century being particularly 'modern' in its thought. Becker argues that the period which was commonly called 'an epoch of reason' in fact did not deserve this name. He argues that Voltaire, Hume, Diderot and Locke still lived – although not consciously – in a world of presumptions from the Middle Ages and that *Les Philosophes* from the eighteenth century, to quote Becker, 'demolished the Heavenly City of St. Augustine only to rebuild it with more up-to-date materials'. Becker can be both extremely precise and sarcastically entertaining. Here is a sample of his style when he writes about *Les Philosophes*:

They denounced Christian philosophy, but rather too much, after the manner of those who are but half emancipated from the 'super-stitions' they scorn. They had put off the fear of God, but maintained a respectful attitude toward the Deity. They ridiculed the idea that the Universe had been created in six days, but still believed it to be a beautifully articulated machine designed by the Supreme Being, according to a rational plan as an abiding place for mankind. The Garden of Eden was for them a myth, no doubt, but they looked enviously back to the golden age of Roan virtue or across the waters to the unspoiled innocence of an Arcadian civilisation that flourished in Pennsylvania. They renounced the authority of the Church and the Bible, but exhibited a naïve faith in Nature and Reason. They scorned Metaphysics, but were proud to be called Philosophers. They dismantled heaven, somewhat prematurely it seems, since they retained their faith in the immortality of the soul. They courageously discussed Atheism, but not before the servants. They defended toleration valiantly, but only with difficulty could tolerate priests. They denied that miracles ever happened, but believed in the perfectibility of the human race ...

Having negated the Christian Creator, they have seen a new Absolute in Posterity – this particular teleology of the eighteenth-century philosophers Becker analyses in a detailed, crystal-clear way. It is important, I dare to think, that Becker is not any camouflaged Christian conservative but quite the contrary; his political views locate him on the progressive Liberal Left side of the spectrum. Telling us with impressive clarity about his understanding of history, Becker knows very well that he is only telling us his own, individual interpretation of history, and not an interpretation representing any ideology standing 'above' him.

Let us try to imagine this situation more closely. It is the year 1931, Hitler is only just preparing himself to grab power, the most horrendous Stalinist 'cleansings' and millions sent to gulags will happen in only a few years' time. The Spanish Civil War – that first 'rehearsal' of the military conflict between two deadly ideologies, which had its roots in the ideas of the eighteenth century – won't happen for another five years. And here, some Carl Becker, unknown to the wider world, some Yankee from Iowa proclaims, 'with relief', that it is 'Everyman', who is 'His Own Historian'. It is as if he already knew in 1931 how both Fascism and Communism will end. It is as if he already knew which 'climate of opinion' (this is an important term in his work) will predominate in 2021.

Would my life choices be different, less intuitive, if somebody had given me Becker's book in my youth? Quite possibly. We were all searching for knowledge about the deadly force of Communism in a very individual way (I would love to write about a 'generation' but, frankly, I cannot remember any 'generation'). The *Main Currents of Marxism* by Leszek Kołakowski, and the works of Karl Popper, were read in underground, samizdat editions. The boorish practices of the real socialism around us were making it possible to guess the rest. Today, after many years, I read Becker's book with unconcealed awe. But this awe mixes with anger — for how was it possible? A full eight years before the start of the Second World War there was somebody who could explain and was able to publish his bitter understanding of the reasons for the bloody madness of the twentieth century. And what, no one in Europe of that time could hear him? No one drew any conclusions? No one understood what he was writing about?

Carl Becker, a historian, a sceptic. A slightly resigned rationalist. At the end of his book, Becker analyses (honestly referring his opinions to the earlier observations of de Tocqueville), the striking similarity of the quasi-religious character of the French Revolution to the analogical symptoms of the October Revolution, which was contemporary for Becker. Communism is a new social religion. 'The Communist faith,' writes Becker, 'exactly like the eighteenth-century religion of humanity, is based upon the laws of Nature revealed by Science.' Should we think, therefore, asks Becker at the end of his book, that the Russian Revolution in the twentieth century, together with the French one from the eighteenth century are the successive steps of humanity toward perfection? Or maybe we should rather assume, following Marcus Aurelius, that a rationalist:

... covers the whole Universe and the void which surrounds it, and sketches its map; reaches into the infinity of time and penetrates, with his thought, the cyclical renewal of everything; engulfs everything in one glance and understands that our children will not see anything new, any more than our fathers ever saw anything more than we can see. Therefore, because of that monotony, a forty-year-old man, if he has a pinch of reason, already has seen everything that is and everything that will be.

59 *Meditations* by Marcus Aurelius: what an incredible book in the European canon it is. That set of notes by the Roman Caesar from the second century AD, written in palaces and military tents, during numerous campaigns in Pannonia and Germania against Marcomanni, Quads and Sarmatii. The lines of the author are precise, well thought out, unrelenting. The arguments engage, the paradoxes glitter, the metaphors delight.

Hippocrates, having healed many, fell ill and died. Chaldeans have prophesied many deaths, and despite of this, destiny took them. Alexander, Pompeius and Gaius Caesar, having destroyed whole cities and slaughtered innumerable numbers of both cavalry and foot soldiers, had to leave life. Heraclitus, who discoursed so much about fire on earth, died swollen with water, after daubing himself with cow shit. Lice killed Democritus; other lice killed Socrates. So what? You stepped on board, you sailed, you reached the port. Get out! If to another life, the gods are everywhere there. If into anaesthesia, you will stop feeling the suffering and pleasures, and you will no longer be subject to this vessel, which is as bad, as what it serves is better.

This 'better' is 'a mind and daimon', that is, the inner, divine element in man. While the 'vessel' for a *daimon*, that is a man's body, is only *'earth and gore'*. On the same theme, more specifically, in the fourth book: *'You are a soul (animula) wrapped in a carcass, as Epictetus said.'*

Nothing indicates that the *Meditations* of Aurelius were written for publication. This is not a philosophical treatise but rather a sort of spiritual diary in which the writer addresses himself. Marcus Aurelius, deeply immersed in Greek language and breathing Greek culture, in his *Meditations* (this title was finally agreed only three centuries ago), is an exemplary stoic, patiently practising everyday virtue (*arete*). Although he never calls himself a stoic, his beliefs qualify him for that particular philosophical school. According to Aurelius, life is – as in a well-known joke – like a child's shirt, short and shitty; its end is rather poor, and it knows it will be so from the beginning. How does one live in these circumstances? Only and exclusively by supporting a *daimon*, that is, our inner, divine voice calling us – despite all the horrible things which happen in our lives – to be good, rather than bad, rational, rather than stupid, doing good, rather than spreading evil.

When meditating, Aurelius is not so much a philosopher; he is dutifully exercising the process of dying, fully according with the postulates of Plato. Aurelius doesn't like the Sophists and doesn't like discoursing for the sake of art. A sophist, according to Aurelius, is 'not an actor, nor a whore'. He says: 'Do everything and talk, and study, as if you were able to leave life in any moment.' Aurelius is not afraid of death; he is ready to defend his deeds in any moment in front of the proper court. Only he does not know where to find such a court: 'Yet if gods do not exist or do not care about human affairs, why should I live in the world in which there are no gods nor a providence?' He convinces himself strenuously to believe in the 'nature of the whole'. He does not want to accept a world which – as in Stanisław Lem – would simply be deprived of sense. 'The nature of the whole would not make such a mistake, permitting both good and bad things to happen to good and bad people with no difference.' Were he alive today, after reading some postmodernist Sophists, he would most probably cut open his veins.

The first commandment of the Stoics was 'life in accord with nature'. The second was the unemotional acceptance of what is necessary, inevitable and independent from us. The aim of life? To discover what kind of good we can desire within the world we live in. And finally, the third essential thing, *philostorgia* – the understanding love, tenderness of feelings, kindness, charitableness.

Marcus Aurelius is really not a bad poet. Let's compare and see: the earlier Caesar Hadrian (AD 76–138) wrote, for example:

> Oh, loving Soul, my own so tenderly,
> My life's companion and my body's guest,
> To what new realms, poor flutterer, wilt thou fly?
> Cheerless, disrobed, and cold in thy lone quest,
> Hushed thy sweet fancies, mute thy wonted jest.
> (Trans. D. Johnston)

And now, Marcus Aurelius (AD 121–80):

> One should also notice that certain things which are additional – along with those directly coming from nature – have a certain grace and seductive attractiveness. For example, cracks show up here and there on baked bread. Despite the fact that they are contingent and somehow opposed to the baker's art, nevertheless they fit, and they whet the appetite. Or figs, for example. When they are almost ripe, they split. And olives, when they ripen on the trees, the very imminence of rotting gives them a particular beauty. And the ears of wheat bent to the ground, and the wrinkly forehead of a lion, and the saliva flowing from the jaws of a boar, and many others …

60 What after me? The majority of the human population, during the course of history, when asking themselves this natural question, simply did not have, and still do not have, enough resources to be able to turn it into concrete fact. I mean, maybe sometimes we have a few material possibilities: well, bequeath the house to Joe, since he is the oldest;

the savings go to Suzie, because she is thrifty; the rings are for Emily and the rest is for the cousins. But very few of us have the resources of Pharaoh Cheops, who ordered a giant pyramid to be built and named after him, or the means of the Chinese Emperor, who left the Terracotta Army to serve him in his afterlife. Very few of us can assure themselves eternal praise among the living, or optimal equipment on the other side of life. An advantageous 'foundation', nobly serving society (named after ourselves, of course), remains a popular, quite rational choice of rich people. This is a choice for those whose numerous properties offer the chance that such a foundation will prosper. But for how long?

What after us? *'Après nous le deluge'* was the call of the French La Boheme over a hundred years ago. Yet, more seriously: what will remain after us when we are gone? The properties (buildings, lots) and money will be taken by children, brothers, sisters, cousins. Manuscripts? The relatives will want to look at them, or maybe will not. Dust to dust; one has to consider such a possibility seriously. Then what? Maybe, if we have any funds at all, maybe we order the construction of a pyramid?

'Exegi monumentum aere perennius,' wrote Horace two thousand years ago, and he was right: his songs survived and, indeed, they are a more enduring monument than any made from marble or brass. The memory of Horace survived and when Shakespeare makes the dying Hamlet ask a character called Horatio to speak 'about him', the faith that 'the song will survive' seems to be unspoiled. Horatio himself eagerly accepts his new role as a storyteller/historian/poet:

> And let me speak to th' yet unknowing world
> How these things came about. So shall you hear
> Of carnal, bloody, and unnatural acts,
> Of accidental judgments, casual slaughters,
> Of deaths put on by cunning and forced cause,

> And, in this upshot, purposes mistook
> Fall'n on th' inventors' heads. All this can I
> Truly deliver.

And what would happen if the new ruler of Denmark, Fortinbras, rejects Horatio's story with contempt? If he prefers to commission a narration about his predecessors from historians of The Institute of Fortinbras's Fame? Hamlet's fear before his death would become frighteningly real in such a case: 'O God, Horatio, what a wounded name, / Things standing thus unknown, shall I leave behind me!' Zbigniew Herbert foresaw such a possibility in his 'Elegy of Fortinbras':

> drum roll drum roll I know nothing beautiful
> these will be my manoeuvres before taking the power
> one has to grip a city by the throat and shake it a little

Apart from the songs which, by a strange fate, survived history, there must be somewhere in the 'otherworld' a body of songs which did not. A set of forbidden songs, of songs burned and stamped into the ground. Also, a set of songs forgotten over the course of time, songs blown away by the winds, songs sung a long time ago in forgotten languages, in idioms which became mute, in dialects which nobody can speak anymore.

> If thou didst ever hold me in thy heart,
> Absent thee from felicity awhile
> And in this harsh world draw thy breath in pain
> To tell my story.

This seems to be more durable and more solid than pyramids. But even words are not eternal, alas.

61 § Audrey was not in London, or in Milan, or in Porto. Umberto was boarding random planes to the last place he dreamt of; there was not much sense in it. He was landing at incidental hotels, with no idea where to go, with no aim. He was wandering the streets, ordering a coffee in a café and sipping it for hours, looking at the streets through the window. He felt an enormous loss, he was incomplete and deeply unhappy. Sometimes he cried during the night, but in the morning he restarted his journey on the pavements.

He did not want to go back to Forlí, there was nothing for him to go back to. He became, not a tourist, but rather a passenger of a lost ark, a follower of a cargo cult, impatiently waiting for the next delivery. Because he was deeply sure that he would see Audrey again. The attack on the Utah desert had separated them. His present timeline had moved on ten, or maybe even fifteen years. But Audrey, a mere thirty-odd years old, red-haired Audrey, was out there, somewhere there, on the orbits of temporal loops and diachronic jumps; he was sure of that. One should wait and one should search for her. He started to make a note of his dreams in a special, green notebook. He caught himself counting the stones on the pavement, an odd number could be a message from her, of course. The channels of communication among wanderers travelling through time can take various forms, he kept explaining to himself.

One morning, he was transferred to Tirgu Mures. He awoke in an unknown hotel room. He could hear the traffic and the cooing of the pigeons on the parapet. He dragged himself to the bathroom and heard the voice of a radio through the half-opened window. He did not know that the language of the speaker was Romanian, but he felt that he had found himself in that other Europe, the one which was more difficult to understand and was almost unknown to him. He washed himself and stepped into Trandafirilor Square. The centre of the square was taken up by an anaemic park in which the number of flower beds dominated the number of dusty fruit trees. The park was surrounded by a wide, one-way street filled with cars, Ladas and Zhiguli, with old Skodas and Dacias, among which a silver Mercedes or a BMW sneaked from time to time. On the other side of the street, the proud houses of the city presented their fronts, all of them from the nineteenth and the beginning of the twentieth century, from the Austro-Hungarian past of Tirgu Mures, from the time when this place in Transylvania was still named Marosvasarhelij.

The pavements were uneven, the grass rather bald, dust was everywhere. He moved to the right and heard Hungarian among the pedestrians. He could identify it but after a short while he heard yet again the former language from the radio; it was clear that he had found himself in some border land. He suddenly saw a group of Roma people in costumes usually seen only in old photos. Large, swinging, black-haired women in splendidly colourful skirts, beside them moustachioed men in hats straight from a Western, and a bunch of small, shouting children. The Sun was burning strongly and in the middle of the day there was already a muggy, Balkan heat hanging heavily over Trandafirilor Square.

He knew that he was in Central Europe, but he did not know whether it was the centre of Europe or its peripheries. There were candidates from many parties who were aiming at the symbolic centre, at the Parliament in Brussels – the fading pictures of their smiling faces were amicably losing their colour on the Trandafirilor advertisement boards. Was it still Europe? Umberto could not see any real poverty here in Tirgu Mures. After sunset, the citizens paraded en masse on the promenade, consuming unthinkable amounts of ice cream. Europe was evidently already present on Trandafirilor Square but it was a Europe – to borrow the term from Bulgakov – of the second sort.

On the second evening, returning from his wanderings,

Umberto sat at the street café close to a group of Italian tourists who were consuming cold prosecco and ice cream.

'Where are you from?' he asked.

'From Rome,' they responded. 'And you?'

'From Rimini,' he answered hurriedly, and asked, 'Where are you going?'

'To Dracula's castle, of course,' they answered and burst into laughter.

'They say that in Dracula's castle the other-Timers regularly show up,' said Laura, freckled and talkative.

'Who?' Umberto asked.

'The other-Timers, as the name tells you, come from a different time, from the Middle Ages for example, or from antiquity. They say that sometimes there are even other-Timers from the future. I suspect that they are all disguised, depending upon tourists.' Laura sipped a gulp of bubbles. Her boyfriend, Maurizio, joined them.

'Laura, they do go there,' he said with authority. 'Timelines different from ours really do exist, but only a very few know how to move along them.'

Laura made a face – 'I won't believe it until I see it.'

Maurizio continued: 'The problem is in the fact that when you are travelling forward you get irrevocably older and there is no way back. Can you imagine? Somewhere there, in a distant, alternative future, thousands of troops, just decrepit greybeards. What if they can go one way and they cannot come back?'

Umberto wished them good night; he felt tired and went to sleep. In the early morning he awoke in an unknown, rather small, dark room. On the bed beside him, covered with a duvet, was Audrey, asleep.

62 § 'Lenin in October' claim the red letters on the white canvas hanging on the school fence. On the industrial grit of the playing field, behind a metal mesh, teenagers are kicking a ball.

Umberto is walking on the pavement with Audrey, passing the odd passers-by. Loud, blue trams are speeding on the street, ringing their bells. There is still light, a warm autumnal afternoon is slowly changing into evening. 'What is it with Lenin?' asks Umberto.

'I don't know, I shall ask Witold,' answers Audrey.

'Are we going to Piazza Centrale?' Umberto asks.

'Yes, to the Main Square. We are in Kraków, remember, in nineteen seventy-four and Lenin is still officially venerated here.'

Witold is a student at the Theatre School whom Audrey met in the canteen of the students' resident block, where she has a small room. Right now, Witold, thin, with a mop of hair, is waiting for them in the side alley near the square. His English is a bit crude, but fluent. In the old, medieval entrance hall is the door to the underground. A crowd of socialites is already swarming in front of it; some are students, some are freaks. Many men have long hair, some of them are dressed in woollen jumpers and look like jazz musicians. A broad-shouldered guard is blocking the gate and he waits for the signal from below.

'This is not the opening. There was no opening yet and nobody knows when it will be. Maybe next week, maybe next month, it depends when it will be decided by Maestro.'

'Maestro?' Umberto questions.

'Well, the Master, Maestro,' agrees Witold. 'This is a preview; yet another one. Gossip says that this show, the first one Maestro has done in two years, is something radically different than his past works.'

'Witold, what is the slogan "Lenin in October" about?' asks Audrey. 'We saw it on some fence.'

'It is about the yearly festival of Soviet films,' explains Witold. '*Lenin in October* and *Cats in March*.'

The guard half-opens the door, the crowd immediately forms a tight group. They squeeze through the entrance one after another. It is dark in the basement. A huge room with some hanging pictures extends to the right. People are going to the brick chamber on the left. In the dimmed light of a projector one can see a stack covered with a white sheet in front of a few rows of chairs.

People are filling the space. Umberto and Audrey find a single chair in the third row. People are whispering, gossiping; there is an aura of anxious expectation. An older, rather short man slowly walks in front of the first row.

'It's him!' Witold hits Umberto in the ribs.

Gradually, silence falls. The man slowly approaches the covered stack and methodically moves it to the side, as if he were unveiling a museum object. Three or four old, worn, wooden school benches from before the war are revealed, simple and modest. Pupils are sitting on them, here two, three there, as if glued to the benches in their dark uniforms, with greasy hair and goggly eyes. They are stiff and immobile like mannequins. Suddenly, a loud, nostalgic music swells from the speakers and the show starts.

It is like a séance, like somebody's dream from the most hidden, suppressed corners of memory. Mannequins are irregularly getting up, raising their hands and wanting to answer. They stutter, intensely, some illogical syllables and recite stupid, short poems. They move like the wooden, mechanical horses of some crazy merry-go-around. Each of them is carrying a corpse of his childhood on his back. It is a doll, maybe half a metre high, pretending to be a boy with similarly goggly eyes and a half-opened mouth. Every few minutes the group of these zombies is put into motion around the benches by – a teacher? – or maybe a custodian of this spectral, black and white classroom. They are dancing incoherently from right to left, turning around ineptly and shaking their tied dolls in the loops of a waltz which is monotonously repeating its first musical phrase. It is as if the vinyl playing the waltz is continuously being stopped (it is the sound of a very old gramophone) and it is repeatedly forced to start again, loudly, boldly and angrily. From time to time behind that procession, in a small window high near the ceiling – the figure of a mourner? – an auntie? – a mother? – is raising its hands and repeating its call:

'Go for a walk, children!'

From time to time a custodian opens fire from a giant machine gun hidden beneath his coat. *Ta-ta-ta-ta-ta!* The boys with mannequins fall to the ground in convulsions. Then the action gets repeated. The action is performed innumerable times, like a copy with very few changes, a copy causing an impression of purgatorial torture which started a long time ago and which will never end. Sometimes the events unexpectedly calm down and a mumbled question from the teacher is heard. One or other of these misshapen Golems then tries to squeeze an acceptable answer out of himself. His whitened mask swells, his suffering grows, his desperation is becoming monstrous. His mouth is mumbling and asking forgiveness, he is trembling, shaking, dribbling, and immediately and irrevocably the swell of the music knocks him down again, like a hellish punishment, throwing him off the bench and forcing him to move.

This is the Theatre of Death, thinks Umberto, biting his lip. This is a lament, a cry, a Kaddish, a funeral mass. After something like this one can only cry helplessly, and then dry one's wet eyes and try to survive, despite the destruction.

The show ends. There is no applause, the spectators sit quietly, totally shocked. The older man, the Maestro, covers the stack with the cloth, with a visible satisfaction.

Umberto and Audrey decide to go for a drink. Witold leads them to Piwnica. Downstairs they enter a bar, which is in a spacious, medieval cellar and is one of the four places in the whole city serving alcohol at this hour. It is rather crowded, but it isn't a day of the cabaret show, which is usually performed in one of the caverns. Natasha is pouring drinks and Audrey is paying with officially non-changeable piles of Polish bank notes ('I am on a temporary scholarship funded by The British Council,' she explains to Umberto). They sit down in the corner. A candle is burning on the table.

'I have never seen anything like that,' whispers Audrey. She is sipping vodka mixed with Dodoni orange juice. 'I feel as if I have been knocked down.'

'Tomorrow, I shall take you to the theatre, to the second dress of *The Liberation*. I have some free student passes. This is going to be something, because it is Swinarski's show, and he is, you know, he is somebody.'

'In Italy we do not even have a place for anything like that. Why do you want to stay in this horrible Republic of Soviets?' asks an excited Umberto.

'That is a very good question, Hubertus,' Witold grins and extinguishes his cigarette. 'When you know the answer, do not forget to share it with me. The day after tomorrow I leave you alone because I am going to see the boss, in Wrocław.'

63 § The streets were grey, the shabby houses and blocks were grey, but people lived among that dullness more or less normally because they had no choice. They lived normally, if normal is the lack of toilet paper in public toilets. This lack was of course combined with the lack of accessible public toilets first of all. They lived normally, if normal is the absence of goods in the shops. But that absence was also connected to the small number of existing shops as well.

People were drinking a lot. Everybody was drinking. The appearance of a heavily tottering drunkard on the street was not so rare. Also, everybody smoked stinking *Sport* or *Club* cigarettes. Life was often dirty, but usually life was also nicely familiar. People were living with their friends; life was messy, but general poverty equalised everybody's chances. There were moments of vivacity because the new Bosses of the Party were intensely borrowing money from the west. So, people sometimes found, quite unexpectedly, lemons in the shop, or – who knows why? – a stash of Japanese cameras.

It was not a fully serious country. A country unnecessarily underdeveloped, dreamy and quite void. A country hanging in the air in expectation, waiting for inevitable transformations, but who knew when and from where they would come? And where could they lead to? There were queues at the tills of the only State Bank. The queues were there to get the right to obtain a tiny *Fiat 126p* car, produced with an Italian licence, the pride of the government. People deposited a lot of money and could get a car after two years.

Audrey and Umberto wander on the streets the next morning and in the evening Witold leads them to the narrow technical balcony, high under the ceiling of the theatre. They are sitting among the electric reflectors, which make crackling sounds because of their high temperature. Below them, on the stage, a panorama of bizarre, historical characters from the nineteenth, eighteenth and seventeenth centuries is unfolding. The characters are circulating downstage in an unstoppable half-dance, half-triumphal march. They exhibit a never-ending cacophony of opinions, beliefs and ideas. This is a marketplace of proclamations and faiths, and the discussion is ferocious. It is like a strange Catholic mass, full of priests and national emblems. It is partly serious, but also partly mocking, tart and acerbic in tone. Every new element of that jigsaw puzzle denies the previous one. No one here can agree with anybody else; no one is able to cooperate. All this mess is whirling around the main character, who is probably some actor. Or perhaps he is some important artist, a poet maybe, who is responsible, or feels himself responsible, for the fate of humanity. His task seems to be to find a way out from the trap of contradicting senses and images. He is emotionally living through that nightmare, and he is visibly suffering. The audience is suffering with him. The general impression is upsetting and quite extraordinary: here, modern Poles from the second half of the twentieth century are absorbing, with every pore of their skin, the shame of their own mass portrait – an extremely unfavourable one. It is a collective self-flagellation. Accusations and derision are flowing from the stage:

'This is who you are!'

The show finishes with a funeral polonaise played by a little orchestra situated on the balcony. This music is the final straw and sees off the audience. It sounds like a sinister tribal curse.

They reach their residence; it is already late but Staszek from room 328 catches them in the corridor.

'Come for a vodka,' he says.

In room 328, an active commune is encamped, with dozens of contradicting political and social views – this much they know. Still, they enter. Parts of the quite spacious room are divided by hanging curtains and bookshelves. The sounds of a whimpering sitar float in the air. Jacek, Leszek, Bronek and Staszek are sitting around the table under a naked bulb. There is a bottle of *Żytnia* and a can of *Dodoni* juice.

'First the flyers,' Leszek is saying, 'flyers, a lot of flyers, a massive action, this is what it has to start from.'

He has small, round John-Lennon glasses, he gesticulates, and is already smashed.

'We need machines, duplicating machines, safe flats and a

whole well-organised network. Well organised, that is, with three levels of precautions, because there will be grasses, there will be arrests.'

'Double agents will be there, too,' adds Bronek, 'even triple ones. Do not trust anyone, I am telling you, this is the only tactic.' He swigs and hiccups.

'Maryna! Shut up with that bloody sitar, I can't stand it! Get "Dazed and Confused"!'

Something clangs, screeches and the voice of Robert Plant roars under the ceiling.

'But why repeat all the time the same patterns, the same repeatable movements, the same mistakes?' asks Staszek. He gets up and starts to circulate around the table. He has long blond hair, not washed recently. 'It may all pan out differently, who knows, maybe nuclear fusion will be discovered. Or we shall land on Mars. Or, who knows, maybe the Ruskies will simply get tired and will leave us alone. It can all still pan out in a completely different way ... What the fuck, Jacek, what the fuck are you reading all the time?'

'I am reading Martin Buber,' answers Jacek: big Afro haircut, yellow bandana.

'It is late. You do not need to finish this bottle, guys.' Leszek grabs the bottle and swallows the rest of it. 'Have you signed?'

On the table is the appeal to the boss of the canteen to change the hours of its operation. Audrey and Umberto sign it, swig a glass each and thank everyone:

'We are tired, we go to sleep, thanks, you are wonderful.'

When exiting, they notice on the wall of the room quotations from *The Master and Margarita* inscribed in green pen:

Manuscripts do not burn.
Yes, man is mortal, but this is nothing. The worst is, that the knowledge of his mortality shows up so unexpectedly, that is the problem!

The second freshness is a nonsense. Freshness is only once – the first one, and because of that, the last one, too. If the sturgeon is of second freshness, it simply means that it is rotten.

64 The influence of *The Master and Margarita* in the middle of the 1970s, among young intellectuals of the People's Republic of Poland, was equalled only by the influence of the prose of Julio Cortazar. Cortazar was widely translated by Zofia Chądzyńska and widely read. But apart from the fashionable literature of magic realism from South America, the important samizdat books were already present, too. Hayek, Popper, the *Main Currents of Marxism* by Kołakowski, smuggled from Paris. The general revolution was gradually germinating in some heads, but still only in the heads of a very few. Such a thought was still like an attack upon the Sun with a hoe; the Soviet Union was supposed to last forever. What writings could open a door to any knowledge of the real world in the 1960s, or 1970s in the PR of P? Since October 1956, young Polish humanists knew very well that the only efficient solution was in maintaining some connection with Paris or London. Jan Błoński knew it very well, as did Ludwik Flaszen. Both Mrożek and Herbert also knew it.

To connect to world trends, one went via Paris, eventually via New York or even Hollywood. Young filmmakers and young writers knew it. Jerzy Grotowski knew it. Konrad Swinarski, because of his bilingual knowledge of both Polish and German, was making his way through Berlin and Tel Aviv – a very tough choice, but a rewarding one too. And yet to translate various cultural trends and changing 'climates of opinion' from the shores of the Seine or the Thames, to the reality of the Vistula River, was an extremely complicated task. Very often it was simply impossible. Western Europe was quickly getting rich while we were becoming poorer and poorer. Western Europe was going through the cultural shock of 1968, it was exploding with flower-power and the sexual revolution. It was saying farewell to structuralism and was gradually preparing itself for the 'Big Change', while we were condemning the 'Zionistic elements' at Party rallies. We were invading Czechoslovakia, bowing our heads in front of Big Brother from the East and irrevocably falling into the trap of financial debt. Western Europe was a rapidly developing world, searching for its new formula, while we were athwart of history. We were in defiance of fashion, with our back to the front and our side turned to the back. Poland was often called 'the most merry barrack in the whole camp' but we, Poles, ourselves, felt quite tragically sad, within it.

The cultural pressure of that unnatural Polish situation was growing continuously and was unstoppable. The 1960s and 1970s were the years of an eruption of talent, of ideas and forms in music, in art, and in the theatre. The sensibility of artists, sharpened in times of economic scarcity, was heightening everything into the grotesque, the expressive, the derisive. For the first time in decades, Polish artists were starting to be present in mainstream world culture. Film, theatre, music, graphic arts came from various directions and intrepidly joined the world-class level. When I think about the set of theatre inspirations accessible in Kraków in the years of my first studies (1973–7) it was simply mind-blowing: Dejmek, Jarocki, Swinarski, Grzegorzewski, Kantor, Tomaszewski, Grotowski and many others. It cannot be denied that there was no better place than Kraków to study theatre at that time in Europe.

No, but daydreaming about changing the system was highly premature before 1978. We did not project too much into the future – looking forward, we were expecting, in our lives, more or less the same that we already had, with some shy hope for 'something better' eventually. Our expectations mainly circulated around professional self-realisation. Well, maybe also around the hope of getting a flat, or maybe even getting a car. And maybe getting some access to the wider world, which meant some necessary funds, of course. But still, our simple life was not oriented around material goods. Art seemed to us the most important thing. What is theatre, what is it for, how to make it most interestingly, most effectively? – these were the questions circling my head in those years. After 1978, after Wojtyła was unexpectedly chosen as Pope (John Paul II), the next twelve years of my life turned out to be heavily political, but up to that moment we, the young, were mostly thinking about theatre.

In June 1975, Jerzy Grotowski managed to host, in Wrocław, the Theatres of Nations – a great assembly of the world's off-theatre. Everyone important and famous was there. Eugenio Barba and his Odin Theatre, Andre Gregory and Joseph Chaikin. Robert Schumann with his Bread and Puppet Theatre came, and also Peter Brook. For a few weeks the city was bursting with performances on the streets and piazzas, with parades of orchestras, with shows, displays and discussions. The wind of historical change was blowing in the warm, summer air. The few thousand young people who arrived there from all over Europe felt themselves to be the avant-garde of the new cultural future of the continent. One was staying with friends in flats hastily made accessible, in student residences, and camping.

I was a member of the after-Brzezinka team of Theatre Laboratorium (my initiation into the 'Holy Time' in Brzezinka village took place the previous November). Together with others, I escorted foreigners to the Brzezinka forest for mad runs up streams and crazy somersaults around bonfires. Peter Brook held – together with Grotowski – a mass rally at the Polski Theatre; Grotowski was translating. The atmosphere was revolutionary. 'All these state dramatic theatres, these bureaucracies, these monsters – will not survive!' thundered Brook. The response of the audience was ecstatic whistling and shouting but Brook remained cruelly sober: 'I wonder, would you clap your hands equally strongly if I said that all the people from those theatres should be executed?'

Participating in Gregory's and Chaikin's workshops was an important experience for me, but the decisive one happened to be a three-day workshop with Peter Brook in the 'black' space of the Theatre Laboratorium. Brook, with his exercises brought from Persia and Africa, became for me a 'gateway' to theatrical initiation. He has made it clear that there is a theatre, and yet another 'theatre'. That it is possible to search, like Grotowski did, some mystic quality beside theatre, some 'Human Mass' or some existential transgression. I understood then – and it was like an epiphany to me – that it is the theatre which interests me. That all that mysticism was not so necessary in my case, that I wanted to make fantastic theatre but I did not want to chase some Moby Dick. This realisation had consequences because Tomek Rodowicz and Włodek Staniewski were starting the Gardzienice experience at that time, and some friends – like Iga Rodowicz, for example – went there. But I did not hesitate anymore and, on returning to Kraków, I joined the professional theatre with full confidence. That very same summer, I managed to travel for a short British Council scholarship in the UK. I visited the RSC in Stratford, the Edinburgh Festival and I also hung out for two weeks, high up in the cheapest seats on the balconies of the West End. I was devouring musicals – *Jesus Christ Superstar*, for example, and others, and I confess that they made a strong impression upon me. The world was wide and open, it was bursting with life, with creativity and with infinite possibilities. And I was only at the beginning of my road, ambitious, and already speaking English.

The Master and Margarita? Surely Bulgakov was somewhere in the back of our heads, in our suppressed subconsciousness.

Bulgakov was asking about Good and Evil, about the survival of the values in a world oppressed by tyranny. He was asking about the highest stakes. Bulgakov was calling from the abyss of the deepest Hell of the twentieth century. He was fighting to save, *excuse moi*, Love and Literature, and to win he was ready to have even a devil by his side. In 1984 I wrote *A Pattern of Metaphysical Proofs* (how and why is another story). Following Bulgakov, among other things, I made Satan the main accuser of the self-opinionated, murderous Enlightenment, whose bastard offspring were stifling our freedoms during martial law. In 1989, a miracle happened and the world changed its countenance. Only a few years earlier, nobody would have believed it possible. We have seen, with our own eyes, how deeply the Captain of *Jacques the Fatalist* was mistaken. The course of events in the world turned out to be undetermined by any *fatum*, and the influence of human free will upon them proved to be dominant. In 1989, in front of our eyes, 'the chains got broken'. In a joyful celebration, we proclaimed that we had overthrown Communism. But from the perspective of the next thirty years, one can see, that in fact it was an irreversible breakdown of the dictates of historical teleology, mentioned above many times. It was that breakdown – nothing was supporting historical teleology anymore – which enabled political change, and not vice versa.

65 I cannot continue this story forever. Maybe Scheherazade could, up to the last line of her history from the *One Thousand and One Nights*, but who wants such a long narrative today? To read – aloud, to somebody, or to oneself, in silence – forever? Sorry, impossible.

Are there any histories which never end? In English I know one, here it is:

It was a dark and stormy night, three men sat around a fire, and one said to the others 'Shall I tell you a story?' And his story began thus:

It was a dark and stormy night, three men sat around the fire, and one said to the others, 'Shall I tell you a story?' And his story began thus:

It was a dark and stormy night …

– and so on. It is a circular story and as such we can, in theory at least, read it or recreate it forever. But, of course, understanding after the third line what it is about, we switch off. A similarly structured verse was used by Jerzy Grzegorzewski in his Krakovian adaptation of *The Death of Ivan Ilych* by Tolstoy in 1990. Jan Peszek, who played the main character, sang it when running along the top of a huge graph of his temperature, which was the stage set.

This circular story, by the way, practically requires inserting inverted commas every second line. One could say that it is a particular, slightly monstrous form of the story-within-a-story. Anyway, it is only a clever trick and not the full answer to the question about the possibility of creating a never-ending story.

However, Stanisław Lem picked up the gauntlet and wrote a convincing sketch of such a situation. This is the sixth sally in his *The Cyberiad* collection of stories (1965), in which the constructors Trurl and Clapautius 'created a Demon of the Second Kind, to be able to defeat the Pirate Pugg'. The Little Demon of the Second Kind (a 'magical, thermodynamic, non-classical and statistical' demon), placed over a little hole drilled in the old barrel, caught with the diamond felt-tipped pen whatever elementary senses were being created from Brown's movements of the molecules of air enclosed within. As a result, Pirate Pugg, maniacally thirsty for knowledge and for any new information:

… sat propped up against the barrel and read, as the diamond pen which the Demon employed to record everything it learned from the oscillating atoms squeaked on and on, and he read about how exactly Harlebardonian wrigglers wriggle, and that the daughter of King Petrolius of Labondia is Humpinella, and what Frederick the Second, one of the paleface Kings, had for lunch before he declared war against the Gwendoliths, and how many electron shells of atom of thermion-olium would have, if such an element existed, and what is the cloacal diameter of a small bird called twit, which is painted by the Wabian Marchpanes on their sacrificial urns, and also of the tripartite taste of the oceanic ooze on Polypelagid Diaphana, and of the flower Dybbu-lyk, that beats the Lower Malfundican hunters black and blue when-ever they waken him at dawn, and how to obtain the angle of the base of an irregular icosahedron, and who was the jeweller of Gufus, the left-handed butcher of the Bovants, and the number of volumes on philately to be published in the year seventy thousand on Mari-nautica, and where to find the tomb of Cybrinda the Red-toed, who was nailed to her bed by a certain Clamonder in a drunken fit, and how to tell the difference between the bindlesnurk and an ordinary trundlespiff, and also who has the smallest lateral wumpet in the Uni-verse, and why fan-tailed fleas won't eat moss, and how to play the game of Fratcher-My-Pliss and win, and how many snapdragon seeds there were in a turd into which Abroquian Phiminides stepped, when he stumbled on the Great Albongean Road eight miles outside the valley of Symphic sighs – and little by little his hundred eyes began to swim, and it dawned on him that all this information, entirely true and meaningful in every particular, was absolutely useless, producing such an ungodly confusion that his head ached terribly and his legs trembled. But the Demon of the Second Kind continued to operate at the speed of three hundred million facts per second, and mile after mile of tape coiled out and gradually buried the PhD. pirate beneath its windings, wrapping him, as it were, in a paper web, while the tiny diamond-tipped pen shivered and twitched like one insane, and it seemed to Pugg, that any minute now he would learn the most fabulous, unheard-of things, things that would open up to him the Ultimate Mystery of Being, so he greedily read everything that flew out from under the diamond nib, the drinking songs of the Quaida-cabondish and the sizes of bedroom slippers available on the continent of Cob, with pompons and without, and the number of hairs growing on each brass knuckle of the skew-beezered flummox, and the average width of the fontanel in indigenous stepinfants, and the litanies of the M'hot-t'ma-hon'h conjurers to rouse the reverend Blotto Ben-Blear, and the inaugural catcalls of the Duke of Zilch, and six ways to cook cream of wheat, and a good poison for uncles with goatees, and twelve types of forensic tickling, and the names of all the citizens of Foofaraw Junction beginning with the letter M, and the results of the poll of opinions on the taste of beer mixed with mushroom syrup … And it grew dark before his hundred eyes, and he cried out in a mighty voice that he'd had enough, but Information had so swathed and swaddled him in its three hundred thousand tangled paper miles, that he couldn't move and had to read on.

The quotation may seem too long, but it cannot be made shorter if the idea and the unbelievable achievement of the author within the art of writing a never-ending story are to be praised. Lem would not be himself, of course, if he did not foresee at the end of this story yet another consequence of his idea:

… and so poor Pugg, crushed beneath that avalanche of fact, learns no end of things about rickshaws, rents and roaches, and about his own fate, which has been related here, for that too is included in some section of the tape – as are the histories, accounts and prophesies of all things in creation, up until the stars burn out; and there is no hope for him, since this is the harsh sentence the constructors passed upon him for his pirately assault – unless of course the tape runs out, for the lack of paper.
(Trans. Michael Kandel)

That 'own fate included in some section of the tape' is, of course, a variant of the 'It was a dark and stormy night'. With such a concept, human language would be some infinitely long, never-ending Möbius strip, a limited collection of syllables which, after a million years, simply cannot avoid combining, statistically, its repetitions. This thought would lead us straight to the repetitive time of the ancients. And also to Laplace's demon, that is, to a theoretically possible abstract being who has knowledge about the position of every elementary particle in the universe and about every force acting upon it. Thanks to such knowledge, a 'Laplace's demon' would be capable of replaying all of the past and would also be able to foresee the movements of every object in the universe in the future. This is the purest possible determinism and the purest fatalism. Luckily, such a prospect is excluded − within the present state of knowledge − thanks to Heisenberg's 'uncertainty principle', which posits that the exact state of a particle cannot be established, and which means that it is not possible to foresee its state in the future.

Therefore, even if the arrival of the end of the 'tyranny of the End' is true, it does not mean that suddenly stories will cease to have final pages. We cannot wait, like Pirate Pugg, for the moment when the paper tape ends on my side (me being in such a case the equivalent of the Demon of the Second Kind) or when the cosmos will stop. This is what I am going to do: I will add a few more speculations which impatiently nudge me to my keyboard and then, after some time, the full stop will come.

66 'What was that performance about?' we sometimes ask ourselves, the next day or some time afterwards. 'What did the poet want to say?' That vexed question of the schoolteacher may even hound us. Well, theatre plays can be about something or about nothing. The latter ones most often are not worth staging, because the most frequent result of staging a play about nothing is a performance about nothing.

Although it is not a rule. I remember an unusual theatre experience at an Italian festival many years ago. A group of talented Spanish actors created a performance based upon some local Spanish telephone book. The show was about anonymity in a big city, about human loneliness and the desperate need for contact. The show provoked both tears of laughter and tears of sadness. Its authors knew how to operate the structure of theatre with the help of the simplest means. Using only the names (often exotic or strange), and surprising combinations of telephone signals, they were able to tell us many unexpected things about modern man. Somebody will say: Well, the telephone book is – in contrast to so many published and staged dramatic texts – *about* something. This is true, but this example proves the creativity of theatre, which always has a chance of saying something important, even from weak material.

On the other hand, there are also plays which are so obtrusively about something that one does not want to stage them, nor to watch them. *An Optimistic Tragedy* (Vsevolod Vishnevsky, 1933) for example, or Karhan Grinder's *Brigade* (Vasek Kana, 1949), or hundreds of other similarly engaged dramatic texts. Engaged politically or religiously. We know it well: whenever the stage becomes a vehicle for propaganda, the spectator longs to see a pantomime or *The Pâté of a Baroness*. What is farce about?

At the beginning of martial law, a certain Party Secretary, responsible at that time for culture, explained to us, the directing students at the theatre school, what our shows should be about. About the spiritual richness of socialist man, he said. And also about the moral rottenness of capitalism – that was how he formulated it. Afterwards, we sang the text of his speech in the school's cabaret. Thanks to this speech that cabaret was decidedly about something.

What is *The Csardas Princess* (Emmerich Kálmán, 1915) about? About nothing. However, for over a hundred years it has been staged everywhere, incessantly, continually. A fabulous nothingness of an operetta? Its 'divine idiotism' – as Gombrowicz put it – its 'heavenly sclerosis?' Most probably, yes. Also, the phenomenally catchy music of Kálmán. And yet it is not the case that all fans of *The Csardas Princess* are, without exception, sclerotic idiots.

Operetta, somebody will say, is a completely separate category, incomparable with dramatic texts. Apart from the music, nothing should really matter in an operetta or a musical. All right, what is *The Comedy of Errors* about, then? And what is *As You Like It* about?

Many years ago, the nothingness of *As You Like It* provoked the anger of a young Peter Brook. In September 1957 he published, in *The Sunday Times*, an open letter to the Bard:

> I don't like your *As You Like It*. I'm sorry, but I find it far too hearty, a sort of advertisement for a beer, unpoetic and, frankly, not very funny. When you have one villain repenting because he's nearly been eaten by a lion and another villain at the head of his army converted from the world because he happens to meet an old religious man and has some question for him, I really lose all patience. So now, dear author, I don't know what to say. I find most of your plays miraculous – except *As You Like It*. The critics find most of your plays a bore – except *As You Like It*. The public loves them all – including *As You Like It*.

Must the theatre necessarily be 'about something'? In one of the main Polish dailies, I have just read yet more solemn praise of new writing by young Polish playwrights. All these new texts, an influential critic writes, although frequently imperfect, deserve praise because they are all about something. They are about drug addiction, about prostitution, about alcoholism, about violence in families, about joblessness and about oppressed sexual minorities. Let us hope, the critic says, that in the next season we continue to have a lot of new texts and that they continue to be about something, that is, about joblessness, about violence, about the oppressed minorities, about drug addiction, about prostitution and about alcoholism.

The formula of the Party Secretary mentioned above seems to me, I confess, more accurate: about something, that is, about the moral rottenness of capitalism. And therefore, I am inclined to propose a staging of at least one play about nothing in every Polish theatre next season (when it is possible in the context of Covid).

The thirty-two-year-old Peter Brook, when provocatively questioning the value of *As You Like It*, knew very well, of course, what he was doing. It was from *As You Like It*, from the long monologue of Touchstone in the fifth act, that he borrowed the polysemous 'If' in the paragraph ending his book *The Empty Space* (1968): 'In everyday life, "If" is a fiction, in the theatre "if" is an experiment. In everyday life "if" is an evasion, in the theatre "if" is the truth.'

67 There's been a lot about the ending; let us then return, for a while, to the beginning. In essence, beginnings in theatre – in literature, too! – are always most interesting because at the beginning everything is possible and therefore everything is good. The curtain rises or opens to the sides, eventually the house lights go down and the stage becomes brighter. Sounds appear, or some shadows flicker, somebody on stage stands immobile, or somebody crosses the space: it's started. We correct our position in our seat, our attention is concentrated at the highest level. We have been invited to an entirely new world; the first seconds and minutes will decide how we see this new world. A whoosh of wind, a thud of metal being torn, a piece of fabric billowing over the board of the stage and a scream: 'Captain, Ahoy!' and we immediately know that we are in the middle of the sea, in the eye of the storm.

Or darkness and some mysterious figures hidden within it, a question delivered with a low voice: 'Who's there?', and then a pressing demand, 'Unfold yourself!' – after a few lines from the sentries we understand that we are on the walls of Elsinore and that midnight has just struck.

During these first minutes of every performance, virtually nothing escapes our attention. The light, the colour of the walls, the shape of the furniture, the kinds of costumes, whispers and sounds – all these elements combine to create the uniqueness of this world. The world which is usually so much more interesting when it is distanced from the everyday world left behind at the doors of the theatre. This new world fascinates us because it is unexpected, it is surprising, it is different. This is a process of learning a new language: A for apple, B for bee, C for cat … the creators of the performance (author, director, actors) introduce us, during the first dozen or so minutes, to an alphabet which was unknown to us until now. They introduce us to a dictionary which is binding in their world. We devour their signals eagerly and usually with no restrictions – our satisfaction in the future minutes and hours of the show will depend upon our fast learning of this code. No, usually we do not resist at all at the very beginning. Everything is possible at the beginning because even the most surprising, inexplicable or shocking event happening at the beginning will find (it has to!) its explanation or solution in the course of further events.

This first quarter of an hour is like charging a battery. Here is a lonely old man on a wheelchair: a whole minute will pass before he removes a stained handkerchief from his face. And another minute will pass before he cleans his dark glasses with the handkerchief, and yet another before he utters, slowly, his first words. In the fourth minute of *Endgame*, we already know that in this particular, extraordinary world, every spoken word will be priceless. The author wanted to awaken precisely such a type of sensibility in the audience and planned the beginning of *Endgame* meticulously to achieve this. A director or an actor who decides to defraud him would be simply ignorant.

This natural lack of resistance among the spectators at the beginning of every theatrical journey is a blessing for the theatre. It permits it to invite the audience into regions which are strange, full of risk, which are even crazy. It permits it to engage the spectators, to fascinate them, to charm them, to woo them. It makes even a well-known text resound with new meanings, unveil new contexts, new senses. It makes every evening in the theatre an unrepeatable event.

But this credit of trust, this unselfish openness of the audience towards the new dictionary, is never without conditions. It is difficult to measure precisely the moment when, like in a game of poker, the audience says: 'I check'. Sometimes it happens in the twelfth minute, sometimes after half an hour, but it always happens. It is a moment, or rather a longer time, while the fate of the performance is being decided. 'I like your alphabet, I got engaged and intrigued by your signals, rhythms, voices and actions, and therefore I shall remain until the end, and I will follow the course of events with great curiosity' thinks a spectator (most often not conscious that he/she does it). And this is when it is good. However, equally often, that 'I check' of the audience comes in the form of impatience, or even of an open reluctance: 'For over half an hour I was diligently learning your alphabet but your letters do not construct any words, your words do not build phrases. In your world I do not find a language, but gibberish; I shall leave during the break.' And then only a quarter of the audience stays after the interval.

It is a quite extraordinary phenomenon that an audience consisting of a few hundred people literally reacts 'like one person'. Whoever has had the chance to be an actor knows it. There are people of different ages in the audience, people of different cultures, diverse passions and interests, and in spite of all that, their reactions, their laughs, their breathing stopping suddenly, or their nervous sniggers are collective, shared together and symbiotic. This does not mean that there is no person among the audience who doesn't like anything, nor a person who is delighted by everything. There are always people from the extremes of the spectrum. But in spite of that, the reception of a show is being decided by the spontaneous, common, strangely democratic, reaction of the majority of the present spectators, almost always unanimously. Whether the performance went 'fantastically well' or was only 'so-so', or went really badly, on both sides of the stage, one simply 'knows' it after the show is over.

After a good performance we exit from the theatre literally 'walking on air' and we want to return there as soon as possible, tomorrow at best. But shows which give wings to the audience do not happen every day. They may happen, sometimes, only once in a few years. Between them we remain condemned to watch a few dozen evidently bad shows. Awaiting their end, we hang our heads, we moan, and we swear to ourselves that we shall never step into a theatre again.

This 'good theatre', so instantly recognised on both sides of the stage – what is it? That theatre which has us walking on air – how does it happen? I will risk an answer: it is the unexpected sharing of a commonly felt emotional and intellectual energy between the actors and the spectators in a given 'here and now'. It is a shock, a jump spark; it is, in a purely Aristotelian sense, a cathartic concussion. It is not important whether it is a tragedy or a comedy: in good theatre, forgotten truths become discoveries, unknown feelings become emotional reality. Our individual place in the universe and in society gains, for a time, completely new coordinates. In society, I insist, because good theatre is never the 'theatre of one spectator', the measure of its artistic efficiency is precisely the ability of unifying, emotionally, a collective, which becomes very diverse again outside of the building. But a theatre without spectators would be a nonsense. It would not be a theatre at all.

§ Pshish-wam, pshih-waash,
Pshesh-wam du-zho,
Du-zho pshesh-wam, no, to zash-wam.
Wad-nesh zash-wa, pshish-wa, nash-wa,
Bo on pshi-shedu, zhe-by zash-wa.
A gje zash-wo to, so pshish-wo,
Ke-dy zash-wash, pshe-che zesh-wo?
Stong zash-wash-chong pshe-he pshish-wo,
Zash-wo bo shong, zneem-o besh-wash.

These chanted sounds were physically pushing an acoustic wave upon the viewers. One could feel it on one's skin. Seven young actors in track suits, arms linked together, moved through the empty space of the stage. They were creating a multi-armed monster with many tentacles, a polymorphous bacterium with a dozen mouths. They were changing places continually, from the back to the front, from the left to the right, like a snow plough. They were consciously bending their arms and their bodies, all the while snorting saliva. Syllables and letters irregularly burst from them like steam from a steam engine. And the syllables were hissing, fizzing, rumbling, purring, and rustling:

Pshesh-washch, pshish-washch, vish- washch, nasch-washch,
Dosh-washch, vish-washch, posh-washch, zash-washch.

I find them once again, my red-haired Audrey and somehow-slightly older Umberto, among a small group of viewers at the matinee show of *Szłość samojedna* by the student Pleonasmus Theatre in the student-residence block. They are both enchanted by the performance. They are not able to hear and to pick up all of the jungle concert of rustling and fizzing Polish, of course, but the ambitious plan of the director connects with them strongly: language as a superior power, primordial and creative. A tsunami of burning sounds pouring from the actors' throats, swamping everything in its way. A victorious cavalcade of human expression, language as the only natural ambience of the human, ravenous protozoan.

It is the autumn of 1974, Audrey and Umberto are immersing themselves in the multileveled climate of Kraków in the years of late, real socialism. Wojtyła is not Pope yet and Poland, at least for now, is for them rather far from the Iron Curtain. Their local friend Witold has just gone to the Brzezinka event of Jerzy Grotowski's to discover there, in the forests and streams, the blasphemous, secular *Holy Times* and *The Mountains of Flame*. I am eavesdropping on Audrey and Umberto and wondering what to do with them next.

Here I am revealing myself, dear reader, whoever you may be, in this moment. Yes, it is I who tangle the threads of Audrey and Umberto and their various adventures. And yes, it is I who remain responsible for the not-very-refined coordination of their travels in time and space. Roughly, I wanted to make them a modern European pair, credibly in love, and I wanted to ask them after some time what would happen if one of them suddenly went missing. Because of an accident, because of illness, because of fate. It is probably clear that I wanted to ask – in the very same way I could ask my beloved – how to live day after day with such a perspective?

But after some time, I confess, I have lost the courage to give any answers to such a question. I do not know whether I am ready to give answers. I do not know whether it would be proper to give them, to fantasise about them. I do not know whether it would be proper to 'measure', even only in the imagination, the variants of a possible future.

Not really knowing what to do, I find a temporary solution. Let the twenty-second ode of Horace, 'To Leuconoe', be the end point:

You should not ask – to know is a sin – which end
the gods have given to me, or to you, Leuconoe, nor
should you meddle with Babylonian calculations.
How much better to suffer
whatever will be, whether Jupiter gives us more winters, or
    whether
this is our last,
which now weakens the Tyrrhenian Sea on the pumice
    stones
opposing it. Be wise, strain the wine, and cut back long
    hope
into a small space. While we talk, envious time will
have fled: pluck the day, trusting as little as possible to the
    future.

Audrey and Umberto are slowly falling asleep in their room, embraced, fatigued with the impressions of the day. I could transfer them now during their sleep to the other side of the globe – do I know where? – to Calgary, or to Pittsburgh, or even to some places to which I have never found a way myself. I could transfer them to medieval Florence, or to ancient Ravenna. To the Venice of Goldoni, or to the London of Shakespeare. I could shoot them to some galaxy a hundred light years away, but I am not going to do it.

'Audrey, we need to talk,' Umberto murmurs, closing his eyes.

'We need to talk, Umberto, we shall do it tomorrow,' Audrey murmurs back.

'We have all the time in the world.'

'Do we? Do we?'

And this is how we shall, temporarily, leave them.

69

The 'passage' described earlier by Salvadori – let us repeat it, a passage from 'the ideology of a totalitarian *"end of History"'* to the 'continually refreshed "beginning of history", understood as an incidental product of many individuals of flesh and blood, given a freedom of action and remaining open to the unpredictable future', inevitably makes us face the problem of relativism. One can even formulate it more strongly: it places us face to face with the perspective of Nietzschean nihilism, whether we want it or not.

Gianni Vattimo, a proponent of 'weak thought', writes: 'There are no facts, there are only interpretations, and this phrase is also an interpretation' (*Beyond Interpretation: The Meaning of Hermeneutics for Philosophy*, 1994). He explains: 'The truth is an interpretation, therefore every verification or falsification of any position must be happening only within a horizon of the earlier opening, which is not transcendental, but constitutes our heritage, and nihilism is a "logical" consequence of this.' Then he adds:

> the 'Nihilistic' sense of hermeneutics: if we do not think that the switch of the metaphysics of presence for the ontology of origins was a correction of the mistake, but rather we think that the switch is an event of the very being, that it is an indication of its 'destiny', which is a tendency to weaken – seen as such exclusively upon a base of the metaphysical category of fullness, of presence – showing up in this way of thinking, then this is exactly the truth of nihilism of Nietzsche, the sense of the death of God and, what follows, the sense of blurring the truth as eternal and 'objective' proof; up till now philosophers believed that they are describing the world, now one needs to interpret it.

The integrity of intentions of 'weak thought' and of an 'ontology of origins' impresses me strongly. But I have an essential problem with these particular 'logical consequence of nihilism'.

This jump seems to me to be too fast, too rapid. Maybe this jump is 'logically consequent' indeed, but its abruptness and bluntness seem to ignore the objective, naked attributes of life.

The next morning, after reading Vattimo, I read, let's say, that two trains have collided. Sixteen are dead, but sixty are fighting for their lives in hospital. I discovered it on the Internet, no doubt, but does it mean that all sixty victims of the accident, from this interpretation, are in the same medical state between life and death? No, clearly some of them are only slightly wounded, and some of them are not alive anymore. The main attribute of reality is the fact that it simply 'is', rather than being an interpretation of what 'being' is. People get born, they live, and they die, in that precise order. At the end, as someone wrote, 'Nietzsche died', and that someone signed this phrase as 'God'. I want to believe that philosophers believe that they interpret the world, but when one describes a railroad accident one wants to get an understanding of it, in a strong, decisive sense, and not a 'weak' interpretation of it.

Is my somewhat desperately invented argument about the train accident convincing enough to weaken the reasoning of Vattimo? Am I capable of undermining his reasoning?

I am looking around me and I find that unexpected help comes from Umberto Eco, in his lecture titled 'An Absolute and Relativity', written in 2007. It was published in the tome *On the Shoulders of Giants*, which presents Eco's lectures given every year at the festival *La Milanesiana*. Eco starts with the extrapolation of Cardinal Ratzinger who, in 2002, in his work *Il Monoteismo*, accused modern philosophical thought of 'rejecting the criteria of truth, of good and of evil'. Its alleged consequence, according to the cardinal, is that nowadays 'there is no place for the idea of God'. 'This extrapolation,' Eco writes:

cannot be defended, unless one identifies all modern thought with a claim that there are no facts, there are only interpretations, from where one can get to the claim that there is no basis of being, therefore God has died and, finally, if there is no God everything is possible.

Afterwards, Eco documents the origin of a key claim by Nietzsche (*About Truth and Lies in the Extra-Moral Sense*, 1896) and its original contexts, and finally he writes:

The view, which proposes that there are no facts but only interpretations, is not shared by all modern thought. Its main part propounds objections against Nietzsche and his followers, such as: 1) Were there no facts, but only interpretations, what would an interpretation of an interpretation be? 2) If interpretations were to interpret one another, there would have to be an object or a first event, which is an impulse to interpreting. 3) Even if being was not possible to be described, one should say who are we who speak about it metaphorically, and the need to say something truthful would move from the object into the subject of cognition.

Finally, Eco concludes:

So maybe the absolute does not exist – or, if it exists, it is not imaginable nor reachable – but there are natural forces which support our interpretations or defy them. If in my interpretation the open door on the illusionistic painting is the real door and if I walk straight into it, then the fact that one cannot go through it will deny my interpretation.

Phew, aided by that authority, I direct a question to Vattimo: briefly, what about the theodicy? I know very well what his answer would be, should he choose to answer. He would say that the question has no sense, that it is badly formulated, that it is not his cup of tea. And should I ask any question about any 'fullness' of being, or about any 'whole', or about any 'presence', he would say I have completely misunderstood his thinking.

In this moment, *Happiness in Unhappiness* – Odo Marquard's words – come to my aid.

70 I like immensely Odo Marquard, who defends human imperfection and who wrote:

> An Absolute – that what is perfect and extraordinary – does not lie within the borders of human possibilities, because people are limited beings. They should not be led in their practice by the motto 'all or nothing': what is human lies in the middle, the truth is a half.

He was born in Stolp, that is, in today's Slupsk. In 1945, in his eleventh year, he became a soldier of the *Volkssturm* and a prisoner of war.

Paul K. Feyerabend, the later author of *Against Method*, also found himself in captivity as a very young official of the *Wehrmacht* at the same time, in Czestochowa. Odo Marquard, only a year later, passed his maturity exam in Treysa (Hessen) and soon became a serious philosopher. His third book, after *Break-up with the Principles* and *Praise of Haphazardness*, I had an occasion to read. This one is about *Happiness in Unhappiness*.

'The fullness of happiness is not for people,' writes Marquard:

> for them – among all the misfortunes – only the imperfect happiness is possible, a happiness in unhappiness. The question about happiness is abstract if we pose it as separated from the question of unhappiness. To have everything beneficial at hand and to not have anything which is harmful, this is simply not possible. Pure happiness is not of this world. In this world, in the world people live in, happiness exists always beside unhappiness, in spite of unhappiness or even because of unhappiness: our own, somebody else's, or both. Human happiness – in the most elementary sense – is always only happiness in unhappiness.

Marquard is a philosopher of human scale. He does not build systems, he does not search for the Holy Grail; he honestly tries to understand whatever can be understood and he transmits his reasoning in simple, clear language. He is an anti-fundamentalist, he does not believe in any 'absolute basics' of knowledge or of cognition. He does not believe in any absolute hierarchies, methods or aims. He emphasises incessantly the contingency, that is, the natural randomness of human existence, and he mocks philosophical projects which try to negate this randomness. Because of that, he does not like revolution nor revolutionaries; he is conservative and he values the old, customary ways of proceeding. The *indispensability of the common practices* is for him a safe port on the ocean of the transitory. He is a sceptic who values a bird in the hand more than the one in the bush. 'Humans are beings who must, who can and who do something for something else; everyone – far from any absolute – originally is shoddy, and therefore a homo compensator.'

Marquard uses the category of compensation in a surprisingly wide way. For example, the birth and development of the modern humanistic sciences represents for him the multi-generational process of the compensation of pre-industrial 'little motherlands', lost by modernity. He is not nostalgic; Marquard treasures and praises modernity and bravely defends it from expected threats. But first of all, Marquard is a philosopher who has his own concept of the history of philosophy, a concept as original as some poet's idea of a poem or some director's concept of a show. In his explanation, he does not lose time on notes or references, he simply knows that it is as he knows, by which he brings his colleagues, other German philosophers – Jürgen Habermas first – to the brink of cardiac arrest.

To present it briefly: according to Marquard, humanity has an eternal problem with God or, more precisely, with the fact that it is difficult to reconcile His eventual existence with the existence of real evil. This is where *Ecclesiastes*, *The Book of Job* and the excesses of *Gnosis* came from. And this is also why the *Theodicy of Leibniz* (1710) had to be written. For Marquard, practically the whole of modernity is a reaction to the defeat of that classical theodicy – that is, the defeat of the effort to justify the existence of evil in the world. The result is that humanity starts to have a problem not only with God but with the lack of God, despite the unchanged reality of evil. All the modern philosophy of history (Hegel, later Marx), says Marquard, used a *teleology of unhappiness* and explained the evil of today with a promise of accounting for it in the future. In fact, all of the modern philosophy of history was for him equally ineffective, like its predecessor, at conducting a successful theodicy. Today we are weaving our contingency, that is, our randomness, on the ruins of that process. And even more: the consequence of the human struggle for the last, almost three hundred years (since Leibniz), with the scandal of evil and with the lack of a possible explanation of its existence, is a continuous, unrelenting 'great modern process of detracting from the evil, the marks of evil'. Marquard describes this great process and documents it in a very convincing way.

I am sorry, but no 'logical consequences of nihilism' by Vattimo can help us here: evil creeps out from life and history like a worm from a ripe apple. It is indelible, it cannot be omitted. It creeps out like the character of the Drunkard in *The Marriage* by Gombrowicz, and it is rooted in us. It keeps marring everything and derailing and destroying. With its thought, with its speech, with its deeds, with its temptation and neglect. When Mikhail Bulgakov makes Satan (named Woland) a conductor of a Moscovian ball of witches, he is following Goethe, of course. He wants to see Voland's role as a 'part of that power which eternally wills evil and eternally works good'.

And yet the fact that evil remains indelible from the rich tapestry of our lives in fact exists in a much more subtle sense than is suggested by this quote. Certainly, its presence is not about taking sides in any fantastical or religious psychomachia. Without evil, goodness becomes more difficult to understand, this is true, but it is the provocative co-existence of both Good and Evil which enables the appearance of a fragile ladder of values. The values which permit us to talk about 'humanity' at all. Gombrowicz was most probably right when he wrote that people 'produce love from themselves, like alcohol from potatoes', but in this landscape of history continually restarting from the beginning, the 'love' in *The Master and Margarita* is nevertheless safe from the perspective of an unforeseeable future.

He is quite an unbelievable philosopher, this Odo Marquard. He knows that he is slightly different, and this is why he values pluralism:

> From the scientific point of view, the most desired situation in philosophy is the one where there are as few needless philosophers as possible. The philosopher is not needless when he is different than other philosophers. Because of that — in the name of true pluralism — there has to be many very different philosophers.

I am only twenty-one years younger than Marquard. In the German Hindenburg, where I was born ten years after the war, all the floors and the walls, all the chairs and the tables in our flat were German. Every person close to me spoke in an Eastern Polish dialect. In the eleventh year of my life, I waved a tri-coloured banner, herded onto the street to welcome the French General de Gaulle. De Gaulle was hailing Zabrze (Hindenburg) as, I am quoting: 'The most Polish of all Polish cities'. When I compare myself to Marquard I dare to think that I was extremely lucky — in my unhappiness. Marquard ends his essay with an anonymous quotation: 'It would be best to be not born at all; well, but who can say he was so lucky?'

71 As an ordinary Doctor of the Theatre Arts with a post-doctoral degree, do I have the right to philosophise? More precisely, when I dare to touch, with my sacrilegious hands, the works of Vattimo, of Marquard, of Agamben or Rorty, do I have the right to have a serious conversation with them? May I comment upon their findings in some mature, philosophical way? Or maybe I am only permitted to quote them from the abyss of my ignorance and, generally, I should just be silent?

Their questions rankle me; what is philosophy for, if it wants to separate itself from my experience in some kind of ivory tower? The reflections of philosophers upon people's self-recognition in the stream of historical time concern me, in my own life, and as such cannot be indifferent to me. Philosophers usually help me to understand my/our situation; with their help I would like to try to move myself out of the proverbial cave of Plato.

Plato's metaphor of the limitation of our cognition (we are like some bound slaves, sitting in the cave with our backs to the exit, and there are flickering shadows on the walls which we follow while we should in fact break away from these constraints and step freely into the world) always struck me with its theatricality. I was not alone; a certain friend of mine, a philosopher from Kraków, regularly created this situation at his seminars with students. The students held strings, handkerchiefs, or whatever there was at hand (these were supposed to be the chains they were in) and looked at the wall. The professor used sunny weather and presented variously shaped shadows on the same wall. The students guessed the objects. For example, they said 'A cat!', while in fact these were scissors; or 'A ruler!', while in fact it was a square. That *limes* of human cognition, shown as a little theatre of treacherous shadows in *modus platonicum*, was very popular for two semesters, until the moment when one of the students suddenly threw away the strings and handkerchiefs altogether and turned around and shouted: 'A professor on a chair, with an umbrella in his hands!'

This is exactly the scale of revolution (but a worldwide one) postulated in the works of Richard Rorty, an outstanding American philosopher, who died in 2007. In the book gathering his last, dispersed articles, titled *Philosophy as Cultural Politics*, his appeal is particularly strong: 'We should not be realists, nor anti-realists; the whole issue of realism–anti-realism should be abolished', writes Rorty. Elsewhere, he adds:

> Those who are on the neo-Kantian side of this split take for granted that Plato was right to postulate a permanent ahistorical matrix for human thought: to attempt to cut things at their joints by making such distinctions as knowledge–opinion, reality–appearance, reason–passion, and logic–rhetoric. Those on the other side follow Hegel in thinking that those distinctions and many others (e.g., mind–body, subjective–objective, transcendental–empirical, realist–anti-realist, representationalist–inferentialist, Kantian–Hegelian, analytic–conversational) are temporary expedients that will sooner or later become obsolete.

Those, who – following Hegel – reject such 'obsolete' tools of thought, according to Rorty, *do* construct 'a new philosophical world'. Rorty explains:

> In this new world, we will not think anymore that thoughts and language include the representations of reality. We shall emancipate ourselves from the issue subject–object, which has dominated philosophy since Cartesius, and from the issue of appearance–reality, which was with us since the Greeks. We shall not feel the temptation of pursuing either epistemology, or ontology, anymore.

Rorty announces a historical decline of philosophy, a discipline called by him *'a temporary genre'* on the human road towards an upcoming 'literary culture'. In this new culture, the narrations called 'philosophical' will lose their privileged status among other kinds of description of reality. The *Ding an sich* of Kant, the '*thing-in-itself*', is just a distant, secularised heritage of Plato and is a pure misunderstanding, says the American. No 'real', ideal reality exists, different from the one which all of us experience and which we describe using the only accessible tools we have: the terms formulated in our ever-changing language. Rorty writes:

> There is no cognitive access to the objects without terms [ideas, concepts]. Our only cognitive access to the beavers, trees, stars, to our subjectivity, or to our transcendent *I* consists of our ability to formulate such expressions as *beaver, tree, star, subjectivity* and *transcendental I*.

Rorty seriously attacks Jürgen Habermas (it is the American's final statement in his decades-long debate with the important European philosopher) for his notorious attempts to connect the 'communicative reason', distinguished in Habermas's *Philosophical Discourse of Modernity*, with the search for '*other than reason*'. Rorty, evidently irritated, writes:

> Habermas uses the latter term to characterise such things as mystic insight, poetic inspiration, religious faith, imaginative power, and authentic self-expression – sources of conviction that have been put forward as superior to reason. ... Both Habermas and I do not trust metaphysics. But where he thinks, that – to avoid the allure of Romanticism – we need to find the interpretation of the concept of universal significance which would be free from metaphysics, I think that such a concept and metaphysics are inseparable.

In Rorty's 'new world', consequently demystified from metaphysics, there is simply no place for any '*other than reason*'. The radical pragmatism of Richard Rorty (he called himself a 'neo-Hegelian holist') may be convincing or not. Yet if one believes in his prognostics – even experimentally – the situation of the Theatre in the age of 'the emancipation of philosophy from the appearance–reality issue' becomes incredibly interesting. That issue is, after all, the core, the very essence, of theatre. Let's add: it is also the essence of all literary fiction. The dance of reality and appearance of truth and fiction is a part of the constitution of every kind of theatre (as well as literature). If Rorty is right, grumpy philosophers will have to forsake, after two millennia, their barren analyses of reality treated as a doubtful show, deliberately performed in front of our eyes by an anonymous producer. Rorty writes with passion about:

> the need of relinquishing the combined ideas of a 'philosophical method' and 'philosophical problems'. In my opinion the popularity of these concepts is an unfortunate consequence of the excessive professionalisation of philosophy, a professionalisation deforming that area since the times of Kant.

After which, he proclaims: 'I do not see any need of any sharp distinction between the works of imagination proposed by philosophers and similar works proposed by non-philosophers.' Enough of the pompous 'distorted speech' of the experts: 'Philosophers – stick to words, and the game of appearances leave to the actors!' Rorty seems to call. In such a view, the Theatre seems to be regaining the primordial glitter of its particular discipline, because it is the one which plays with fire. But also, this is an 'impure' discipline, one which openly and shamelessly deals with a lie.

Would the Theatre accept at any time the status implied by Rorty's ideas, the status of a discipline 'of openly untrue, illusionistic tricks'? Theatre, apart from all its possible technical tricks, always was, and still invariably remains, the proponent of the unnamed, the speaker of the unspoken, the medium of the unknown. The postulated, radical breaking of the spell between reality and its fictional representations in Rorty's version looks to me a bit like an overly strong emetic.

Therefore, while listening with the greatest curiosity to his ideas about the 'historical decline of philosophy', I would rather reserve some scepticism towards such a possibility.

72 We need to say something more about ghosts and, concretely, about the ghosts in *A Midsummer Night's Dream*. How did Pedro de Uzeda explain ghosts in Jan Potocki's *The Manuscript Found in Saragossa*?

> Señor, huge changes, huge changes take place in the netherworld! Empuses, larvae and lamias were appearing from the most ancient times, but ghouls for example, belong to the new discoveries. I distinguish two different kinds between them, the Hungarian ghouls and the Polish ones. Both are simply corpses exiting from their tombs to suck human blood. But there are also the Spanish ones, which – entering the first encountered body – shape it into whatever form and – belonging to the kin of Satan – cause the most horrible tortures to the living.

Let us look around, for a while, at the spirit world of the Athenian Forest. When the madness of Midsummer's Night in the forest reaches its zenith, when half-conscious lovers stray in the deep thicket and Titania pulls Bottom-morphed-into-a-Donkey to her bed, Puck, the main culprit of this whole mess, urges Oberon to take action:

> My fairy lord, this must be done with haste,
> For night's swift dragons cut the clouds full fast;
> And yonder shines Aurora's harbinger,
> At whose approach ghosts, wandering here and there,

Troop home to churchyards. Damned spirits all,
That in cross-ways and floods have burial,
Already to their wormy beds are gone,
For fear lest day should look their shames upon;
They wilfully themselves exil'd from light,
And must for aye consort with black-brow'd night.

Oberon answers his servant with surprising assurance: 'But we are spirits of another sort.'

Of 'another sort' – therefore of which particular sort? If the 'Damned spirits all' are all damned, their proper place is in Hell. They should not be 'in cross-ways' or in 'floods'. The saved souls stay in Heaven, while the damned souls fry in Hell. What kind of spirits fly away so hurriedly from the light of the morning – what's more, what kind of spirits are so basically different ('another sort') from Puck and Oberon?

Well, those 'ghosts ... wandering here and there' and 'trooping home to churchyards' are exactly like those in *Forefathers' Eve* by Mickiewicz – the souls suffering the tortures of Purgatory. The souls which, in late Renaissance England, were subdued by radical persecution. 'There is no single word about Purgatory in the whole Scriptures!' – Simon Fish, one of the early Protestant agitators, thundered in 1529 – 'Purgatory was invented to convince people that the Pope has the power to absolve every felony. Not only here, where people live, but also after Death.' There was no place for Purgatory in the doctrine of the victorious Anglican Church.

Purgatory is a fraud, it is an 'illusion and phantasy', it is a 'whimsy of the poet', as the preacher William Tyndale put it (Tyndale who, by the way, suffered a martyr's death for attacking Purgatory). This is why, at the end of the sixteenth century, the souls from Purgatory must hide outside Athens in 'crossways and floods'. The 'whimsies of the poet' were exiled to their proper place – to the Theatre.

The key role of Purgatory in the Protestant revolution is widely described in the works of Stephen Greenblatt, the prime mover of the so-called 'New Historicism' in contemporary literary research. The doctrine of Purgatory was adapted by the Catholic Church rather late. 'Purgatory did not exist before the year 1170 and this is the earliest possible date', acknowledges Jacques Le Goff, a well-known Medievalist. In that period, the concept of Purgatory as an intermediate place between Heaven and Hell, and the system of indulgences which were supposed to help the souls imprisoned in that place, started to seem, to the faithful, necessary for the institutional structure and for the authority of the Church. The theological intricacies were not important, Purgatory became necessary as a part of a wider understanding of the existence of the nature of faith and of the structure of the family and of the parish.

The possibility of helping the dear deceased with a prayer, of breaking the chains in which their souls were held, the possibility of helping them pass from suffering to the land of eternal joy, became part of common faith. 'Purgatory created a distinct channel of communication between the living and the deceased, or rather permitted the deceased to be not fully deceased' writes Greenblatt. It also enabled – through the course of time – the flowering of a whole industry of indulgences, intercessions, prayers and masses for the dead, for which one paid with serious currency. For example, King Henry VII, the father of Henry VIII, took care to have 10,000 masses celebrated immediately after his death for the absolution of his sins and for the peace of his soul. Ten thousand masses!

To ardent Protestants, the concept of Purgatory and the elaborate ceremonialism of the Roman liturgy, the golden array, paintings, votive offerings and statues, seemed the tools of some treacherous Theatre. The heavily decorated copes, albas and stoles were sold directly to the theatre on the dissolution of the monasteries, Greenblatt reminds us. The actors of the

Globe Theatre were most probably acting in authentic liturgical robes in the Chronicles. In the desacralised robes, of course, but the robes were still endowed with some symbolic power from their former usage. Therefore, they were costumes which were attractive for the theatre. 'When in 1603 Samuel Harsnett whipped the exorcisms towards the theatre (a publication of his was *A Declaration of Egregious Popish Impostures*)', Greenblatt notes, Shakespeare was already using this text at the Globe. The exorcism, that deceitful 'ceremony of playing the holy miracles' (Harsnett's words), that almost open 'Theatre of Satan', had to share the fate of Purgatory in Protestantism. However, Edgar – Mad Tom in *King Lear* – when simulating his state of possession speaks to Gloucester using phrases borrowed straight from these 'Popish Impostures'! The possession and the exorcism, expelled from theology, radically changed, were reconstructed to find shelter in the theatre, that land of false appearances.

That 'another sort' of Oberon and Puck, what is it about? How are they different from the spirits of Purgatory? Greenblatt explains that:

> Shakespeare writes for the glory and for the praise of the theatre – of that deceitful institution, which never pretends that it is not; the institution, which openly shows what it is not, which expresses the nothingness, which transfers literality into metaphor, which denies everything it represents. ... The Shakespearean theatre survived the institutions to which it was paying homages and it still exists, paying homages to other, rivalling institutions, alternatively representing them and depriving them of meaning ...

This is why Puck, at the very end of the Athenian Midsummer's Night, turns directly to the audience, not in the name of 'spirits', but of 'shadows':

Think but this, and all is mended,
That you have but slumb'red here
While these visions did appear
And this weak and idle theme
No more yielding but a dream

73 So, how is it in the end with the 'Truth', I ask. Is it that it simply is, objective and unyielding in any discussion, or only that various interpretations of it can exist?

When I have a choice between something and nothing, my intuition decidedly pushes me towards something. It is better to be, than not to be, isn't it? What 'is' seems to me to be usually docile and quiet. What 'is' does not need to brag that it exists. By contrast, 'nothingness' is bold and loud, because what does it have apart from its cry? Nothingness loves to parade, to gloat, to complain, to direct, to declare and to proclaim. It is incessantly media-savvy and sells fantastically today. This is the seemingly accidental, damned fate of nothingness – in a strange way, it is always loud.

In *Much Ado About Nothing*, the beautiful Hero, publicly accused by Claudio of debauchery and therefore publicly dishonoured at the church altar in Messina, manages – in the face of this slander – to utter a few uncoordinated, defensive words, and faints. Her 'something' remains helpless in front of the loud nothingness of Claudio's accusations. Her truth is incapable of shouting, of screaming; blessed are the meek. Claudio bellows his accusations (one can see it and can hear it particularly well in Branagh's film), formulating not only his personal disappointment as a groom (Claudio is in this moment absolutely sure of Hero's guilt) but also informing the whole society of Messina that Hero is an ordinary whore. What is the motivation of Claudio? My own shame doesn't matter, let everybody know about it! The real director of all that shameful intrigue, the brother of the prince, the bastard Don Juan, rubs his hands.

Slander – the very definition of that word – is always about falsehood. Aspersion is always premeditated. But there is also – and its author is always difficult to identify – gossip, rumour and hearsay. Finally, there is misinformation divulged on purpose, a reinterpretation of the truth (Pontius Pilatus: 'What is truth?'); particularly abhorrent because consciously committed *insinuation*. Do we not recognise it?

Behind this trivial story about multi-levelled insinuation, Shakespeare hides a question about the conditions of the existence of good, which we call truth. A question particularly important for our time. Truth? 'It simply exists' – an idealistically oriented fundamentalist will say (there were always some of them, and there still are). 'The objective truth does not exist' – the relativist will answer (there were always some of them, and there still are). Peter Brook has written, in *Empty Space* (1968), that the truth, at least in the theatre, of course exists, and that we all know about it, but an interesting attribute of truth in the theatre is that 'it stays in constant movement'. Brook's dynamic concept of the truth is not a Platonic one (a Platonic truth, as an ideal one, cannot move, tremble, shiver; any 'moving truth' would be imperfect for Plato). Yet Brook's formula is not an Aristotelian one either (the truth as a correspondence of the fact and its description). Brook's intuition about truth 'in constant movement' attempts to express the phenomenon of the theatrical 'here and now'. Everyone, even in their best performance, must attempt each evening (with the active help of the viewers) to risk reaching the best 'truth' on that day and the best 'good' on that day. Let's note: actors and spectators in innumerable theatres all over the world believe in Brook's concept every time they perform.

When we ask a modern philosopher about the existence of truth, the radicalism of his answer may surprise us. Here again is Richard Rorty and his essay 'The Decline of the Redemptive Truth and the Rise of Literary Culture':

> The question 'Do you believe that truth exists?' is shorthand for something like 'Do you think that there is a natural terminus to inquiry, a way things really are, and that understanding what that way is, will tell us what to do with ourselves'. Those who, like myself, find themselves accused of postmodernist frivolity, do not think that there is such a terminus. We think that inquiry is just another name for problem-solving, and we cannot imagine inquiry into how human beings should live, into what we should make of ourselves, coming to an end.

In *Much Ado About Nothing*, the truth (and Hero's reputation) are saved by the so-called 'simple people'. It is saved by, among others, a certain Dogberry, the Head of the City Guard, a local, particularly dull policeman, half-idiot, half-fool. And yet the level of Dogberry's intelligence is completely unimportant. What is important is the fact that no angel (after all, an angel could, let's say, have flown down to testify the truth, couldn't they?) nor any democratic vote (the majority wants it, therefore it must be the truth) saves the truth here. It is saved by a concrete human action.

Let me reiterate this: the truth exists and the truth can be saved by a concrete human action. Because of this, let us do whatever we have to do. And let us do something, rather than nothing.

74 A concrete action can save the truth and the similarly concrete – although not always fully conscious – collaboration of a theatre audience can help in making the scenic world more credible.

In *The Comedy of Errors*, there are two pairs of twins, separated a long time ago, who do not know each other. The first pair are rich merchants both named Antifolus, one from Syracuse, and one from Ephesus. The second pair are two Dromios, their servants. It would be quite natural to cast these roles with two sets of real actors' twins, and such a solution has already been tried in the history of the theatre. But what to do when we do not have actors who are twins? Since the times of Plautus (*The Comedy of Errors* is Shakespeare's remake of *Menaechmi*, that is, *The Twins* by Plautus) the theatre has solved this problem in two ways. Either the two actors alternately played the two different twin brothers (only in the end, when all four of them are on stage, was a pair of similarly dressed doubles added), or by giving all four of the (nominal) twins similar costumes, or similar shapes, and leaving the rest to the intelligence of the audience.

Antifolus and Dromio from Syracuse appear in Ephesus, which is absolutely alien to them, in the second scene of the play. Dromio says one line and exits. His twin from Ephesus enters the stage literally moments later and, for the next quarter of an hour, explains to his master that his wife is waiting for him with a meal at home. We, the spectators, together with Antifolus from Syracuse, are forced to examine reality: either Dromio (strangely similar to himself, who has just left the stage) for some unknown reasons is talking rubbish (maybe he is inventing? or lying?), or he speaks truly, but in such a case it must be a completely different Dromio than the one who just left. Antifolus chooses the first interpretation (the scene ends with Dromio being heavily beaten by his angry master), while we cunningly choose the second and we become, as a result, 'the cheated, who are more wise than the cheating'.

The machine of 'errors' starts to turn: by accepting two different, incredibly similar Dromios, we also agree with their scenic affinity and therefore we co-create with this acceptance the world of the witchy Ephesus, full of traps. The level of likeness between the two actors playing the Dromios ceases to be relevant in this moment. Now the two Dromios are twins because we want them to be. And when, at the beginning of Act III, Antifolus from Ephesus finally appears on stage, a simple similarity of costumes or of haircut will be enough for us to see in him, with no reservations, the twin brother of the Antifolus we already know.

'No reservations', 'Because we want it' – the wildest improbabilities of the scenic world become probable thanks to our (the spectators') active collaboration. In *A Midsummer Night's Dream*, Puck remains invisible to Demetrius and Lisander because we, the spectators, have agreed to treat him as such (we also agree that he is invisible for them, not for us). In *Measure for Measure*, Angelo goes under cover of darkness to the bed of Mariana, absolutely sure that he is bedding Isabella. Against all reason, we accept this trick of the switch because without it the final denouement of the whole plot would lose all sense. It is a bond; had we not agreed at the beginning of the play that the disguised prince remain unrecognisable for his subjects, the whole plot of the play would dissolve into dust. 'We agree', 'We believe', 'We co-create' – the active acceptance of the proposed, often quite refined rules of the game, remains a condition of our satisfaction with the whole story completed by the actors. This is a game called 'What would happen if?' What would happen if the Athenian Forest was full of invisible ghosts? What would happen if the ship got wrecked at the shores of a mysterious island? What would happen if an appalling spectre appeared at midnight on the walls? What would happen if King Claudius rose with his heart full of remorse during a show reminding him of his former crimes?

This 'if' seems to be a tenet necessary for the phenomenon of the theatre. Years ago, searching the Sahara's wasteland among the local population, who never had anything to do with the theatre, Peter Brook observed that all the 'theatrical' scenes played to them by the actors remained completely incomprehensible. However, the most vivid, spontaneous reaction the viewers had was to the situation improvised by the actor: 'What would happen if suddenly the brown shoe box captured my left foot?' The childish instinct of play, present in all of us, the sense of playful suspension of everyday rules, permits us – in a most elementary sense – to participate in the theatrical event. It is Touchstone, the fool in *As You Like It*, who speaks about that 'if' most fully at the end of the play. Here, a quarrel between two nobles, which threatens to bring them to a deadly duel, is only prevented when one of them discovers the resources of 'if': 'If you said so, then I said so', and they see that they can reach a reconciliation. Touchstone sums it up: 'This "if" is the only peace-maker; much virtue in If.'

Very well, but what would happen if this 'if', somehow a little childish, as if from a fairy tale – and therefore ideologically suspect – was once and for all forbidden to the audience? This question was asked by the intrepid Austrian innovator Peter Handke in his *The Public Offended*, a text faithfully in accordance with its title. Three actors, for two hours, curse the audience, using the most offensive words possible – 'You bourgeois pigs, hungry for the narcotic of the happy end!' and so on. This interesting text has already been staged in Poland four times, so the next opening will probably be soon. If anybody is brave enough. If anybody possesses enough of 'if'.

75 Texts love to talk to texts, but because very often they happen to be written in different languages, they are also condemned to the infinite perturbations and demands of a perfect translation. *Traduttore, traditore*. Translators, for centuries accused of a lack of care, of sloppiness, or even of betrayal, finally got the proper recognition of their work in the famous text by Walter Benjamin, 'The Task of the Translator' (1921). To make it clearer, let's start with an example.

After numerous 'Fuck you's and 'Fuck off's directed at various, often incidental interlocutors, a certain Traveller, hired to kill in the thriller *Collusion* by Stuart Neville (2011) utters a weak, almost innocent 'You fucking bastard' minutes before shooting his victim in cold blood. He will call his next victim, just before their death, 'You dirty fucker!' The detective Jack Lennon, who chases the Traveller to the very end of the thriller, after their unfortunate brawl in a dark alley in Belfast, curses himself: 'Fucking stupid arsehole'. Yet the Traveller is linguistically much more innovative: 'Grumpy auld pishmire' he will say about his meeting with some gangster's sister. In the next chapters, the Traveller decidedly develops his vocabulary: from 'Fucking cock-pulling arsehole' (this about a victim who has managed to run away from him in the last moment), to 'Bastard cunt of a motherfucking whore's son!', after noting that another victim has also managed to slip away.

The task of the translator is to translate these curses roughly into everyday language. Translating slang is the most difficult part of the work of every translator and unfortunately most of them have serious problems with it.

'The task of the translator ... is in finding such an intention directed upon the final language of the translation, which will make in this language the echo of the original resound' writes Walter Benjamin in his legendary essay, an essay enriched with hundreds of learned commentaries. As Paul de Man, the high priest of modern linguistic expression, observes:

> 'The Task of the Translator' is a text that is very well-known, both in the sense that it is very widely circulated, and in the sense that in the profession you are nobody unless you have said something about this text.

The essay by Benjamin is intricate and tangled, it is a real 'cascade of metaphors', as Adam Lipszyc, who translated it into

Polish, says. These words, he says, 'reflect not only the unthink-able level of metaphors in the text, but also the speed in which one metaphor is substituted by another'. The problem is, in fact, that Benjamin, inspired by the tradition of the Kabbala, gen-erally assigns to the translator a messianic aim. He wants the translator to achieve in the translated text the 'reine Sprache', a sacred, pure language, identical with that of the pure names of the Torah.

Benjamin writes:

> In all languages, apart from that which is communicative, there remains something which is non-communicative. Something, which is, depending upon its context, symbolising or being a symbol of ... To free that imprisoned language, to save it in one's own language, to free that pure language in the process of translation – this is the task of a translator.

'Oh, merdre', as King Ubu would say. Just think that, for decades, hundreds of philosophers of language were ineffec-tually developing the non-existing mirage of 'pure language' invented by Benjamin. Paul de Man, once considered to be a guru by contemporary linguists, writes authoritatively: '... absolutely nothing like the "reine Sprache" exists. A "pure lan-guage" exists only as a permanent disjunction colonising all the languages as they are, particularly the language which man calls his own.' The utopia of a pure language is also torn to shreds by Giorgio Agamben, a prominent Italian philosopher: 'Mod-ern thought has reached the knowledge that any meta-language, absolute and ultimate, does not exist and that every construction of a meta-language joins the backward movement *ad infinitum*.' Agamben draws from this fact some radical conclusions:

> The archetypical character (*archē*) of logos was fully revealed and no new figure of deity, no new historical fate can result from language.

... There is no name of the name, there is no meta-language, even in the shape of a non-significant voice ... The epiphany which language achieves is a speech totally abandoned by God. Man was precipitated into language with no voice, nor God's word, which could guarantee to him the possibility of an escape from the infinite game of significant phrases. Therefore, we shall find ourselves finally alone with our words, for the first time alone with language, abandoned by any fundamentals.

If we are to believe Agamben, there is no excuse for a poor translator. What if – let us imagine – there is a deadline in the publishing house and the fantastic curses of the Traveller have to be translated! The curses are uppermost in the translator's mind. He opens the YouSwear.com website (there is such a one) and he starts. In the beginning he finds a juicy Latin phrase: '*Futete! Futete te ipsum! Irrumator, mater tua lupa est! Ut felacio! Coitus te, scronium!*' And then in Swahili: '*Kuma Mamako! Kuma wewe, mbwajike, nenda kajitombe! Unatombwa na farasi, wewe malaya!*' Or in Guarani: '*Yapiro, aña rako peguare! Ejapiro tuna ari, jaguarembo! Terehó na ejapiro túnare ...*'

76 Texts come from texts and they feed on texts. Texts gorge on texts, like a mite satiating itself upon the rotting wood of a fallen forest. Like the young shoots of a blackberry bush spring from the earth, they colonise every clearing, every meadow, they climb upwards, clinging to each other; they grow. Texts spread out into tracks, into chains, strings, into stories. And newly minted stories and their protagonists immediately go through a process of multiplication. They do it as fast and as efficiently as DNA or RNA. They multiply, they copy, they double, they imitate, they repeat, and they mock, giggling.

'That Carl is a total mindfuck. To kill his own fiancée? A strong man, but a nutter.'

Jack Reacher and Spenser sit having a beer at the Angel's in Ashland, Oregon, and browse through *The Robbers* by Friedrich Schiller.

'They don't say which gun he fired,' Reacher continues, 'but it could have been a Heckler and Koch, nine millimetres. Very fast, light, half-automatic.'

Spenser looks at him leniently.

'Jack,' he says, 'that was the eighteenth century. Even the Colt wasn't in circulation then.'

Spenser reads quite a lot, and it may be that he can quote Milton from memory. Reacher does not read anything, even the newspapers. Spenser has a flat and his private gumshoe's office in Boston, Massachusetts. Reacher does not have any fixed address and does not even have a car. He wanders across the whole of the US on Greyhound buses or hitchhiking, and the most incredible adventures happen to him in various places. He emerges from all of them unharmed, of course, but the corpses around him are usually numerous. In *Persuader*, for example, particularly at the end, it is a slaughterhouse.

'On the other hand,' Reacher says, 'that Amalie was asking for it.'

Reacher, the son of a soldier, spent most of his life in the US Military Police as a prosecutor and, because of that, very few can stand up to him. Fired from the army some time ago, Reacher deals nowadays with various *Mafiosi*, psychos and other whackos, with whom neither the police nor the Feds can cope. In *Without Fail* he even had to stake out two guys who were attempting to kill a vice-president, at the request of the Feds.

'Women,' sighs Reacher.

'Women,' Spenser repeats and sips a swig of *Budweiser*.

Women pursue Reacher like bees around a honeypot because Reacher is, of course, handsome as hell. Only extraordinarily sexy women pursue Reacher, of course, and usually he sleeps with them once or twice, *charmant*, usually in the middle of the story. Soon afterwards, they usually become the victims of some unspeakable crime and Reacher has to chase their killers with clenched teeth and with a wound in his heart. It was only the policewoman Roscoe, I think, from *Killing Floor*, who managed, despite the romance with Reacher, to stay alive.

Women, of course, pursue Spenser in their masses as well, but Spenser remains faithful to his Susan in every book. Spenser is six feet high and looks like a professional boxer, which he once was in fact. Nowadays he shoots gangsters professionally, he breaks their ribs and jaws, puts dozens of bullets into them or runs over their bodies in his beloved *Subaru*. Afterwards, as if nothing has happened, he rushes home to Susan and pours out his worries. Susan finished Harvard and runs a swanky psychotherapeutic practice. And when Spenser feels particularly bad, because he has, let's say, had to finish of some gang of guys, in two rounds, from behind a wall, Susan patiently explains to him that there was no other option, or something like that. Having quietened Spenser's delicate ego this way, she quickly drags him to bed to heal his libido.

'The beloved of Carl Moor can only die by the hand of Moor' – Spenser reads aloud one of the last lines of Carl, the robber. 'What is your problem, Jack? He couldn't let his fellow gang members finish her. The chap had no choice.'

Exactly like Spenser himself in *Thin Air*. Or in *Total Mischief* when Susan had a romance with a certain rich buster from California. There was no choice; she had a crush on him, and the guy had to die. Or like Jack Reacher in *Echo Burning*. The whole big farm in Texas had to burn, with all the bad guys shut inside.

'Chap had no choice,' Reacher agrees, 'like you in *Chance*.'

'Like you in *Die Trying*,' continues Spenser. 'Carl Moor found himself in a tragic situation, which finished for him badly, only because Schiller was not planning a sequel. There was no demand. The market was too small.'

The evening falls slowly over mountainous Ashland.

Another hour until the beginning of the show. The waitress brings another beer for each of them.

'Isn't it strange,' asks Reacher, who reads little, 'that two hundred years after Schiller both you and me, the heroes of mass culture, repeat incessantly his literary invention?'

'Not so much his invention, it came generally from the gothic novel,' explains Spenser, who has also read *The Roots of Romanticism* by Isaiah Berlin. 'Carl Moor and both of us, we all fulfil the pattern of the so-called "virtuous villain". Carl became a robber, not from choice, but because his horrible brother Franz manoeuvred him into such life. You and I, we also operate on the verge of the Law. Sometimes even outside the Law. The imperfection of our society pushes us into this dirty work. The Feds lack proper resources and yet somebody has to kill all those horrible, unpunished murderers and permit the reader to regain the moral balance. We have merciless fists, but we also have golden, Romantic hearts, Jack. Unlike Carl Moor, we give the reader comfort. There has to be a continuation; therefore, from the very beginning, everyone knows that we will win. Unlike Carl, we are not tragic, but luckily we still exist in the next episode. Although your author, that Lee Child, may get bored with you and may kill you in the next book.'

'Rather your author, Robert B. Parker, might do such a thing to you; he is a Yankee,' barks Reacher, while paying the bill. 'My author is a Brit, a gentleman.'

And they both saunter slowly to the nearby Oregon Shakespeare Festival for a performance of The *Robbers* directed by Maciej Prus, with set design by Jan Polewka.

77   'Tosca, finally mine!' – triumphs Scarpia at the end of the second act of Puccini's opera. He moves towards Tosca to embrace her – and he becomes impaled upon her knife. His first reaction is – as Puccini wants – 'un grido terribile', a

horrible scream: 'Maledetta!'. For the next minute and a half, he will sing a monotonous refrain: 'Aiuto ... muoio ... socorrso ... muoio' (Help, I am dying, help me, I am dying). Contemporaneously, with these last spasms of Scarpia, Tosca enjoys her deed: 'This is Tosca's kiss!', and she repeats a few times: 'Muori dannato! Muori! Muori! Muori!' (Die, condemned, die, die, die!). At the end of the second minute, Scarpia finally goes quiet and falls on the boards of the stage. The next comments by Tosca are probably not very revealing, but absolutely appropriate to the situation: 'È morto ...' (He is dead).

Le strage non si tocca is the old, still current, proverb of Italian actors. In a free translation it means literally: 'Director, stay away from death scenes.' From the moment the poison enters the bloodstream of the character, when the blade of the knife or rapier hits its deadly blow, presenting the physiology of dying is still, for an actor in the Italian theatre, a privilege. It is seen as a professional display, as the stunt of a magician. The wobbly knees, the hands desperately clutching the fresh wound, unsure, the stumbling last steps – all this repertoire of images of giving up the ghost – is used with knowledge and also with great pleasure. The key moment is the moment when the character falls to the ground. First to the knees, then to the floor. There is also this superhuman effort of raising the head from the boards with the help of weak elbows. Convulsions are possible, as well as cramps, quivers, bloody spews from bitten, hidden pouches of paint and finally – because it has to come – the final spasm, the last moan and, at last, quiescence. Tosca thinks about such a masterfully executed, totally theatrical act of dying when she informs her lover, Cavaradossi, in Act III about the necessity of going through his faked death. There will be no real bullets in the carbines of the execution platoon and the task of Cavaradossi will be to effectively convince the uninitiated soldiers that his death is real. 'Like in the theatre?' – Cavaradossi wants to be sure – 'Exactly like that' answers Tosca. And when, at the command of an official, the shots are fired (unfortunately real shots) and Cavaradossi falls to the ground, Tosca – still certain that this is fake – shouts openly with admiration: 'How beautiful my Mario is! Go, and die! Here is a real artist!' We are on a higher level, a Pirandellian one of the Italian love of a scenic death: the theatrical one appears real, while the real one still takes place in the theatre.

As the example of Cavaradossi shows, firearms kill immediately and do not leave time for any last words for the modern victims of murderous violence. In the times of poison and daggers it was very, very different. The agony had then its scenic time of duration. Life fading away in front of the eyes of the audience allowed playwrights to write life summaries, dramatic confessions, and some important warnings for the living. *Le strage*, the scenes of dying, do not do well in modern dramaturgy. Gombrowicz's Yvonna, for example, cannot say anything because she is choking on a fish bone. And Hamm from *Endgame* cannot even decently die on stage. How fascinating, in comparison, is Mercutio's dance of death in *Romeo and Juliet*, from the first sight of a naked blade, through the bluster and braggadocio addressed to Tybalt. Afterwards, there is the mad scramble of the fight, a thrust of Tybalt under Romeo's arm, a stupid scrape – and the young Mercutio, bursting with life, with wit and poetry, in a dozen angry, hastily spoken lines, has to reach his inevitable end. Shakespeare will save him from dying on stage (the wounded Mercutio, both in a literary and in metaphorical sense, exits from the stage), but when a moment later Benvolio informs Romeo about his death, the impetuosity of this completely unexpected event will leave the audience in a state of shock.

The death of a character is a separate area of art for Shakespeare. The baroque variety of forms of death in his plays would be worth a special dissertation; it is enough to mention the formidable slaughterhouse at the end of *King Lear* or the final composed concerto of falling bodies in *Hamlet*. The most effective (in the sense of most shocking) suicidal death that I have ever seen in the theatre was Goneril, played by Irene Worth in a black-and-white TV version by Peter Brook from 1966. Black-haired, not so young anymore, and totally defeated, she kneels on a stony slope. Slowly, methodically, she swings her body to the left, and to the right, like a pendulum. Then, accelerating the movement, she hits her head against the stones.

Death has always been presented in the theatre, in the same way as conception and birth, because conception, birth and death are inseparable from our lives. The most extreme conclusion from *le strage*, from the Italian tradition of dying on stage, was presented by Eugène Ionesco in his drama *Exit the King*. The king of the title is dying for more than two hours — the subtitle of the drama is '... or ceremonies'. Ionesco boldly wrote a baroque score, and has transferred rhythms, phrases, and intonations from his own funeral celebration. He cast himself in the leading role, appropriately for the 'King of Creation', and analysed, in writing, everything until his end (he must have been anticipating, when writing, his own demise).

Is it better, I wonder, to anticipate, to imagine this moment, to savour it, to 'play' it almost? Or should one rather ignore it; leave it for the future? Or maybe one should even forget about it altogether with no regrets?

78 § Basically, one could foresee the second vanishing of Audrey. If only Umberto had ever thought about it. He did not have time for it; he devoured the gift of her person without distance, without reflection. He breathed with her being, he fell asleep and awoke filled with her intense existence, her laughter, her glances, the rhythm of her unexpected reveries. From the moment of meeting Audrey, his life divided itself into two blurry oceans of impressions and images. One of

those was his past without Audrey, some time ago. A past which merged into one continuum of grey, non-interesting being which he had lived for years, not even conscious of its grey quality. The second ocean was an astounding galaxy of co-existence with Audrey, an ocean of experiencing her delights, her discoveries, her surprises. A cosmos of never-ending emotions and never-ending joys. Only the second ocean was important. It was borderless and infinite.

The second vanishing of Audrey, unannounced, and totally unexpected, left Umberto in Kraków as a castaway on the sands of an unfamiliar, hostile land. One morning, she was simply not there, she was missing for the whole day and the whole night and after a few days of her absence, Umberto suddenly heard that he was howling. A whine was gurgling in his throat, a choked moan which he could not stop.

He found Witold and explained, with a lot of trouble, what had happened. For the next eight, maybe ten weeks, all the universities in the country were looking for a red-haired girl matching the description of Audrey. With no results. During that time, Umberto drank a lot (he loved to drink together with Staszek in room 328), and he slept until midday. Then he went to the coach station and looked for Audrey among the alighting travellers. After a few months, he was thrown out of his residence, and he slept for a few nights in a somewhat suspect squat. One early morning, he awoke on a bench in the middle of the Villa Borghese.

He stayed in Rome, he did not want to return to Forlí or to go anywhere else. He found a job as a night guard at some construction site. They gave him a caravan for himself, with running water and some meals in the canteen. That was fine for him. During the night, he walked along all the gates and fences of the site, which were packed with electronic sensors and cameras. During the day, he slept in his caravan or wandered for hours around the city.

He became dishevelled, unkempt. He had long, tangled hair, he shaved irregularly and rarely changed his clothes. Old jeans, a T-shirt, a dingy blue sports coat; it was not a problem for his employer, as long as he started his shift on time and did not create any incidents. He bought a second-hand mobile phone because everybody had mobile phones and it was becoming impossible to live without one. For unknown reasons, he had landed in Rome in the same year in which he had been transferred to Palermo for the first time. However, after all the temporal transfers, Umberto was physically older by a quarter of a century. Something was aching in his knee, and he did not run up the stairs anymore.

He talked to himself practically with no breaks, although this was not a monologue audible to everyone. He kept explaining why he loves her and why he will never stop loving her. I am worrying about you, do you understand? – he continually repeated – I am worrying that whoever controls these kidnappings across Time will hurt you. They are playing with us like children play with toys, they murder us like flies. But I cannot complain; had they not transferred me that time to Palermo, I would never have had a chance to meet you. We are created for ourselves, Audrey. Audrey, where are you? Audrey, come back.

After the end of the night shift, he liked, when coming back to his place, to sit for a while on the back of the national 'piano' in Piazza Venezia. The view wasn't bad and stretched from almost the top of Campidoglio to the Forum Romanum below. A Franciscan house for pilgrims was nearby and he started to meet an older pensioner there regularly. The man exited every morning from the building for his first cigarette; they became friendly and started to enjoy their morning chat. His name was Francesco. He was a bit old-fashioned: an ironed shirt, a bow tie, a satin jacket despite the time of day. After a few meetings, Francesco revealed his secret.

'I am from the past century, Signor Umberto,' he was smiling. 'Something transferred me in an incomprehensible way to your times, but my times were more interesting, I'm telling you. People were slightly different, more friendly'.

'Who transferred you, Signor Francesco?' Umberto asked.

'Who? They did. I saw them a few times, always blurry. I think that they come from a distant future and that they do with us whatever they want. They do not want us to see them. They are playing with us. They are checking how we shall behave in various epochs, and therefore they transfer us, they experiment with us.'

'What do they look like, Signor Francesco?' continued Umberto.

'All of them look very young. They are all young and very handsome. Because they do not get old, Signor Umberto, I tell you. And this gnaws at them, this destroys them, their artificiality, their falseness. They want to know through us, through our feelings, what it means to live, to get old, to suffer or to be happy. Bloodsuckers. Immortal ghouls, merciless, jealous, wretched. They do not know what it is to love, what is it to desire. They will never understand my fatal history, full of deadly accidents, my history with my niece. Two innocent children had to lose their lives; do you understand? They will never understand. I was personally present at the opening of Tosca and I understand Puccini and I feel for him. They cannot feel anything, I tell you.'

She appeared to him a few days later in a narrow alley in Trastevere. He was returning from a longer walk in the city, evening had just fallen and the streetlights were glittering. She looked like a teenager, she had not changed at all, her red hair was spilling out onto the collar of her blue coat. She had a book in her hands. She was serious. She was looking at him steadily, her eyes wide open, but she kept a few metres' distance between them. He blinked and froze.

'I had to see you one more time, Umberto. I had to check if you were all right.'

'Audrey,' he whispered, 'Audrey, come back to me, please.'

'I am with you all the time, Umberto. Not right beside you, but a little further away. You do not see me, but I am.'

'Audrey, come back. Please.'

'It is a long time. You should start to forget me. You should already have new friends.'

They were silent. The sounds of traffic were coming from the nearby Viale di Trastevere, but in the alley it was all quiet. He looked at her voraciously, devouring her with his eyes. He stepped forward.

'Come back,' he said. And at that moment she vanished.

That night he could not sleep. It was a phantasm, he kept repeating, that was simply a dream, I wanted to see you so badly, he thought, and finally I have seen you. You did not say anything that I could not have known before. This only confirms to me that I dreamt you.

After two years, he moved to the northern suburbs near the Priscilla Catacombs. The firm which hired him was building a huge shopping centre there. They offered him a room near a Romanian family. It was not large, but it had access to a bathroom and a separate entrance. It was further to the centre of the city, but it did not matter. He travelled to the other end of the city by metro whenever he wanted. He still believed that Audrey would come back, and although he did not think about it every day, the certainty that one day it would happen had not left him.

He almost missed it when she appeared the next time. He was on the tube, it was late; half-dreaming, he was leaning against the window of the carriage. He felt that somebody was looking at him and he slowly opened his eyes. Audrey was glued to the back door of the previous carriage. She spread her hands high on the glass and she was looking straight at him. The carriages were shaking, they clickety-clacked. He rapidly left his place and reached the closed, glass door. She ran away immediately to the centre of her carriage and was lost amid the other people. At the nearest station, he jumped onto the platform and was able to see how her blue coat vanished at the turn of the stairs. He threw himself into the chase, but he could not find her upstairs among the crowds of people and cars.

Someone must have been telling tales about Umberto Enea, because three years later, when – returning from wandering round the city – he was turning from Via Foscolo into the Viale Val Padana, when he suddenly saw, on the other side of the street, the house number 17 at Via Vespucci in Forlí, tucked between two other inconspicuous grey houses. His first impulse was to stop right there, and immediately he understood that everything was coming back to its place. And that inside he would find Mr. and Mrs. Calendra, as well as Mr. Palomini, and that Audrey, the red-haired Audrey, was waiting for him there, impatiently. He moved towards the gate and turned the door handle.

79 Such a story: they killed him, but he managed to escape. We look at James Bond: how they try to kill him cruelly in the most elaborate ways, and how they dust themselves off after a job well done, and in the next take he is obviously alive, escaping by fantastical means and preparing some form of vengeance which his persecutors have not dreamt of.

This is a particularly unwise story: they killed him, but he managed to escape. It is watched every evening on every possible channel by several billion people connected to the TV or Internet (at least for now) – almost half the Earth's inhabitants. Of course, it is not only Bond that they are watching, but also all those other spin-offs, series and films related to Bond by genre. Look, they killed him again; one wonders, will he escape? Look, he escaped again; what will happen next?

TV series, computer games and paperback thrillers seem to play a role in our lives every day, every evening, Scheherazade. They killed him and he escaped – this somewhat strange story, openly appearing as if on an industrial conveyor belt, helps half of humanity to go to work the next morning and is also useful to the unemployed (and to those who do not need to work, or cannot).

The original Scheherazade told the stories of *One Thousand and One Nights* for the sake of her survival: 'As long as I keep telling, I will not die.' But why do we – viewers, listeners, players, readers – so desperately need the thousand and one fragments of an openly nonsensical story? Because our parents told us fairy tales in bed in our childhood? Because we remember that it was always warm, good and safe then? One cannot exclude it. Parents knew very well that they had tell stories to make their children feel good and safe. In their own childhood, they were told stories too, as were their parents and their parents' parents. There lingers in all of us an elementary hunger for stories – universal, by the way, for all humanity. Scientists maintain that this hunger is genetic. The concrete 'generative structures', as Noam Chomsky called them (a concrete language, for example), are not innate, but a tendency to build such structures and to develop them genetically, is, scientists say. A story in a series, episodic TV or a box set would, then, all be forms of 'generative structures' of whatever level. Therefore, it may be that Scheherazade is not only telling, but also listening, to the story for the sake of her own survival.

The convincing story – unfortunately, practically every story, even the most absurd ones – consolidates the world and explains it. A truly founding story, myth, or history permits everyone to find his/her place on the map of creation. The absence of such a story literally 'smashes' the world, breaks it into pieces which do not fit, one with another. A broken mirror instead of a reflection.

There is nothing to look into, there is nothing in which to understand oneself. The story about the end of stories, which appears more and more often, is – paradoxically – yet another story itself. Nevertheless, it is a fact that the narratives surrounding us nowadays rabidly compete between themselves, exclude themselves, undermine one another. The world around us is seriously broken, more difficult to express in words, therefore more difficult to understand.

Should one fall into despair? Should one take Prozac? Surprisingly, many behave like in that old joke: 'The wife thinks I am at the lover's, the lover thinks I am with the wife, while I have just trotted off to the library.' We cultivate a classic escapism when we reach for a thriller, or we start a new TV episode. The rules here are clear and simple: although he will get killed yet again, he will manage to escape. It is obvious that everything will end well, and it is obvious that the next episode will follow. A substitutive, yet infallible, narrative paradise.

James Bond, the famous 007 agent in the Secret Services of Her Majesty, is probably a particular case, because he remains eternally alive. After the death of Ian Fleming in 1964 (the original author and inventor of this character) sequels of Bond's adventures were written by Kingsley Amis, John Gardner and Sebastian Faulks, with mediocre results. Despite this, the estate of Ian Fleming turned, some time ago, to an American specialist of psychological thrillers, Jeffrey Deaver, for yet another sequel. In this way, a surprisingly fine Bond story, titled *Carte Blanche*, was born. Deaver is successful in an extraordinary way: Fleming's hero acts, in his book, in our modern world (he uses mobile phones and the Internet), while maintaining all the chivalrous grace of his 1952 predecessor. Interestingly, Deaver does not attempt to imitate the literary style of Fleming, even for a moment. He invents his own mixture of flashy dialogue and shocking turns of action. He seems to understand very well that in Fleming's books and the films based on them, successful impersonations of Bond emerged over the decades into the mass imagination of one continuum of car chases, technical fireworks and love conquests; he consciously plays with these after-images. It also reads very well, because Deaver has given a credible psychological character to his Bond. Deaver dedicates his work to Ian Fleming, of course, who 'taught us that we still can believe in heroes'.

A sequel is an old and well-known invention in literature – what sold well the first time should sell just as well the second. How surprised is Don Quixote when in the 'Second Part' of his adventures he comes upon their 'First Part' in one of the bookshops in Madrid. Although Deaver's James Bond does not attend the films about him, his world of fast cars and beautiful, treacherous women almost begs for such a joke in one of the next adventures. The sequel in drama happens decidedly less frequently, for no clear reasons. Is it because in the theatre, unlike in popular literature, we are less prone to 'believing in heroes'? The strongest, the most important sequel in Polish drama is probably *Liberation* by Wyspiański, embedded in *The Forefathers' Eve* of Mickiewicz. But also *The Wedding* of Wyspiański had a number of new versions, in the theatre and on film. Some time ago, I was thinking about the possibility of the continuation of the life of Henryk in *The Marriage* by Gombrowicz. After many years, let's say, Henryk is liberated from his prison and enters today's world. This world, meanwhile, has been underpinned by Derrida and Lacan. Would Henryk want to marry at all in such a world, or would he rather prefer to dream another story? And what would a younger generation of 'Yvonne, Princess of Burgundy' look like? What new scandal would King Phillipe's son, Prince Carl, create when his parents greet the Nation on the National Day? And Beckett? Can one imagine the next day of Estragon and Vladimir? Yes, one can, and I would love to see such a *Godot II*, but the sequel to *Endgame* is beyond my imagination.

The sequel remains a rare phenomenon in the theatre maybe because successful stagings of an original play continuously change. We are ready to see such a title for a third, or even for a fifth time, because we are intrigued by its different, possibly unexpected, interpretations. And, of course, we may have bad luck. Someone may have already done it this way, so I will go to an entirely different production. The director dresses the actors in jeans, for example, or perhaps they add their own text and here it is: *Hamlet – a Reactivation*. Modernisations of this type are usually born from the understandable desire to avoid any kind of theatrical mothballs, but also very often they come from an unjustified, overwhelming wish to be radically 'original'. Yet, after all, the main property of the sequel is not originality but, on the contrary, the intended replicability of the behaviour of the hero or the group of characters, in changed circumstances. Just as in the case of James Bond, it is the success of the first version with an audience which suggests to the author to write a sequel. Because the character of Falstaff was so incredibly successful with audiences, Shakespeare had no choice and simply had to write *The Merry Wives of Windsor* for the actor who played Falstaff.

Shakespeare had no problems with writing a sequel, because – like Fleming or Deaver – Shakespeare was a professional writer, earning his money by writing, and earning quite a lot. No one could have understood better than him the infinite journeys created by the vehicle called Theatre – these journeys have nothing whatsoever in common with mere cheap commerce. And yet he knew very well that, whenever the professional theatre started to sell tickets (they cost one penny at the Globe), the public would buy them, and then, inevitably, the theatre would also become a commodity, and the viewer a customer.

To think that Balzac, Dostoevsky, Dickens, Tolstoy and Flaubert all wrote their novels in episodes. The nineteenth century introduced that habit in the daily and weekly newspapers, together with the growth of the press and of journalism. The readers were akin to fans, as authors were pushed to the finishing post, as if on a racetrack.

From at least the end of the eighteenth century, serialised stories and never-ending sequels helped enable the existence of a mighty, and profitable, international publishing industry. All those *thrillers* and *harlequins* were produced in a mechanical way. Every author gifted with a relatively recognisable name hired an army of assistants and copyrighters who planned the plot, invented the characters, the extras, the landscapes and all the details. Eventually, the author would add some characteristic expressions himself, in the last, final edition. These massively published products form stacks in every bookshop in every country, and in every language. Right beside them are piles of their innumerable screen versions – both Hollywood and Bollywood are factories belonging to the same industry. This is the gradual decline of *The Gutenberg Galaxy*. If the process of reading the printed word becomes too problematic for someone, they can receive some colourful, gracefully flickering images instead.

This description of the 'factory-of-stories' industry is depressing, I think. Yet it is, I am afraid, also true.

80 In the nineteenth century, the century of steam and electricity, literature became a market commodity, subjected to the brutal laws of supply and demand and conditioned by the costs of massive reproduction. When one wanted to sell for more money, the prices of the original idea and of its renditions, rose. When one wanted to sell more, ironically, demand also rose: a 'happy end'.

'*Happy end*' meant – and still means – that the novel, story and film will all end 'fine'. However complicated the earlier action and adventures of the main heroes were, in the final happy end, all those separated by fate will be happily reunited; others, lost, will happily be found; the lovers will be bound by the knot of marriage and all of them will live happily ever after. A happy end is like the guarantee of sugar in the cake we buy at the shop: we assure you, dear customers, that the consumption will end sweetly, with no unneeded bitterness. The guaranteed happy end does not have anything in common with the work of art. On the contrary, the guaranteed presence of a happy end is often proof of the transformation of the former work of art into a purely market-based object of consumption.

The phenomenon named happy end started to flourish at the same time as the so-called 'well-made play'. The French were responsible for the development of the genre called 'la piece bien faite' by Eugène Scribe, Victorien Sardou, Alexandre Dumas (the son), or Emile Augier. It was a dramatic form with a precise dramatic plot, basically maintaining the principles of Greek tragedy described in the *Poetics* by Aristotle.

The plot of the well-made play usually depends upon a key element of information, unavailable to some characters, but known to others (and known also to the audience). Most of the plot happens even before the action of the play. The exposition in the first act builds sympathy towards the main hero (*vel* hero), but not towards their rival (or rivals). The whole thing aims towards an obligatory culmination in which the hero triumphs. The plot ends with an explanation in which all the elements of the intrigue are revealed and explained. The prop most often used in the well-made play is a letter, or a whole series of letters, which fall into the wrong hands. The letters are usually connected with a rapid change in the fate of the character, who often happens to be not the person he/she claims to be. The hidden or mysterious identity is often the basis of complications called *quid pro quo*. Here's another piece of information about this particular genre, borrowed from the encyclopaedia: 'Eugène Scribe has written over three hundred plays and librettos for opera. Thirty-five of them are considered "well-made".'

I started to have difficulties with the problematic end of the well-made play when I directed *Happy End* by Bertolt Brecht and Kurt Weill, in 2003 at the Shaw Festival in Canada. Brecht 'borrowed' the story, with no scruples, from earlier authors and, having radically changed it, he combined, in its final denouement, gangsters from Chicago and Chicago's Salvation Army. There are two wedding ceremonies at the end of the play and a revolutionary parade. As we might remember, at the end of Brecht's *Threepenny Opera* (1928), the professional thief, Macheath, asks the audience: 'What is robbing a bank, when compared to the founding of a bank?' In *Happy End* (1929), Brecht pushed this provocation much further: 'Breaking the safe is nothing. We must break those guys who keep the cash. Put on the knuckle dusters and learn where to hit!' *Happy End* finishes with a fiery call to start the revolution immediately; a strictly Marxist revolution, of course. 'Forget your fear and march with us! Let the tanks and cannons roar!' I can imagine the euphoria of Comrade Weigel, the freshly married partner of Brecht, when she sang those words (she played Lillian, the main female role) at the Berlin opening. She added her own fiery speech, full of agitation, and threw a pile of revolutionary leaflets into the crowd. The audience reacted with an angry commotion and the show was shut down after only two performances. Well, the noble aim sanctifies the means, they say, and the aim was particularly ambitious: 'To fight for a bowl of soup for a poor man!'. The Communist doctrine saw in the use of violence the only effective, morally justified tool for a final salvation for the starving masses of the workers. On the day of the Berlin opening, Comrade Weigel and Comrade Brecht probably honestly believed, I think, that robbing the bank was indeed nothing when compared to the good that such an act could bring.

In 2003, the naïve faith that any political ideology could build a 'paradise on Earth' was practically extinct. The Communist utopia, after robbing what it could, was sadly petering out in North Korea and in Cuba. It was dying, together with millions of its fusilladed, starved and tortured victims, for whom no tribunal like the Nuremberg trials had ever attained justice. But did this mean that we were not supposed to perform *Happy End*? That we were supposed to forget that wonderful piece of theatre? To forget 'Surabaya Johnny?' To forget 'Mandalay Song?' That is simply impossible. Those singing gangsters from an openly fictional Chicago and those amorous sisters from Chicago's Salvation Army, all of them entered the history of theatre a long time ago. *Happy End* by Brecht and Weill is a classic, a classic of the highest level.

All right, but what to do with the happy end of *Happy End*, with that propagandistic ending? At the beginning of the new millennium, the play was staged by the main theatre in Gdansk. I did not see the show. I read in the press that the American director, Marjorie Hayes, hired some unemployed workers from the Gdansk shipyards. They greeted the audience as they arrived with billboards: 'I do not have work' and 'My children starve'. Did Marjorie want to call the Poles back together under the red banner? I know nothing about it, but slowly my 2003 Canadian dilemma becomes clearer. My Canadian actors in *Happy End* somehow naturally (always and everywhere) leant to the Left, and were absolutely eager to sing, in harmony, the song praising the robbing of the banks (ironically sponsored by the Bank of Montreal). It seems that our audience was eager too because the show sold out ten days before opening. Yes, but those spectators were paying seventy dollars for a ticket and to buy a house for under half a million, within a radius of thirty kilometres from Niagara-on-the-Lake, was practically impossible. By waving the red banner in this geographical and political context, I would have made a total idiot of myself.

Also, as a well-experienced child of socialism from the PRL (Polish People's Republic), I did not want to do it for purely personal reasons. The wealth and affluence of Canada were the best proofs of the pertinence of avoiding historical shortcuts.

In the end, we finished the performance with the frame of 1929, referring the audience to the times of the Great Crash. But another possible solution – which I have not used (the name Stalin was familiar to Canadian viewers, but rather exotic) – could have been to use a phrase spoken by Joseph Vissarionovich.

I found the historical recording of Stalin's speech on some Internet website. He spoke slowly, the year was 1936. The show trials were going on, the Gulag archipelago was working at full throttle. It was a tired, slightly whisky baritone. He was saying: 'You may be sure that Comrade Stalin will fulfil his duty to the nation [loud applause]. To the workers' class [loud applause]. To the peasants [loud applause]. And to the intelligentsia [enthusiastic applause].'

81 The prehistory of the libretto of *Happy End* by Brecht and Weill is a perfect example of the possible, tangled connections between various literary sources and their interaction across two continents. Everything started from George Bernard Shaw (GBS). Were it not for Shaw, Marlon Brando would never sing and dance *I've Never Been in Love Before* in a duet with Jean Simmons in *Guys and Dolls* by Frank Loesser (1955). In 1905, in his *Major Barbara*, Shaw introduced to the London stage an extraordinary female character named Barbara Undershaft, a lady from a very good background and an officer in the Salvation Army. Barbara was defending, with socialist passion, the rights of the poor; fighting with her father, an arms producer based on the figure of Siegfried Krupp. *Major Barbara* was a deserved success and it remains one of the most frequently staged of Shaw's plays to this day. It was from this

play that Damon Runyon borrowed an idea. Runyon was a journalist in New York, a sports commentator and writer who, at the end of the 1920s, wrote a short story titled 'The Idyll of Miss Sarah Brown'.

Until his death in 1946, Runyon remained a one-man New York institution. A confirmed gambler, a fan of baseball and of Havana cigars, he described in his stories the colourful, uneasy life of the New York underworld, the adventures of actresses from Broadway, or of clever thieves from Brooklyn. He faultlessly imitated the characteristic New York drawl and the unique slang of these figures. He knew how to present the rhythm and pulse of the night life of that grand metropolis. The word 'Runyonesque', meaning something or somebody slightly mad and not fully legal, entered everyday usage. In 'The Idyll of Miss Sarah Brown', Runyon made the main character (very beautiful, naturally) a boss of a branch of the Salvation Army, right on Broadway. And he had the local, stunningly handsome king of racehorse betting, Sky Masterson, woo Miss Sarah intrepidly.

In 1929, after the mind-blowing success of *The Threepenny Opera*, Bertolt Brecht and Kurt Weill were looking for material for a sequel in Berlin. Elisabeth Hauptmann, a collaborator and lover of Brecht, found 'The Idyll of Miss Sarah Brown' by Runyon. All three of them went for a vacation in Provence and this is how the libretto of *Happy End* was written. The action was transferred to Chicago, Sky Masterson's name was changed to Bill Cracker – a gangster and bar owner, while Sarah Brown morphed into Lillian Holliday. In the Salvation Army she enjoyed – because of her fieriness – the nickname 'Hallelujah Lil'.

Chicago, the gangsters and pseudo-philanthropists, enabled Brecht to make his final appeal to rob the banks in *Happy End*. The appeal was much more provocative than the end of *The Threepenny Opera*. The Berlin opening resulted in scandal, the show closed rather swiftly, but the topic of the combative, beautiful woman fighting with the injustice of the world did not leave Brecht. He borrowed once more from GBS and soon *Saint Joan of the Stockyards* was written – yet another of his plays set in Chicago. The titular Joan is here called 'Dark'. She leads the brotherhood of Black Caps which defends the poor, while Andrew Undershaft from *Major Barbara* morphs into Pierpont Mauler, an awfully rich pursuer of poor workers from a preserve factory. In 1932, Radio Berlin managed to transmit *Saint Joan of the Stockyards* as a radio play, but the full theatrical version of the play opened only in 1959, in Hamburg. After the death of Damon Runyon in 1946 (from throat cancer) his ashes were thrown from a plane over Broadway by Captain Eddie Rickenbauer, yet another legendary figure – an Air Force ace from the First World War, a star of car racing and the founder of the very profitable Eastern Air Lines, besides being a gambler and a womaniser.

A freshly demobilised New Yorker, Frank Henry Loesser, songwriter, was looking for a new job. Born in 1910, he did not finish any musical studies but had already managed to write music for Hollywood filmmakers before the war. During the war, he was despatched to the Special Unit in the Army, where he composed simple theatre pieces and simple musicals. These were then sent to the trenches with full instructions on how to sew the costumes and how to build the sets. It was there where he composed his first melody, a song called 'Praise the Lord and Pass the Bullets', which became a huge hit. Encouraged by such applause, Loesser soon wrote his first Broadway success, a musical called *Where's Charley?* (1948) and then – searching for a 'really, really New York' topic – he turned to the works of Runyon. 'The Idyll of Miss Sarah Brown' served as a base for the whole work, but Loesser also used other stories by Runyon: 'Pick the Winner' and 'Blood Pressure' (for the famous scene featuring the dice) and in this way, in 1950, *Guys and Dolls* appeared on Broadway. A legendary musical, staged continuously since that opening run of 1,200 performances on every possible stage in America and all over the world to this day.

In Loesser's *Guys and Dolls*, New York is emerging from pre-war Prohibition. The USA is searching for a new social balance in a new, changed world (with a TV set in every household). Sky Masterson, a master of dice, a legend of the casinos of Nevada and Havana, is being dragged to the altar by an undeterred Sarah Brown. His friend, Nathan Detroit, a specialist in illegal gambling on Broadway, is being tamed, for a change, by a certain Adelaide, a star of the 'Hot Box' cabaret. Loesser's music explodes with joy and ease, the dialogues are extremely funny, the adventures of the heroes and heroines are crazy. The America of that time, a world hegemon charting trails of the future, looks at itself in the mirror in *Guys and Dolls*. In 1955, Joseph L. Mankiewicz wanted to direct *Guys and Dolls* in Technicolor, and he needed stars. Masterson was played in the (not fully satisfying) film by Marlon Brando, while Frank Sinatra played Nathan Detroit. And Brando sings in the film! He doesn't sing very loudly, but he sings and dances with grace.

The genealogy of the story: this theme travels from continent to continent, across decades. Characters change their names, authors are superimposed over one another, places change their names. Texts talk to earlier texts, they twist and misstate them, they illegally deform them, very often changing them so radically that they become unrecognisable.

82   A *crime story* is a particular example of a story massively disseminated during the last two centuries. The incomparable success of its formula seems to be based upon the success of the invention of the riddle, unchanged for millennia. To unravel a mystery of a refined murder is to reach – against all

probability, against the hopes of the murderer – a deeply hidden truth. Revealing the truth, even if it is a shocking truth, means enhancing the rationality of the world, means an increase in man's control over the unpredictability of events in the world. Within the genre of the crime story, truth is redemptive and rational.

The Sphinx, the winged monster with the body of a lion and the head and breasts of a woman, guarded the entrance to Thebes. She sat on a rock and devoured people who were not able to solve her riddle. She asked: 'What is an animal that walks on four legs in the morning, on two legs at midday and on three legs in the evening?' After a prophetic dream, Oedipus solved the riddle. 'A man' was the solution – man crawls in infancy, walks on two legs as an adult and uses a stick in his old age. Solving the riddle caused the death of the monster, who fell into the abyss.

Another riddle is posed to the younger companion of the First Gravedigger in *Hamlet*: 'Who builds stronger than a mason, a shipwright, or a carpenter?'

After a while, he answers himself: 'A grave-maker. The houses he makes last till doomsday. Go, get thee in, and fetch me a stoup of liquor.'

Every crime story asks us, in a more or less honest way, a question: whodunnit? An author who is relatively 'honest' (the classics of this genre were seen as such: Poe, Conan Doyle, Christie, Simenon) leaves us numerous traces, references and clues; numerous signs which – at least in theory – can help the reader solve the riddle by themselves. Nevertheless, the crime story, despite unbelievably successful literary achievements, seems closer to *sudoku*, to crosswords, or a chess problem, than to serious literature.

83 The inquiry about truth, which in the nineteenth century was still seen as the natural and basic remit of science and of every police department, in the twentieth century becomes much more complicated. The truth, being difficult to grasp, often flickers in continuous movement, but also, equally often, remains unknowable.

The optimistic positivists and their sociological scientism gathered under the banner of Auguste Comte and came to be questioned more during the second half of the nineteenth century. The Enlightenment programme of recognition and disenchantment with the world is often defective, because although the reign of knowledge continually grows, the range of questions without answers grows even faster. After decades of pressure from Romantic influences, a new discipline was born – anthropology. Its influence is the reason why cognition and knowledge are seen as more and more problematic. Sometimes it is simply better 'not to know'. And sometimes, despite one's will, 'one cannot know'.

With 'Whereof one cannot speak, thereof one must be silent' Ludwig Wittgenstein ends his *Tractatus Logico-Philosophicus* (1921). The ghastliness of the First World War decidedly accelerated the turn towards the 'unspoken'. But despite that, the proud banner of modernity – as opposed to the emptiness of the *Stunde Null* – flew over the trenches of Positive Science for quite a long time. For example: it may be surprising, but in 1966 Jerzy Grotowski, a graduate of the Moscovian GITIS, named his new outpost in Wrocław as *The Institute for Studies of the Method of Acting*. For him, it was like Bohr's Institute in Copenhagen. It seemed that the possibility of widening human knowledge in anything other than a 'scientific' way was still unthinkable for that young engineer of human souls. A process of approaching a scientific truth, in geology, let's say, or in cultural anthropology, was needed, according to him. He wanted a disciplined, verifiable 'method', exactly like in the times of Konstantin

Sergeyevitch Stanislavski. That 'scientific' solution of the stat-ute and terminology of his theatre permitted Grotowski to lead 'practical research of the technical rules of the Art of Theatre, in the centre of which is the creative technique of the actor'. It also freed him from the necessity of producing shows.

I must repeat an opinion already expressed: it was the apoca-lypse of the *Stunde Null*, from 1945, experienced on a worldwide scale, which caused the questioning of the 'progressive' and 'developmental' character of human society. That questioning started quite cautiously at the beginning but soon grew to be a loud and conscious process. It is instructive to see how the accu-mulating doubt in human cognitive capabilities was formulated after the Second World War by consecutive, often accidental victims like, for example, Stanisław Lem. In such novels as *The Investigation* (1959), *Eden* (1959), *His Master's Voice* (1968) or *Fiasco* (1987), the frantic process of getting to the scientific, irrefutable truth (about the world, about society and finally about 'aliens' from a different planet) becomes discredited as an unfounded haughtiness, as the arrogance of fools. The unknown and unrecognisable force, which avoids the simple division into rational or irrational phenomena, moves the corpses waiting in cemetery chapels in *The Investigation*. It is a force most likely connected to Probability Calculus and to the Law of Huge Numbers, but it cannot be defined – at least for now – with any mathematical equation. And the grotesque world of madness in Lem's *Memoirs Found in the Bathtub* can only be compared with the spectral and hellish worlds of Franz Kafka.

84 One can wander through the Land of Fiction forever. This is an edifice strangely similar to the 'Library of Babel' of Jorge Luis Borges – full of amazing spaces, corridors, secret chambers and unexpected enfilades. This is a building like the 'Carceri d'invenzione' of Piranesi. Its successive levels

vanish somewhere high under the sky, its multileveled basements and dungeons stretch deep in the abysses of canyons and bottomless crevasses.

Umberto Eco managed to make a similar excursion in his *Six Walks Through the Land of Fiction* (1994). The level of this work was set very high, of course – those lectures were given at Harvard, after all. We have there the scientific terms of 'a model reader' and 'an empirical reader'. In Eco we have a cascade of flamboyant, yet precise analyses, we have jokes, irony and a deeper meaning. I have to admit, I would never dare to fly so high. And we are not doing that, because in our stroll through the Land of Fiction, I have underlined the Theatre (which Eco did not) and this way, I want to believe, I have avoided the trap of repeating something after somebody else. A narrative fiction widened by theatrical worlds; this is my secret weapon.

A perambulation, even the longest one, has an aim (otherwise it would be a peregrination, in which a description stops halfway). Am I announcing the end of this journey right now? True, I do so, because the end seems almost visible on the horizon, and at the same time no, I do not announce the end ceremonially because – as I wrote above – one can wander through the Land of Fiction forever.

A few points are still left to make: a 'library' is one of them. Yet it is not that Borgesian one, loaded with symbols and metaphors, which is on my mind, but a concrete, earthly, incredible library planned and constructed in Seville by Hernando Colón (1488–1539), the illegitimate son of Christopher Columbus. Hernando's mother was named Beatriz Enriquez de Arana. As a young man, Hernando accompanied his father on his fourth voyage to the New World (1502), where he sailed along the shores of Honduras, Nicaragua, Costa Rica and Panama. He was an admirer and a propagator of the achievements of the Admiral. He wrote a biography of his father and struggled, all his life, for his good opinion, often against enemies at the

Spanish Court. He was exquisitely educated and was awarded very high positions. He was the author of a Spanish dictionary and of a cosmographic description of Spain. He was the supervisor of the publication of a number of important maps of the world and of other cartographic materials. He founded a botanical garden, one of the first on the continent, and he amassed substantial wealth. But first of all, Hernando was a pioneer of the gathering and cataloguing of printed works, a visionary of the use of information.

Printed books in the sixteenth century were still a rather costly novelty. Hernando was one of the first people to understand the importance of the preservation of the printed word and he invented new, efficient methods for their storage, enabling fast access to their content. He travelled across the whole of Europe, buying thousands of freshly printed books in many different countries. He gathered over 20,000 of them. His ambition was to create a library which would have a copy of every book published on Earth. If the land of narrative fiction resembles the Library of Borges, the Seville library of Hernando Colón (who named it himself Columbina), remains a concretised dream of human omniscience.

A shrine of human omniscience? Absolutely, and what's more, Hernando Colón was not the inventor of that idea. Let's start this story, somewhat perversely, at the beginning of the twentieth century.

After winning a competition by correspondence for his prestigious position, John Gabbert Bowman, the tenth Chancellor of the University of Pittsburgh, Pennsylvania, came to the city by train from Iowa University in 1921, and he asked the taxi driver to take him to the centre of the town. The driver was completely stupefied because no one in Pittsburgh has ever heard of anything like a downtown. However, a desperate Bowman took an oath: I shall build a centre for Pittsburgh, and even more than a centre, I shall create 'a building exemplifying the dreams of the lives that the citizens of Pittsburgh have always wanted to live'.

The Pittsburgh of that time – one can see it in old photographs – was a colossal industrial, coal and metallurgical area deprived of high buildings – a place like Manchester or the Ruhr area in Germany. There were innumerable steelworks, mining towers, shipyards and docks (the Ohio River starts its course there). The officials of that time, it is remembered, used to change their shirts for clean ones around midday. They were born, they worked extremely hard and soon they were dying amid the omnipresent smog (the chronicles are tactfully silent about the shirts of the working class). The energetic Bowman presented his idea to the local industrial moguls (Carnegie, Heinz and many others), the necessary funds were collected quite quickly, and a renowned architect, Charles Klauder, from Philadelphia, was hired. The preparation of the plans took only two years and in 1926 the construction of the Cathedral of Learning, of the highest university building in the world, started. It was finished, after bravely overcoming the difficulties of the Depression, in 1936.

A tower of knowledge, a tower of wisdom; well, a Cathedral of Knowledge and Wisdom at once, with capital letters! The construction of the building is of steel, of course; the sandstone brought from Indiana is only glued to this skeleton of steel in a clever way, but all these stone gargoyles, arches, ceilings, and keystones are much more laboriously carved than in Notre Dame or in Cologne. They look more Gothic than the oldest buildings in Oxford or in Cambridge.

Bowman and Klauder, hired by him, were not the first to build in this style. In 1913, the Woolworth Building was opened with great pomp on Broadway in New York. Two high towers in the style of the French Gothic, connected as one by an even higher, elaborate crown. New Yorkers immediately christened the Woolworth Building as the 'Cathedral of Commerce'.

'Cathedral' and 'commerce' on that continent – unlike in Europe – never were, and still are not, extreme opposites. Together, they are a divine unity, a perceptible proof of the rightness of the doctrine of predestination.

In an architectonical sense, the Cathedral of Learning develops and repeats solutions introduced by the architect Cass Gilbert in the Cathedral of Commerce. But the ambitious concept which it embodies – the shrine of human cognition, a sky-reaching edifice of human knowledge – comes from the Italian Renaissance. Antonio Averlino, called Filarete, described his vision of the House of Virtue, of a tower reaching the sky in his *Trattato* in the middle of the fifteenth century. Averlino, a sculptor and builder, served the Sforza family and therefore the ideal city described by him is named *Sforzinda*. He imagined powerful city walls within an octagonal plan of eight city gates. In the middle of the piazza there is The House of Virtue. Inside it, on the first floor, are 'dwellings for prostitutes and the headquarters of the police'. Then, floor after floor is dedicated to the 'teaching of every handcraft', from pottery to tanning; then, even higher, the fine arts and a separate floor for every one of the sciences. At the very top there is an astronomical observatory, from which one should contemplate 'the perfection of Heaven and the perfection of Creation'.

The Cathedral of Learning must have given the 'Great Linguist' (Stalin) a lot to think about because already, in the year 1953, the edifice of Moscow University became the tallest university building in the world. Two hundred-and-forty metres high, the fake Gothic ornamentation was substituted by numerous 'Russian and Soviet motifs' and the whole complex was designed by Lev Vladimirovich Rudnev. The same Rudnev who, even before finishing construction in Moscow, became the head of the team designing a twin building, a gift from Stalin to the 'brotherly Polish Nation': that, is the Palace of Culture and Science in Warsaw (1955). It's not only books and theatre performances that talk passionately between themselves. Paintings and symphonies, sculptures and installations, frescos, friezes and palace gardens do it, too. Also, and maybe most often, buildings do it.

In the theatre on the lowest floor of the Cathedral of Learning in Pittsburgh, I directed *Endgame* by Samuel Beckett in 2006; we even got a prize for the best show of that season. We put the audience on the stage, the action took place at the edge of the stage, and the background of the action was a huge auditorium, disguised as a ruin and half-buried by sand. On the abandoned director's table among the seats, one could see, among some papers and drawings, a white model of the Cathedral of Learning, about a foot high. One could see it from a distance; a helpful prop or maybe a memento of the long absent, forgotten, director.

Columbina, the Library of Hernando Colón in Seville, began to be dispersed a few years after his death, but luckily, thanks to the care of the Church, it survived and still exists to this day. It currently holds 7,000 books. It was spared the fate of the Library of Alexandria. Which is not, unfortunately, a frequent outcome in history. Libraries, and the goods collected in them, always draw the attention of fanatics and inquisitors.

> For the Inquisitors of every epoch, every race and every religion, fire purges not only human beings, but also books. There are numerous cases of burning the books; it happened because of negligence, but also for the sake of cleansing and of destroying the specimens of degenerated art – as in the case of Nazi pyres ...

writes Umberto Eco (*On the Shoulders of Giants*).

The zealous friends of Don Quixote, worrying about his morality and about the health of his mind, burned his library full of romances. At the end of *Auto Da Fé* by Elias Canetti, the library of Professor Kien is on fire. This pyre resembles the sacrifice of Empedocles ('When the flames finally reach him, he starts to laugh as loud as never before in his life'). Also, the books condemned to vanish burn in *Fahrenheit 451* by Ray Bradbury, as well as the library in the monastery in *The Name of the Rose* by Umberto Eco.

A commentary by Fernando Báez, from his book *Historia universal da la destruccion de libros* (2004) states:

> Fire is a redemptive element and because of this almost all religions use it when worshiping their idols. But that power guarding life is also – let's remember – a destructive power. When destroying, with the help of fire, man plays God, the Master of Life and Death. The reason to use fire is obvious: it reduces the spirit of the work to pure matter.

85   I was saving the important fragment of *Don Quixote*, in which the Knight of the Rueful Countenance refutes the accusations of the improbability of Romances, for the end of this discourse. When all the different combinations, configurations and comparisons of various narrative fictions had already been discussed, I thought that the speech by Don Quixote, in which he colourfully defends Romances, monsters, dragons and sorcerers, might be interesting. In this, he defends, generally, the world of phantasy from attacks by the party of non-believers.

When I finally re-read this fragment, that is, the wordy conflict between Don Quixote and the Canon (page 196 in the Polish edition, translator Walenty Zakrzewski), a huge disappointment awaited me. Don Quixote, existing in my memory as a Romantic defender of poetic phantasy, turned out to be somebody completely different in the actual phrases of Miguel de Cervantes. That real Don Quixote, from his novel, does not defend any 'phantasy' but, instead, the alleged truthfulness of openly nonsensical legends. He does not support or praise any 'Romantic visions' but supports a set of long-dead formulas, which he repeats in a mechanical way. In my memory, the Romantic stereotype of Don Quixote – borrowed straight from the musical *The Man from La Mancha* – destroys the real Don Quixote, that is, the particular case of a person with a deranged perception of the world.

Let us look at his key conversation with the Canon. The Canon has many arguments, and he has them all well prepared. The sick state of Don Quixote's insanity irritates him, personally. It complicates his understanding of the world and of human nature. Therefore, the Canon rolls out his accusations on every possible occasion, like guns on the walls of a defensive outpost in some decisive battle. They have just stopped for a break and permitted Don Quixote to go to the bushes. Don Quixote returns much lighter and in very good humour, and the Canon begins his attack:

> Is it possible, Gentle Sir, that the nauseous and idle reading of books of Chivalry can have had such an effect on your Worship as to upset your reason, so that you fancy yourself enchanted, and the like, all as far from the truth as falsehood itself is? How can there be any human understanding that can persuade itself there ever was all that infinity of Amadises in the world, or all that multitude of famous Knights, all those Emperors of Trebizond, all those Felixmartes of Hircania, all those palfreys, and damsels-errant, and serpents, and monsters, and giants, and marvellous adventures, and enchantments of every kind, and battles, and prodigious encounters, splendid costumes, love-sick princesses, squires made counts, droll dwarfs, love letters, billings and cooings, swashbuckler women, and, in a word, all that nonsense the books of Chivalry, contain?

These are just two questions, but they are asked with such viciousness, such derision and audacity that Don Quixote does not have enough strength to answer. Meanwhile the Canon, energised by this silence, continues:

> For myself, I can only say that when I read them, so long as I do not stop to think that they are all lies and frivolity, they give me a certain amount of pleasure; but when I come to consider what they are, I fling the very best of them at the wall, and would fling it into the fire if there were one at hand, as richly deserving such punishment as cheats and impostors out of the range of ordinary toleration, and as founders of new sects and modes of life, and teachers that lead the ignorant public to believe and accept as truth, all the folly they contain.

It is interesting that the Canon experiences 'a certain amount of pleasure' for as long as he takes the written word as truth. The Canon seems to hate sheer fiction, while 'truths' and news from the paper, he accepts with no hesitation. Let us also note that fire and a stack of burning books are the images closest to his imagination. Then the Canon throws the last fatal punches, which – according to him – should finish the battle:

> Come, Señor Don Quixote, have some compassion for yourself, return to the bosom of common sense, and make use of the liberal share of it that heaven has been pleased to bestow upon you, employing your abundant gifts of mind in some other reading that may serve to benefit your conscience and add to your honour. And if, still led away by your natural bent, you desire to read books of achievements and of Chivalry, read the Book of Judges in the Holy Scriptures, for there you will find grand reality, and deeds as true as they are heroic. Lusitania had a Viriatus, Rome a Cæsar, Carthage a Hannibal, Greece an Alexander, Castile a Count Fernando Gonzalez, Valencia a Cid, Andalusia a Gonzalo Fernandez, Estremadura a Diego García de Paredes, Jerez a García Perez de Vargas, Toledo a Garcilaso, Seville a Don Manuel de Leon, to read of whose valiant deeds will entertain and instruct the loftiest minds and fill them with delight and wonder. Here, Señor Don Quix-

ote, will be reading worthy of your sound understanding; from which you will rise learned in history, in love with virtue, strengthened in goodness, improved in manners, brave without rashness, prudent without cowardice; and all to the honour of God, your own advantage and the glory of La Mancha, whence, I am informed, your Worship derives your birth.

The Canon ends by puffing himself up and I bet that he is very satisfied, reading in the eyes of the Curate, who listens to the argument, an admiration for such elaborate reasoning.

'Don Quixote listened with the greatest attention to the Canon's words, and when he found he had finished, after regarding him for some time, he replied to him:'

Cervantes writes, 'listened with the greatest attention', so we can presume that Don Quixote fully understands the words directed to him, as well as the intentions of those words. His answer is very clear; one cannot maintain that it is the answer of a madman who does not understand what he is talking about. Don Quixote answers:

It appears to me, Gentle Sir, that your Worship's discourse is intended to persuade me that there never were any Knights-errant in the world, and that all the books of Chivalry are false, lying, mischievous and useless to the State, and that I have done wrong in reading them, and worse in believing them, and still worse in imitating them, when I undertook to follow the arduous calling of Knight-errantry which they set forth; for you deny that there ever were Amadises of Gaul or of Greece, or any other of the Knights of whom the books are full.

It is all exactly as you state it – said the Canon; to which Don Quixote returned – You also went on to say that books of this kind had done me much harm, inasmuch as they had upset my senses, and shut me up in a cage, and that it would be better for me to reform and change my studies, and read other truer books which would afford more pleasure and instruction.

– Just so – said the Canon.

– Well then – returned Don Quixote – to my mind it is you who are the one that is out of his wits and enchanted, as you have ventured to utter such blasphemies against a thing so universally acknowledged and accepted as true that whoever denies it, as you do, deserves the same punishment which you say you inflict on the books that irritate you when you read them. For to try to persuade anybody that Amadis, and all the other Knights-adventurers with whom the books are filled, never existed, would be like trying to persuade him that the Sun does not yield light, or ice cold, or earth nourishment.

'Whoever denies it, as you do, deserves the same punishment which you say you inflict on books that irritate you when you read them' – if, in the eyes of the Canon, books about chivalry deserve the pyre, in the eyes of The Knight of Rueful Countenance, it is the Canon who should be burned.

What wit in the world can persuade another that the story of the Princess Floripes and Guy of Burgundy is not true, or that of Fierabras and the Bridge of Mantible, which happened in the time of Charlemagne? For by all that is good it is as true, as that it is daylight, now; and if it be a lie, it must be a lie too that there was a Hector, or Achilles, or Trojan War, or the Twelve Peers of France, or Arthur of England, who still lives changed into a raven, and is unceasingly looked for in his Kingdom. One might just as well try to make out that the history of Guarino Mezquino, or of the quest of the Holy Grail, is false, or that the loves of Tristram and the Queen Yseult are apocryphal, as well as those of Guinevere and Lancelot, when there are persons who can almost remember having seen the Dame Quintañona, who was the best cupbearer in Great Britain. And so true is this, that I recollect a grandmother of mine on my father's side, whenever she saw any dame in a venerable hood, used to say to me, 'Grandson, that one is like Dame Quintañona', from which I conclude that she must have known her, or at least had managed to see some portrait of her.

If the story of the Princess Floripes and Guy of Burgundy is not true, there was no Trojan War? – I am very sorry but that argument, as well as most of the following arguments, is completely false. What does the existence or non-existence of the Twelve Peers of France have in common with Princess Floripes? And what does Arthur, the mythical King of England, have in common with it either? The arguments of Don Quixote are a classical hotchpotch. It is a mixture of the crumbs of legends, names, alleged events and mythical facts – a mixture in which elements, maybe real sometimes in the past, are equated with pure phantasies, with fairy tales told to children. The words of Don Quixote only simulate rational argument while in reality they reject the possibility of rational discussion.

For Don Quixote it is merely a question of lack of belief. Look what an oddball he is, stubbornly wanting to convince us that two and two makes five. So, this perverse Don Quixote continues: the reference to the testimony of his own grandmother is the strongest example of his possible proof. If his grandma has seen Quintañona with her own eyes – or even if she has only seen her portrait – it means, without a doubt, that dragons exist, and that wandering knights definitely exist. Don Quixote is so certain of himself that he enjoys copying the Canon's exuberant style ...

Then who can deny that the story of Pierres and the fair Magalona is true, when even to this day may be seen in the King's armoury, the pin with which the valiant Pierres guided the wooden horse he rode through the air, and it is a trifle bigger than the pole of a cart? And alongside of the pin is Babieca's saddle, and at Roncesvalles there is Roland's horn, as large as a large beam; whence we may infer that there were Twelve Peers, and a Pierres, and a Cid, and other Knights like them, of the sort people commonly call Adventurers. Or perhaps I shall be told, too, that there was no such Knight-errant as the valiant Lusitanian Juan de Merlo, who went to Burgundy and in the city of Arras fought with the famous Lord of Charny, Mosen Pierres by name, and afterwards in the city of Basle with Mosen Enrique de Remesten, coming out of both encounters covered with fame and honour; or adventures and challenges achieved and delivered, also in Burgundy, by the valiant Spaniards Pedro Barba and Gutierre Quixada (of whose family I come in the direct male line), when they vanquished the sons of the Count of San Polo. I shall be told, too, that Don Fernando de Guevara did not go in quest of adventures to Germany, where he engaged in combat with Micer George, a Knight of the House of the Duke of Austria. I shall be told that the jousts of Suero de Quiñones, him of the 'Paso', and the emprise of Mosen Luis de Falces against the Castilian Knight, Don Gonzalo de Guzman, were mere mockeries; as well as many other achievements of Christian Knights of these and foreign realms, which are so authentic and true, that, I repeat, he who denies them must be totally wanting in reason and good sense.

The certainty of Don Quixote is invulnerable. It resembles the invulnerability of yet another character, similarly incorrigible, in *Bartleby, the Scrivener* by Herman Melville (1853). Some commentators maintain that the famous phrase that equates to, 'I'd rather not' the ('I prefer not to') of Bartleby's, repeated so many times, is the undeterred expression of his free will and the only way of expressing his humanity. Others say that his attitude is an expression of extreme stubbornness, that Bartleby is unable to respond to any persuasion and that his recalcitrance is inexplicable and absurd. 'He who denies the achievements of Christian Knights must be totally wanting in reason' – there are no halftones; for Don Quixote it is the end of the conversation.

Don Quixote reveals himself as a fundamentalist unable to reach any rational compromise, a fundamentalist with a deeply flawed sense of reality. Earlier, he took for a real event a fictional story represented with the help of puppets. The real, wooden windmill was for him an attacking dragon. Don Quixote seems not to know any principle of Coleridge's 'willing suspension of belief'. More precisely, he does not know, and does not understand what narrative fiction is.

Umberto Eco writes:

In some phenomenologies of the lie narrative fiction is being enumerated as a secondary and acceptable case. But narrative fiction is <u>not</u> <u>a lie</u>. Manzoni is not lying when he writes that a certain vicar was threatened by two robbers at Lake Como; he pretends that what he is telling us about actually happened and he asks us to participate in his fiction by suspending – as Coleridge wanted it – disbelief. He asks us to do exactly what a child does, when he grabs a stick and pretends that it is a gun and when he asks us to participate in the game and to pretend that we fall like a shot lion.

In narrative fiction one does not say an untruth to make anyone believe it, nor to harm anyone. In narrative fiction one builds a possible world and invites the reader or the viewer to live in it as if it was a real world, that is by accepting its rules as credible (talking animals, works of magic, superhuman acts).

(Umberto Eco, *On the Shoulders of Giants*)

86 C, a doctor, says: The first week of April has ended and the Covid disease seems to be petering out, at least in the UK. In about a week, pubs, restaurants, cinemas and bookshops will open. Vaccinating over half of the population is bringing results, it seems. Everybody is afraid, but also everybody is so fed up with the lockdown that they are dreaming about even partial freedom. Partial, because travelling abroad still remains restricted. H, a publisher, comments: People were writing, are writing and they will keep writing. One cannot deny that they were writing more than usual during lockdown. They wanted to get rid of it, to get it down on paper. Now we are overwhelmed in the publishing houses, we are late reading

everything. They've been writing down their memoirs, adventures, achievements. They've been writing down thoughts, reflections, prognoses. They've been writing diaries, in masses. *What will remain after myself?* they kept wondering. Well, maybe a book, on decent paper, from a decent publishing house. And this is pure despair for the publishers, because all these works from lockdown are very similar.

C: It will be roughly as it was before the lockdown but in many departments it is going to be different. We shall all see each other less frequently, we shall meet in much smaller groups. Many will continue to work online, the cost of renting an office will keep falling.

H: A book about storytelling? Why not, it sounds as good as a book about painting or a book about playing the trombone. Partly a guide, partly a list of experiences? As long as it is readable. As long as it is written in a way which engages the reader.

C: We shall live, and we shall multiply. We shall build cities, we shall fly to the stars, we shall change borders and habits. We shall do it for many generations and one day it will be over. Because one day, somehow, in some way, it has to end. In some distant future. After all, we all know that:

> The cloud-capped towers, the gorgeous palaces,
> The solemn temples, the great globe itself,
> Yea, all which it inherit, shall dissolve,
> And, like this insubstantial pageant faded,
> Leave not a rack behind.
> (Shakespeare, *The Tempest*)

Index

Adorno, Theodor 57
Agamben, Giorgio 192, 207, 208
Aeschylus 100, 101
Agathon 15
Alighieri, Dante 22, 65, 97, 134
Amis, Kingsley 221
Apollodorus of Athens 15
Appel, Libby 119
Arana, Beatriz Enrique de 235
Ariosto, Ludovico 20, 88, 96, 97, 98
Aristodemus 15
Aristophanes 135
Aristotle 22, 225
Atossa 100
Augier, Emile 225
Augustine of Hippo 5
Aurelius, Marcus 38, 151, 152, 153, 154
Austen, Jane 20, 21
Averlino, Antonio di Pietro (Filarete) 238

Baez, Fernando 240
Ballard, J. G. 120
Balzac, Honoré de 223
Barba, Eugenio 169
Bayley, John Oliver 67
Becker, Carl L. (Lotus) 149, 150, 151
Beckett, Samuel i, vii, 4, 6, 21, 57, 64, 222, 239

Benjamin, Walter 121, 205, 206, 207
Bergerac, Cyrano de 134
Berlin, Isaiah 211
Berman, Jakub 51
Berman brothers 53
Białoszewski, Miron 23, 63
Bloom, Harold 21, 22, 101, 102
Blok, Alexander Alexandrovich 74
Błoński, Jan 167
Boccaccio, Giovanni 17, 20, 123
Bohr, Margrethe Norlund 99
Bohr, Niels 99, 233
Borges, Jorge Luis 234, 235, 236
Bowman, John Gabbert 236, 237
Bradbury, Ray 240
Branagh, Kenneth 200
Brandon, Marlo 228, 231
Brecht, Bertolt 35, 59, 75, 120, 147, 226, 227, 228, 229, 230
Breton, André 60
Broniewski, Władysław 51
Brook, Peter vii, 82, 115, 169, 170, 177, 178, 201, 204, 214
Brown, Lancelot (Capability) 123
Buber, Martin 166
Büchner, Georg 137, 138, 146
Bulgakov, Mikhail 158, 170, 171, 190
Burton, Robert 20
Byron, George Gordon 20, 106, 107

Cade, Jack 11
Calderón de la Barca, Pedro 78
Campanella, Tommaso 134
Camus, Albert 4
Canetti, Elias 239
Capek, Karel 139
Carnegie, Andrew 237
Carroll, Lewis 134
Cervantes, Miguel de 11, 12, 13, 17,
 19, 20, 24, 27, 28, 29, 54, 88, 240,
 243
Caesar, Julius Gaius 99, 152
Chaikin, Joseph 169, 170
Chandler, Raymond 9
Chaplin, Charlie 74
Charlemagne, Emperor 27, 88, 244
Charles V 66
Chateaubriand, François-René de
 108
Chaucer, Geoffrey 17, 20, 97
Chadzyńska, Zofia 167
Cheops (Chu-fu) 155
Child, Lee (Jim Grant) 211
Chomsky, Noam 220
Christie, Agatha 232
Coleridge, Samuel Taylor 9, 247
Colón, Hernando 235, 236, 239
Comte, Auguste 233
Cortazar, Julio 167
Craig, Gordon 73
Chekhov, Michael 3

Dante (Alighieri, Dante) 22, 65, 97,
 134
Danton, Georges 146, 147
Darius, King 100
David, Jacques-Louis 58
Deaver, Jeffrey 221, 222, 223

Debourau, Jean-Gaspard 74
Dejmek, Kazimierz 168
Democritus of Abdera 152
Derrida, Jacques 222
Descartes, René 82
Deutscher, Izaac 51
Dick, Philip K. 39
Dickens, Charles 111, 223
Dickinson, Emily 110
Diderot, Denis 23, 77, 104, 149
Donne, John 46
Dostoevsky, Fyodor Mikhailovich
 vii, 7, 11, 12, 23, 99, 100, 223
Doyle, Arthur Conan 232
Dumas, Alexandre 225

Eco, Umberto 186, 187, 235, 239,
 240, 247
Ecclesiastes 38
Empedocles of Akragas 240
Epictet of Hierapolis 152
Epicurus 17
Espronceda, José de 108
Evans, Arthur 121, 122

Faulks, Sebastian 221
Fellini, Federico 38
Fénelon, François (François
 De Salignac de la Mothe) 99
Feyerabend, Paul Karl 57, 188
Filarete (Averlino,
 Antonio di Pietro) 238
Fish, Simon 197
Flaszen, Ludwig 167
Flaubert, Gustave 11, 223
Fleming, Ian 9, 221, 222, 223
Fontenelle, Bernard le Bovier de 99
Fraser, James George 44

Frayn, Michael 99, 148
Fredro, Aleksander 64, 131
Freud, Sigmund 21, 22, 44, 102
Fromm, Erich 102
Frederick II 173
Fukuyama, Francis 55, 56

Galileo, Galilei 46
Gardner, John 221
Gaulle, Charles de 191
Gilbert, Cass 238
Glaucon 15
Goethe, Johann Wolfgang von 190
Gogol, Nikolai 100
Goldoni, Carlo 74, 75, 184
Gombrowicz, Witold 5, 14, 16, 21,
    50, 52, 65, 66, 125, 147, 148, 177,
    190, 191, 213, 222
Gounod, Charles 107
Greenblatt, Stephen 198, 199
Gregory, Andre William 169, 170
Grotowski, Jerzy vii, 82, 167, 168,
    169, 170, 183, 233, 234
Grzegorzewski, Jerzy 168, 172
Gutenberg, Johannes 8, 224

Habermas, Jurgen 189, 194
Hadrian, Publius Elius 154
Handke, Peter 92, 93, 205
Harsnett Samuel 199
Hart, Moss 39
Hauptmann, Elizabeth 229
Hayek, Friedrich August von 167
Hayes, Marjorie 227
Hegel, Georg Wilhelm Friedrich
    48, 56, 80, 121, 137, 146, 147, 190,
    193, 194
Heine, Heinrich 108

Heinz, Henry John 237
Heisenberg, Werner 99, 175
Henry VII 198
Henry VIII 198
Henry of Navarre 45
Heraclitus of Ephesus 152
Herbert, Zbigniew 156, 167
Herodotus of Halicarnassus 20
Hippocrates of Kos 152
Hitler, Adolf 150
Hogg, James 9
Homer 16, 20, 129, 130, 145
Horace (Quintus Horatius Flaccus)
    155, 183
Hume, David 149
Huxley, Aldous 139

Iambulus 16
Ionesco, Eugene vii, 214

James, Henry 67
Janion, Maria 77)
Jarmusch, Jim 110
Jarocki, Jerzy 168
Jarry, Alfred 147
Jasiénski, Bruno 51, 52
John of Patmos 37, 38, 39
Joyce, James 20, 21
Jung, Carl Gustav 44, 102

Kafka, Franz 234
Kálmán, Emmerich (Imre) 176, 177
Kana, Vasek 176
Kant, Immanuel 53, 81, 193, 194
Kantor, Tadeusz 168
Kaufman, George S. 39
Keaton, Buster 74
Kierkergaard, Soren 54, 81

Kieślowski, Krzysztof viii

Klauder, Charles 237

Kochanowski, Jan 96

Kochanowski, Piotr 96

Kojève Alexandre 55

Kołakowski, Leszek 151, 167

Kott, Jan 146

Kozak, Jolanta 43

Krajewski, Stanisław 52

Krasicki, Ignacy 99

Krupp, Siegfried 228

Kuhn, Thomas 49, 57, 136

Kundera, Milan 11, 12, 77

Kyd, Thomas 101

Lacan, Jacques 102, 222

Laclos, Pierre Choderlos de 7

Laërtius, Diogenes 17

Laplace, Pierre Simon de 175

Le Goff, Jacques 198

Leibniz, Gottfried Wilhelm 47, 190

Lem, Stanisław 9, 39, 61, 134, 139,
    153, 172, 174, 234

Lenin, Vladimir Ilych Ulanov 59,
    160, 161

Lennon, John 165

Leopardi, Giacomo 111

Lewis, C. S. 97, 98

Lipszyc, Adam 124, 206

Locke, John 149

Loesser, Frank Henry 228, 230, 231

Lorris, Guillaume de 97

Lucian of Samosata 16, 20, 99, 134

Luxemburg, Rosa 52

Maestro (Tadeusz Kantor) 160, 162

Malinowski, Bronisław 44

Mancuso brothers (Lorenzo and

Francisco) 87, 88, 95, 110

Mankiewicz, Joseph L. 231

Mann, Thomas 64, 65

Man, Paul de 206, 207

Manzoni, Alessandro 247

Marat, Jean-Paul 58, 59, 147

Marx, Karl 49, 50, 51, 52, 53, 56, 58,
    59, 121, 147, 190, 226

Marquard, Odo 137, 188, 189, 190,
    191, 192

Masters, Edgar Lee 99

Mayakovsky, Vladimir 49

McCarthy, Cormac 41, 120

Melville, Herman 246

Miciński, Tadeusz 21

Mickiewicz, Adam 109, 110, 137,
    197, 222

Miéville, China Tom 36, 37

Miller, Walter M. 120

Milton, John 21, 209

Miłosz, Czesław 97

Mitchell, Joni 110

Möbius, August Ferdinand 175

Montaigne, Michel de 45, 47, 99

Morris,William 122

Mrożek, Sławomir 167

Napoleon Bonaparte 59, 64, 136,
    137, 146

Neville, Stuart 206

Nietszche, Friedrich 51, 67, 185, 186,
    187

Orbán, Viktor 76

Orwell, George 139

Parker, Robert B. 9, 211

Pasek, Jan Chryzostom 21

Pater, Walter Horatio 67

Peszek, Jan 172

Pilatus, Pontius 201

Pinter, Harold 39

Pirandello, Luigi 74, 75

Piranesi, Giovanni Battista i, 234

Plato 8, 15, 22, 38, 53, 69, 79, 108, 134,
153, 192, 193, 194, 201

Plautus (Titus Maccius Plautus) 73,
203

Plutarch of Chaeronea 69

Poe, Edgar Allan 9, 232

Polewka, Jan 211

Popper, Karl 151, 167

Potocki, Jan 9, 19, 134

Proust, Marcel 67, 131

Prus, Maciej 211

Przybyszewska, Stanisława 147

Przybyszewski, Stanisław 21

Pseudo Dionysius the Areopagite 8

Pseudo-Philo 8

Pseudo-Plato 8

Ptolemy, Claudius 46

Puccini, Giacomo 211, 217

Pushkin, Alexander Sergeyevich 108

Racine, Jean 101

Ratzinger, Joseph 186

Riccoboni, Antoine-François 104,
105

Rickenbauer, Edward 230

Robespierre, Maximilien de 147

Rodowicz, Iga 170

Rodowicz, Tomasz 170

Rorty, Richard 54, 55, 192, 193, 194,
195, 196, 202

Rosendorfer, Herbert 123, 124

Rossini, Gioacchino 107

Rousseau, Jean-Jacques 5, 108

Różewicz, Tadeusz 57

Rudnev Lev Vladimirovich 238

Runyon, Damon 229, 230

Rymkiewicz, Jaroslaw Marek 79

Rzewuski, Henryk 21

Sade, Donatien Alphonse François
de 58, 59, 147

Salvadori, Roberto 55, 75, 76, 78,
82, 185

Sardou, Victorien 225

Scherillo, Michele 73

Schiller, Friedrich 106, 209, 210, 211

Schlink, Bernhard 62

Schumann, Peter 169

Schumann, Robert 107

Scribe, Eugène 225

Sebald, Winfried Georg 57

Seneca the Younger (Lucius Anneaus
Seneca Minor) 99, 100, 101, 109

Sforza de, Alessandro 238

Shakespeare, William 9, 17, 20, 21,
22, 45, 54, 70, 71, 72, 73, 102, 104,
105, 146, 155, 184, 199, 201, 213,
223, 248

Shaw, George Bernard 228

Shelley, Mary 138

Shore, Marci 50–1, 52

Sienkiewicz, Henryk 21

Silverberg, Robert 41, 141

Simenon, Georges 232

Simmons, Jean Merilyn 228

Sinatra, Frank 231

Słowacki, Juliusz 97, 108

Socrates 54, 152

Sondheim, Stephen 39

Spenser, Edmund 20, 97

Spielberg, Stephen viii
Stalin, Joseph Vissarionovich 51, 53, 150, 228, 238
Stande, Stanisław Ryszard 51
Staniewski, Włodzimierz 170
Stanislavski, Konstantin Sergeyevich 234
Sterne, Laurence 14, 20, 108
Strehler, Giorgio 112
Stryjkowski, Julian 51
Swift, Jonathan 134
Swinarski, Konrad 59, 163, 167, 168

Tasso, Torquato 97
Tchaikovsky, Pyotr Illych 107
Tocqueville, Alexis de 151
Tolkien, J. R. R. (John Ronald Reuel) 20, 97, 98
Tolstoy, Lev Nikolayevich 51, 172, 223
Tomaszewksi, Henryk 168
Toulmin, Stephen 45, 46, 47
Trump, Donald 76
Tyndale, William 197

Vattimo, Gianni 81, 82, 120, 121, 124, 139, 185, 186, 187, 190, 192
Voltaire (François Marie Arouet) 149
Virgil 39, 44, 130

Wajda, Andrzej, viii
Warski, Adolf 52
Wasilewska, Wanda 53
Wat, Aleksander 51, 52
Ważyk, Adam 51
Weigel, Helene 226
Weill, Kurt 75, 226, 227, 228, 229
Weiss, Peter 57, 58, 59, 60, 147
Wells, H. G. (Herbert George) 138
Wilde, Oscar 67
Witkiewicz, Stanisław Ignacy 4, 21, 49, 52
Wittgenstein, Ludwig 233
Wojtyla Karol (Pope John Paul II) 169, 183
Wordsworth, William 21
Worth, Irene 214
Wyspiański, Stanisław 105, 222

Xerxes 100

Yeats, William Butler 41, 43

Zakrzewski, Walenty 240
Zanussi, Krzysztof, viii
Zapolska, Gabriela 68

Żeromski, Stefan 60

Acknowledgements

KATE SINCLAIR

Sadly, Tadeusz is not here to thank the countless kind people who have helped, read, and supported the English edition of *The End of Ends*, so it falls to me to do this in his stead.

Many thanks go to:

Charles Boyle of CB editions for working so tirelessly to help bring this iteration of the book to life. And copy-editor Simon Barraclough and proofreader Karen Atkinson.

Mike Sims from the T. S. Eliot Prize who has been a rock and an inspiration in helping me in the process of setting up a literary award in Tadeusz's name to create a further legacy for him. From the very beginning, Krzysztof Zanussi has always been key to this endeavour, and generously and importantly continues to help me with this.

All who worked on the Polish edition of the book and its journey into print: Dariusz Kosiniski, publisher of Żywosłowie Press, and Tadeusz's original editors, Dorota Buchwald and Janusz Legon.

The important first readers: Staszek Radwan, Krzysztof Zanussi, the extraordinary Sarah Lotz, who has been a Super Rock to Tadeusz and I throughout all, Jan Polewka, Simon Bradbury, Jacek Filek and Declan Donellan.

And later, equally important ones: Thomas Keneally, Francis Spufford, Daniel O'Connor, Paul Lacoux, Donato Santeramo, Pawel Dombricki, George Crisp, Mike Sims, Franco Palmieri, Dominique Probst, Krzysztof Babicki, Tadeusz Słobodzianek, Ryszard Skrzypczak and Andrew Paul.

Tadeusz's theatre colleagues, friends, and students, too numerous to name individually, who read *The End of Ends* in Polish. All at AST (the State Theatre School in Kraków) who supported and honoured his work, and his many valued compadres in Canada, the US and Italy.

Tadeusz's family, British and Polish: beloved children Gosia and Janek; wider family, Jurek, Wojtek, Basha and Marta; and the wonderful British family - John, Janet, Jonathan and Penny.

Tadeusz loved so many people, and was so beloved himself, that it would be impossible to mention everyone who deserves our gratitude. Please humbly forgive me if I have accidentally missed any of you. You know who you are, and the thanks are still just as heartfelt.